D1603616

Exploring Christian Holiness

Volume 1
The Biblical Foundations

Volume 1
THE BIBLICAL FOUNDATIONS
by W. T. Purkiser, Ph.D.

Volume 2
THE HISTORICAL DEVELOPMENT
by Paul M. Bassett, Ph.D., and
William M. Greathouse, M.A., D.D.

Volume 3
THE THEOLOGICAL FORMULATION
by Richard S. Taylor, Th.D.

Exploring Christian Holiness

Volume 1
The Biblical Foundations

by
W. T. Purkiser, Ph.D.

BEACON HILL PRESS OF KANSAS CITY
KANSAS CITY, MISSOURI

ISBN: 0-8341-0843-7
    0-8341-0842-9 (set)

Printed in the United States of America

10   9   8   7   6   5   4

Contents

Foreword

John Wesley is the principal forebear of what is commonly called the "Holiness Movement." Although he was obviously not the originator of the doctrine of Christian perfection (as he chose to call it), he was the one who retrieved from theological limbo this biblical truth so positively enunciated in the Scriptures but so greatly neglected since apostolic days.

It is recognized, also, that Wesley did not come forth with a full-blown doctrinal statement that comprehended all aspects of holiness belief and practice. Indeed it remained for such associates as John Fletcher and Adam Clarke to "fine tune" the doctrinal structure, even introducing some nuances not found in Wesley's writings or only lightly alluded to by him. The matter of "Spirit baptism" is perhaps the most crucial of such extensions. Certainly they did much to clarify the practical matters of secondness and how to attain entire sanctification, since Wesley's emphasis had been upon the experience itself.

Nor has the elaboration of holiness doctrine ceased. As various concepts and interpretations have been added, and aberrations introduced, splinter groups have proliferated, each emphasizing some specific point or points of belief or conduct. The result has been some confusion and even contradiction among groups which claim a common Wesleyan ancestry.

The consequent need for a comprehensive and definitive summation of the doctrine of holiness or entire sanctification has long been recognized. Although numerous, competent works have been written on the subject, it appears that no complete study of all aspects of the doctrine has ever been attempted before. The publishers have undertaken this task with some sense of obligation, representing as they do the largest extant holiness body. But there has also been a sensitivity to the variant interpretations of equally knowledgable and devoted believers who share our doctrinal heritage. These resultant volumes are neither a polemic nor a studied attempt to establish consensus. Rather they simply present an in-depth study of the three areas which form the foundation of holiness theology—Scripture, history, and doctrine.

The writers of this work are highly respected scholars and exponents of the truth of holiness. Although all are members of the Church of the Nazarene, this is in no sense a sectarian presentation. Indeed it is the hope of the publishers that this work may stand as the best possible statement of holiness doctrine to which the broad spectrum of "holiness people" can heartily subscribe.

—The Publishers

Preface

This is the first volume of a three-volume work under the general title *Exploring Christian Holiness*. It is a survey of the biblical foundations of the doctrine, experience, and life of holiness. The second volume, authored by Doctors Paul M. Bassett and William M. Greathouse, deals with the historical development of holiness teaching through the Christian centuries. The third volume by Dr. Richard S. Taylor takes up the present theological formulation of the doctrine.

One can only offer a work such as this with a certain degree of diffidence. There is so much more that could be said, and there are some nuances of interpretation which may have been omitted. The treasures of the Word are inexhaustible and succeeding generations of Christians will ever be mining new riches. It is not that God's truth changes; it is that we hope to understand it better.

There are many ways the results of a study of biblical materials on holiness could have been presented. I have chosen the most simple possible outline following the canonical order of the books of the Bible. In the nature of the case, major space is given to the doctrinal sections of the New Testament. The basic text used is the *New International Version*, but any good translation of the Scriptures will yield the same results.

What is offered here is not a series of "proof texts" abstracted from their contexts. As always, "a text without its context is only a pretext." What is offered here is a survey of some of the biblical evidence underlying the Wesleyan understanding of entire sanctification. Others will read the evidence in different ways, but space does not permit extensive consideration of such alternative views.

The concept of holiness in the Scriptures is vast and comprehensive. In its broadest meaning in Christian experience, holiness is life under the Lordship of Jesus Christ in the power and purity of the Holy Spirit. As such, it relates to every other major biblical doctrine: the Trinity, Incarnation, Atonement, grace, faith, justification, the church, Christian ethics, and on and on. Holiness teaching is not a line running through the Bible. It is a vast network of interconnecting truths that pervades the whole.

The major source for the material on the following pages is the Bible itself. However, a wide variety of sources has been consulted covering a broad spectrum of theological positions, older as well as contemporary. It should go without saying that the citation of an author's views on a given text or subject is not to be taken as an endorsement of his entire doctrinal stance or his opinions on other texts or other subjects. Many scholars, for example, whose theological orientation would be described as Calvinistic or as "liberal" become almost Wesleyan in the exegesis of biblical materials, a phenomenon from which I have not hesitated to profit.

We may and do come to the Bible from a variety of theological directions. We come closest together when we bow in humility to the absolute authority of the Word of God for faith and life. When we meet at the Word we should meet not to argue but to worship and adore Him who "chose us in him before the creation of the world to be holy and blameless in his sight" (Eph. 1:4). In His light is our life.

—W. T. Purkiser

Acknowledgments

Permission to quote copyrighted materials is gratefully acknowledged:

Abingdon Press, from *The Interpreter's Bible,* vols. 2, 9, 10, and 11; and *The Interpreter's Dictionary of the Bible,* vol. 4; and from L. M. Starkey, *The Work of the Holy Spirit.*

Christianity Today, column by Gerrit C. Berkouwer, "What Difference Does Faith Make?"

Wm. B. Eerdmans Publishing Co., from F. F. Bruce, *The Book of Acts;* and C. Leslie Mitton, *The Epistle of James.*

Harper and Row Publishers, Inc., from William Barclay, *The Apostles' Creed for Everyman;* L. Harold DeWolf, *A Theology of the Living Church* (rev. ed.); and C. H. Dodd, *The Epistle of Paul to the Romans,* in the Moffatt New Testament Commentary series.

Presbyterian Publishing House, John Knox Press, from George A. F. Knight, *A Christian Theology of the Old Testament.*

Charles Scribner's Sons, from Henry Van Dusen, *Spirit, Son, and Father.*

Westminster Press, from Charles R. Erdman, *The Epistle of Paul to the Romans;* and William E. Hordern, *New Directions in Theology Today: Introduction.*

Abbreviations

AB—*The Anchor Bible*
BBC—*Beacon Bible Commentary*
BBE—*Beacon Bible Expositions*
BDT—*Baker's Dictionary of Theology*
DSB—William Barclay, *Daily Study Bible*
EC—*The Evangelical Commentary on the Bible*
EDNTW—W. E. Vine, *Expository Dictionary of New Testament Words*
ERE—*Encyclopedia of Religion and Ethics*
IB—*The Interpreter's Bible*
IDB—*Interpreter's Dictionary of the Bible*
ISBE—*International Standard Bible Encyclopedia*
LBC—*The Layman's Bible Commentary*
NBC—*New Bible Commentary*
NICNT—*New International Commentary on the New Testament*
TDNT—*Theological Dictionary of the New Testament,* Kittel
TNTC—*The Tyndale New Testament Commentaries*
WesBC—*Wesleyan Bible Commentary*
WTJ—*Wesleyan Theological Journal*

1

What Is Holiness?

Holiness is a term with wide application and rich and varied meaning. The English words "holy" and "holiness" come from the Anglo-Saxon roots of our language. The old English form of "holy" is *hālig* from *hāl* meaning "whole"—akin to "hale, heal, health, and hallow."[1] Holiness is the state or condition of being holy, whole, healed.

The context of "holy" and "holiness" with which we are concerned is the usage found in biblical and particularly Protestant Christian sources. However, the terms have a broader application. India knows its "holy men" whose lives are devoted to meditation and Hindu piety. Concepts of taboo and mana in primitive cultures have affinities with ideas of holiness. The Roman pope is known as "His Holiness" and addressed as "Your Holiness," and the manner of life that characterizes Catholic devotion is described as holiness. But in their most distinctive use, "holy" and "holiness" are terms based on the Judeo-Christian Scriptures and used chiefly in reference to Christian experience and life as understood in Protestant circles.

A twin term is "sanctification," used as a synonym in some English translations of the Bible. With its related forms, "sanctify" and "sanctified," it comes from the Norman-Latin roots of our

---

1. Cf. O. R. Jones, *The Concept of Holiness* (New York: Macmillan Co., 1961), p. 89.

language. The Latin verb *sanctifico* is derived from *sanctus*, "holy" or "set apart for the service of the gods"; and *facio*, "to make." To sanctify is defined as "to make holy or sacred; to set apart for holy or religious use; to hallow; to purify from sin; to make the means of holiness."[2] *Sanctus* is also the source of "saint," a term applied in the New Testament to all the people of God.

As used in English versions of the Bible, "holiness" and "sanctification" are in the main alternate translations of one group of Hebrew and one group of Greek terms. As such, there is no clear distinction in Scripture between them. In theological use, however, holiness is regarded as a condition or state which results from the act or process of sanctification. This distinction is implied by the difference in the use of "ness" as an English suffix denoting quality or state, and "tion" as expressing action.

I. AN IDEA WHOSE TIME HAS COME

An important note in current religious thought is a revival of interest in the concept of sanctification and holiness.

A. The Rediscovery of Sanctification

William E. Hordern is general editor of the series titled *New Directions in Theology Today*. Dr. Hordern wrote the first volume, *Introduction.*[3] Of special interest is the chapter on "Sanctification Rediscovered."[4] Hordern opens the chapter with the words:

> An important development in recent theology is a renewal of interest in sanctification. The theological analysis of Christian salvation is often divided into justification and sanctification. Justification deals with how a man becomes a Christian. It describes God's forgiving acceptance of the sinner and the sinner's response of faith. Sanctification is the act of God whereby the forgiven man is made righteous, it describes how a man grows in his Christian life. Although for the purposes of analysis these may be separated, in actual life they cannot be sharply separated. When a man accepts God's forgiving love he trusts God and puts his life into God's hands.[5]

---

2. *The New Grolier Webster International Dictionary of the English Language* (New York: Grolier, 1976), 2:849.

3. (Philadelphia: Westminster Press, 1966). Used by permission.

4. Pp. 96-113.

5. Ibid., p. 96.

Hordern notes the appropriateness of such a rediscovery. The church today is faced with widespread criticism of its life and practice. During the 1950s, in America at least, the church "sailed on a wave of popular approval."[6] Church membership was at an all-time high. The only charge against the churches that "could hope to be respectable were those which claimed that the churches had been infiltrated by communists," which, Hordern says, did more to discredit the attackers than to harm the church.[7]

The scene has changed. There are a growing number of voices raised in criticism not of the faith of the church but of its life and practice. He recalls Rolf Hochhuth's play *The Deputy* with its scathing criticism of Pope Pius' failure to protest the Nazi slaughter of 6 million Jews. Protestants have come in for their share of criticism in Pierre Burton's *The Comfortable Pew*—and to these titles might be added Gregory Wilson's *Stained Glass Jungle* and *The Suburban Captivity of the Church.*

Even before criticism became widespread, theologians were beginning to "take a new look at the doctrine of sanctification."[8] Illustrating the trend was Dietrich Bonhoeffer's *The Cost of Discipleship,* Emil Brunner's third volume of *Dogmatics,* Tillich's doctrine of the New Being, and L. Harold DeWolf's claim from a liberal perspective that "sanctification is the forgotten doctrine."[9] The "new conservatives" likewise have been concerned with rediscovering sanctification.[10]

A major treatment in our time has come from Karl Barth, who in volume 4 of his *Church Dogmatics* "has developed one of the most extensive treatments of sanctification since the work of John Wesley."[11] Far from a previously suspected antinomianism, Barth asks: "What is the forgiveness of sins (however, we understand it) if it is not directly accompanied by an actual liberation from the committal of sin? . . . What is faith without obedience?"[12]

Hordern notes that early 20th century liberalism said much about the Christian life and ethic. But its thought was always

---

6. Ibid.
7. Ibid., pp. 96-97.
8. Ibid., p. 98.
9. Ibid., p. 99.
10. Ibid., pp. 74-95.
11. Ibid., p. 99.
12. *Church Dogmatics,* vol. 4, pt. 2, p. 505; quoted, ibid.

against the background of optimism regarding human nature. Jesus was sought in history as an inspiring example and leader. Liberals hoped "that a combination of evolutionary development, education, reason, ethical exhortation, and an effort by the will of man, would lead to the good life."[13]

Conversely, the neoorthodox emphasis was on man's inability to save himself, requiring the free grace of God's forgiveness and justification by faith alone. But many theologians of neoorthodoxy made little attempt to move beyond this to a doctrine of sanctification. Bonhoeffer spoke out against any form of "cheap grace" which promises forgiveness without calling for the living of a new life.[14]

Hordern sees three basic themes in the current emphasis on sanctification: "It accepts a basically pessimistic view of human nature, but a highly optimistic view of the power of God's grace; it emphasizes the uniqueness of the Christian ethic; and it recognizes that sanctification must be deeply rooted in the church."[15]

We must recognize in this a broad use of the term "sanctification," a use that will be considered at length later. Hordern's closing paragraph is also noteworthy:

> The concern for sanctification, as we have discussed it, transcends theological schools of thought. Those who are dedicated to it are not in complete agreement with one another. But the fact that men of differing theologies and backgrounds are converging on this doctrine indicates that it represents an area of vital concern to theology and the church today.[16]

B. The Difference Faith Makes

Three years after the publication of Hordern's *Introduction* to *New Directions in Theology Today*, Gerrit C. Berkouwer, a leading Reformed theologian, published an essay in *Christianity Today* titled "What Difference Does Faith Make?" He opens his discussion with a series of questions:

> Does Christian faith really make a difference in real life? Does it actually have the power to grab hold and set life on a new course? Or is the vocabulary of faith a mere set of pious

---

13. Ibid., p. 100.
14. Ibid., pp. 100-101.
15. Ibid., p. 101.
16. Ibid., p. 113.

phrases? Questions like this fill the air these days, and they need tending to. For they touch the vitals of *sanctification;* they call into question its possibility and its reality.

What sort of pretension does the Church make by calling itself the communion of the *saints?* Has it made good, at any time, on this title? Or has nothing really changed? Are we the same people we have always been, living our unchanged lives in an unchanged world? Was Martin Buber right when he said that the Messiah could not have come because human life has not yet been fundamentally changed?[17]

These questions, Berkouwer says, are important in theology. The biblical idea of redemption suggests a radical alteration, a thorough rerouting of life, "an about-face of human existence." The reality of this change, he says, "implies a crisis for the future: without being sanctified, no one shall see the Lord (Heb. 12:14). We are therefore obliged to strive toward holiness, toward peace and sanctification."[18]

Nor is it possible to relegate sanctification to what happens after this life. "The Christian walk has to be made on this earth (I Pet. 1:15 f.), and it must here and now contradict the former way of life."[19] The church's teachers, says Berkouwer,

> have sometimes been too quick in their judgment of perfectionism. In doing so, they usually point to the obvious weaknesses in Christian people, and they recall what James said about all of us stumbling, in many ways (Jas. 3:2). But we should not forget that James meant this as a confession of guilt; he would be amazed if his words were quoted as an excuse. In fact, he meant to urge his readers on toward obedience to the perfect law of liberty and so to the achievement of active and practical holiness (Jas. 1:25).[20]

Perhaps what we are seeing in our day, Berkouwer comments, is a new awareness "that God wills us to be *actually* sanctified, *actually* to change, and *actually* to be new creatures."[21]

Again we note the broad use of the term "sanctification." But the plea is basic and timely and serves to reinforce the truth that sanctification is a doctrine whose time has come.

---

17. *Christianity Today,* vol. 14, no. 5 (December 5, 1969), p. 52. Used by permission.

18. Ibid.

19. Ibid.

20. Ibid.

21. Ibid.

II. BIBLICAL TERMS

We have seen the derivation and meaning of the English terms "holiness" and "sanctification." When we turn from English to the Hebrew of the Old Testament and the Greek of the New Testament, we find much to enlarge our understanding of holiness. As we have seen, the two groups of English words (that is, "holy, holiness"; and "sanctify, sanctified, sanctification") are used basically to translate one family of Hebrew terms (the *q-d-sh* family) and one set of Greek terms (those formed from the *hag* root).[22]

The source and original meaning of *q-d-sh* is not known with certainty. One view traces it to an Assyrian root meaning "bright, clean, pure."[23] Others find its source and original meaning in a Semitic root for "separate" or "cut off,"[24] or "to divide, set off or apart."[25] It is used only in a religious context, in relation to what is deemed divine. The Old Testament uses other terms for "separate" or "set apart" in other circumstances. What is called holy in the Old Testament is not holy because it is separated; it is separated because it is related to God and therefore holy.[26]

The Hebrew word opposite in meaning to "holy" stands for what is common, "what pertains to ordinary life."[27] Holy in this sense comes close to what we should call sacred: "More than any other term, 'holiness' gives expression to the essential nature of the 'sacred.'"[28]

---

22. There are infrequent but important exceptions that will be noted later in context.

23. Cf. George Allen Turner, *The Vision Which Transforms* (Kansas City: Beacon Hill Press of Kansas City, 1964), p. 16; Alfred Edersheim, *The Bible History: Old Testament* (Grand Rapids: William B. Eerdmans Publishing Co., 1949 reprint), 2:110; James Strong, *A Concise Dictionary of the Words in the Hebrew Bible* (reprint ed., Nashville: Abingdon Press, 1890; n.d.), p. 102.

24. Turner, ibid.; cf. Robert Young, *Analytical Concordance of the Bible,* 22nd American ed. rev. (Grand Rapids: William B. Eerdmans Publishing Co., n.d.), pp. 487-89, 834-35.

25. Otto Procksch, "*Hagios,* etc." in Gerhard Kittel, ed., *Theological Dictionary of the New Testament,* trans. and ed., Geoffrey W. Bromiley (Grand Rapids: William B. Eerdmans Publishing Co., 1964), 1:89—hereafter cited as TDNT; cf. James Muilenberg, "Holiness," *The Interpreter's Dictionary of the Bible,* George Arthur Buttrick, ed. (Nashville: Abingdon Press, 1962), 2:617—hereafter cited as IDB.

26. Cf. Jones, *Concept of Holiness,* p. 107.

27. Procksch, TDNT, 1:89.

28. Muilenberg, IDB, 2:616. Cf. Robert F. Davidson, *Rudolf Otto's Interpretation of Religion* (Princeton: Princeton University Press, 1947), p. 79. Otto's coined word *numinous* is almost an exact equivalent of the English word *sacred,* for which there is no German counterpart.

The New Testament family of words growing from the *hag* root has a similar meaning in its earliest usage. It stands for that which is the object of awe, whether in reverence or fear. It was applied to shrines, sanctuaries, and gods before it was used in the New Testament. It is a religious term first of all, and should be understood as such.[29]

While the sources and original meanings of biblical terms are important, even more important is the way they are used. For this reason, a concordance may be a better guide to word meanings than a dictionary or lexicon. Biblical materials for the study of the meaning of holiness are abundant. *Q-d-sh* is used in the Old Testament more than 800 times, and *hagios* and related terms occur in the New Testament some 302 times.

III. THE HOLINESS OF GOD

There is widespread agreement among Bible scholars that holiness in Scripture takes its essential meaning from what God is. God alone is holy in himself. All other holiness is derived from a relationship with Him.

Therefore, to understand the full scope of holiness in Scripture, we must recognize that its essential meaning is derived from the nature and character of God. For people in biblical times, the question rarely was, "Does God exist?" The fact of God was a "given" in Hebrew thought. The question rather was, "What kind of God exists?" To this, the first answer was, "the *holy* God."

Holiness, says James Muilenberg, is "The 'given' undergirding and pervading all religion; the distinctive mark and signature of the divine. . . . It is therefore to be understood, not as one attribute among other attributes, but as the innermost reality to which all others are related."[30] Holiness is the essential nature of God.

A. In the Old Testament

While the term "holiness" as related to God does not occur in the first book of the Bible, the idea is clearly expressed and begins to pick up some of its full meaning. Adam and Eve walk with the

29. TDNT, 1:88-89; Rudolf Otto, *The Idea of the Holy*, trans. John W. Harvey (London: Oxford University Press, 1946), p. 5.

30. IDB, 2:616.

Lord in the Garden until rebellion breaks their relationship to Him and they hide themselves in fear (Gen. 3:1-10). The increasing wickedness of Adam's descendents provokes God to destroy the race. The exception is Noah who "found favor in the eyes of the Lord" as a "righteous man, blameless among the people of his time" who "walked with God" (6:5-9; cf. cc. 6—9). The presumptuous pride of man led to the confusion of languages (11:1-9).

The true God called Abram away from the many gods of Ur in Chaldea and led him to the land of Canaan. Twenty-four years later the Lord appeared to Abram and said, "I am God Almighty; walk before me and be blameless" (11:31—12:4; 17:1; cf. Acts 7:2-3).

Jacob's reaction to his vision of the ladder reaching into the heavens illustrates the response of the human to the divine: "How awesome is this place! This is none other than the house of God; this is the gate of heaven" (Gen. 28:17). "Wherever God's presence is felt, there men encounter the wonder and mystery of holiness."[31]

All through Genesis, God acts in creation and providence as sovereign Lord, transcendent or separate from the ordinary ways of life.

The distinctive words for "holy" and "holiness" are used freely in Exodus with the covenant of Sinai in view. The ground around the burning bush is "holy ground," and Moses is bidden to take off his sandals (Exod. 3:5). God is

> *majestic in holiness,*
> *awesome in glory,*
> *working wonders* (15:11)—

the first explicit statement of the holiness of God in the Bible.

Leviticus stresses a note picked up in the New Testament: "I am the Lord your God; consecrate yourselves and be holy, because I am holy. . . . therefore be holy, because I am holy. . . . Be holy because I, the Lord your God, am holy" (Lev. 11:44-45; 19:2; 1 Pet. 1:15-16). "You are to be holy to me because I, the Lord, am holy, and I have set you apart from the nations to be my own" (Lev. 20:26). "I the Lord, who sanctifies you, am holy" (21:8, NASB).

---

31. Ibid.

Joshua proclaims the Lord as "a holy God" who cannot be served by a disobedient people (Josh. 24:19). Devout Hannah says,

There is no one holy like the Lord (1 Sam. 2:2).

The survivors at Beth Shemesh asked in terror, "Who can stand in the presence of the Lord, this holy God?" (6:20).

The holiness of God is a recurrent theme throughout the Psalms:

> *Let them praise your great and awesome name—*
> *he is holy. . . .*
>
> *Exalt the Lord our God*
> *and worship at his footstool;*
> *he is holy* (Ps. 99:3, 5).

The concept of the holiness of God is central to Isaiah's whole theology:[32]

> *But the Lord Almighty will be exalted*
> *by his justice, and the holy God will show himself*
> *holy by his righteousness* (Isa. 5:16).

No passage in the Old Testament says more about the nature of God's holiness than Isa. 6:1-8, the record of the prophet's crucial Temple experience. The cry of the seraph is picked up again in the song of the four living creatures in Rev. 4:8:

> *Holy, holy, holy is the Lord Almighty;*
> *the whole earth is full of his glory* (Isa. 6:3).

As Otto Procksch comments, whereas God's glory appears in all the world "as in a transparency, His holiness denotes His innermost and secret essence."[33]

We will come back to these verses later in connection with the growing richness of the idea of the holy in the Old Testament. At this point, Isaiah's holy awe in the presence of the divine shows his awareness of the essential nature of God.

It is Isaiah who uses most freely the phrase "the Holy One of Israel"; Isa. 1:4; 5:19, 24; 10:20; 12:6; 17:7; 29:19, cf. 23; 30:11; 31:1;

---

32. Cf. TDNT, 1:93.
33. Ibid.

37:23; cf. 40:25; 41:14; etc. (Cf. also 2 Kings 19:22; Ps. 71:22; 78:41; 89:18; Jer. 50:29; 51:5; Ezek. 39:7.) The Hebrew original in this expression actually lacks the substantive "One" that is necessary in the English translation, and reads as *qadosh Yisrael,* "the Holy of Israel."

Closely related to the nature of God is the name of God. The holiness of His name indicates the holiness of His nature. To have anything to do with idols is to profane God's "holy name" (Lev. 22:2, 32). In a triumphant psalm composed on the occasion of the return of the ark of the covenant to Jerusalem, David glories in and gives thanks to God's holy name (1 Chron. 16:10, 35; Ps. 105:3; 106:47).

The Psalmist describes God's name as great, awesome, and holy (Ps. 99:3; 111:9) and often extols God's holy name (33:21; 103:1; 145:21).

Isaiah speaks of "Holy" as being the name of God, reminiscent of his favorite phrase "the Holy [One] of Israel":

> For this is what the high and lofty One says—
>   he who lives forever, whose name is holy:
> "I live in a high and holy place,
>   but also with him who is contrite and lowly in spirit,
> To revive the spirit of the lowly
>   and to revive the heart of the contrite" (Isa. 57:15).

The combination of transcendence ("the high and lofty One says: . . . 'I live in a high and holy place'") and immanence ("but also with him who is contrite and lowly in spirit'") makes this a key verse in understanding the holiness of God.

Ezekiel and Amos share a common concern that God's holy name will be profaned by the sin and immorality of the people (Ezek. 20:39; 36:20; 39:7, 25; Amos 2:7). "With the emphasising of the name holiness becomes far more personal than cultic. . . . In the process, however, the concept of holiness merges into that of divinity, so that Yahweh's holy name contrasts with everything creaturely. . . . God's holiness thus becomes an expression for His perfection of being which transcends everything creaturely."[34]

---

34. Ibid., 1:91.

B. Components of God's Holiness

The "holy, holy, holy" of Isa. 6:3 and Rev. 4:8 suggests a threefold analysis of the holiness of God. There is the holiness of His exalted majesty. There is the holiness of His infinite radiance. And there is the holiness of His spotless purity. Each has meaning for the full scope of the term both as applied to God and as extended to people.

1. *The holiness of God's exalted majesty*

Isaiah "saw the Lord seated on a throne, high and exalted" (Isa. 6:1). Implicit in biblical concepts of the divine is the sense of God's "otherness," His transcendence, His apartness from all He has created. God stands over against the world and human society as its Creator and Sovereign Lord. Man must always be willing to "let God be God."

In the human response to the divine there is the element of mystery and awe, a combination of dread and fascination.[35] The idea of the holy—a unique experience of the human spirit—points to a reality transcending that which is an object of scientific study.[36] Even as "our Father," God is "in heaven" (Matt. 6:9).

Yet God's transcendence is not the sole fact. He is also immanent. "The train of his robe filled the temple" (Isa. 6:1), so near one could almost reach out and touch it. In the words of J. W. Harvey, translator of Otto's *The Idea of the Holy,* God is not *wholly* "Wholly Other." The "high and lofty One" dwells "in a high and holy place, but *also* with him who is contrite and lowly in spirit" (Isa. 57:15, italics added).[37] Even "in heaven," God is "our Father" (Matt. 6:9).

There is therefore in God's holiness that blending of transcendence ("otherness") and immanence ("inwardness") which characterizes a true biblical theism. God is the transcendent Being who in the beginning "created the heavens and the earth" (Gen. 1:1). He is also the immanent Being who "upholds all things by the word of His power" (Heb. 1:3, NASB).

2. *The holiness of God's infinite radiance*

God is "the Lord seated on a throne, high and exalted," yet

---

35. Cf. Otto, *Idea of the Holy,* pp. 8-50 for a classic analysis.
36. Davidson, *Otto's Interpretation of Religion,* pp. 11-14.
37. Otto, *Idea of the Holy,* translator's preface, p. xviii.

"the whole earth is full of his glory" (Isa. 6:1, 3). Closely related to the exalted majesty of God is His glorious radiance. When the Lord appears to Moses, the sign of His presence is the fire that burns in but does not consume the desert bush (Exod. 3:2-6). God's presence on Sinai and in the Tabernacle and Temple is symbolized by fire (19:18; 40:34-38; 2 Chron. 7:1). "It is in fire that Yahweh manifests himself most characteristically" in passages "often directly related to holiness."[38]

The term "the radiance of God's glory" is used of Christ in Heb. 1:3, but it fairly describes the whole biblical idea of the glory of God. Its symbol is fire and light. God covers himself "in light as with a garment" (Ps. 104:2). His glory "shone around" the shepherd band when the birth of the Messiah was announced (Luke 2:9). He is "the blessed and only Sovereign, the King of kings and Lord of lords; who alone possesses immortality and dwells in unapproachable light" (1 Tim. 6:15-16, NASB).

The Lord is "the Father of the heavenly lights, who does not change like shifting shadows" (Jas. 1:17). He "is light; in him there is no darkness at all" (1 John 1:5) and His Incarnate Word is "the true light that gives light to every man" (John 1:9).

3. *The holiness of God's spotless purity*

Isaiah's response to the Temple vision was not chiefly the result of his sense of being finite in the presence of the Infinite. It was his sense of being sinful in the presence of divine purity. Procksch writes, "Most closely related materially to *qodesh* or holiness is the term *tohar* ('purity')."[39]

The purity implied in God's holiness is His ceaseless opposition to evil. His

> *eyes are too pure to look on evil;*
> *[He] cannot tolerate wrong* (Hab. 1:13).

It is God's total aversion to sin and unrighteousness that makes holiness practically synonymous with moral purity in later Old Testament writings and throughout the New Testament. O. R. Jones says, "Much is made of the contrast between holiness and impurity in the Old Testament. There, holiness is closely associated

---

38. IDB, 2:617.
39. TDNT, 1:89.

with cleanness and is taken to be incompatible with uncleanness. Indeed it often appears that holiness simply is cleanness. (Lev. 10:10; Gen. 8:20)." He cites John Calvin's remark (*Institutes* [Edinburgh: T. and T. Clark, 1949] 2:3): "When mention is made of our union with God, let us remember that holiness must be the bond . . . because it greatly concerns his glory not to have any fellowship with wickedness and impurity."[40]

C. In the New Testament

The holiness of God is a pervasive truth in the New Testament and includes the holiness of Father, Son, and Spirit. God's very name is hallowed (Matt. 6:9; Luke 11:2). Jesus addressed the Father as "Holy Father" (John 17:11). Peter echoes Leviticus with its affirmation of God's holiness in his call to his followers: "As obedient children, do not conform to the evil desires you had when you lived in ignorance. But just as he who called you is holy, so be holy in all you do; for it is written: 'Be holy, because I am holy'" (1 Pet. 1:14-16).

We have already noted that the Trisagion (the threefold affirmation of the holiness of God) in Isaiah is picked up by the living creatures in Rev. 4:8 who join with it ideas of God's omnipotence and eternity:

> Holy, holy, holy
> is the Lord God Almighty,
> who was, and is, and is to come.

The Book of Revelation concludes with a vision of the "Holy City, the new Jerusalem, coming down out of heaven from God" in which the Lord God is enthroned and where there is no need for the light of lamp or sun because the Lord himself is the Light (21:2; 22:5).

"The holiness of God the Father is everywhere presumed in the NT, though seldom stated. It is filled out in Jesus Christ as the *hagios tou Theou* ('the Holy One of God') and in the *pneuma hagion* ('the Holy Spirit')."[41] "The NT reaffirms the OT confession: 'The Lord our God is holy.'"[42]

---

40. *Concept of Holiness,* p. 100.
41. TDNT, 1:101.
42. IDB, 2:623.

Jesus Christ is specifically described as holy in the New Testament some nine times, and the idea of His holiness is constant throughout. Luke related the holiness of the Son of God to His miraculous conception by the Holy Spirit in the womb of the Virgin Mary: the angel Gabriel tells Mary that "the Holy Spirit will come upon you, and the power of the Most High will overshadow you. So the holy one to be born will be called the Son of God" (Luke 1:35).

Demons acknowledge the Son of God as the "Holy One of God" (Mark 1:24; Luke 4:34). Peter speaks for the disciples: "We believe and know that you are the Holy One of God" (John 6:69). He charges his people with having "disowned the Holy and Righteous One and asked that a murderer be released to you" (Acts 3:14). The Church in prayer spoke of the persecution and power of the Father's "holy servant Jesus" (4:27, 30), a clear reference to the Messianic Suffering Servant of Isaiah (Isa. 42:1; 61:1).

The illumination of believers by the Holy Spirit comes as the result of their "anointing from the Holy One" (1 John 2:20). Jesus introduces himself to the church in Philadelphia as the One who is "holy and true, who holds the key of David" (Rev. 3:7).

In all these passages, says Procksch, "*hagios* [holy] is used to describe the deity of Christ."[43]

An additional point is made in Heb. 2:11 (RSV, NASB) when Christ is said to be the One "who sanctifies" His brethren. He sanctifies His brethren by His sacrifice (10:10) in which He enters the holy of holies with His own blood and thus opens the way for those who follow Him (vv. 14-22). He who sanctifies others must himself be holy.

D. The Spirit of God

The Spirit of the Lord God had already been introduced in the Old Testament as the "Holy Spirit" (Ps. 51:11; Isa. 63:10-11). In the New Testament, this becomes His regular designation. While the phrases "Spirit of God," "Spirit of the Lord," "Spirit of Christ," "Spirit of his Son," and "the Spirit" are used, the designation "Holy Spirit" occurs a total of 93 times in the New Testament literature.

That the personality of the Holy Spirit should not have been stressed in the Old Testament ought to be no surprise. For Old

---

43. TDNT, 1:102.

Testament man, with the constant appeal of pagan idolatry around him, the emphasis must be on the unity of God. The Shema of Deut. 6:4-5 is the distilled essence of Old Testament theology: "Hear, O Israel: The Lord our God, the Lord is one. Love the Lord your God with all your heart and with all your soul and with all your strength."

It was with the coming of the Son as God incarnate and the teaching of the Son as to the promised Holy Spirit that the truth of God as Three in One could be made known. The Father is God, holy in all His being; the Son is God; the Spirit is God. The doctrine of the Trinity is not a theological abstraction; it is our attempt to put together the biblical data concerning the deity of Christ and the deity and personality of the Holy Spirit with the admitted unity of the Godhead. Father, Son, and Spirit are Three in person but one God in nature and substance—and that nature and substance is holy.

E. God's Essential Nature

In summary, it is fair to say that biblically defined, holiness is close to describing the very nature of God. It is "the sum of the attributes," the essence of Deity, the "godness of God." The uniqueness of God is "the uniqueness of his holiness."[44] Holiness is a theological category, a term we use in thinking and talking about God and therefore never completely definable. Our human response to the holiness of God is a sense of wide-eyed awe and wonder. We find ourselves in the presence of a "mysterium tremendum," to use Rudolf Otto's phrase.[45] God alone is holy in himself.

There is wide agreement at this point among biblical scholars. John Wesley wrote: "When God is termed holy, it denotes that excellence which is altogether peculiar to Himself; and the glory flowing from all His attributes conjoined, shining forth from all His works, and darkening all things beside itself."[46]

Hermann Schultz described holiness as "the perfect fulness of

---

44. IDB, 2:619.

45. *Idea of the Holy,* p. 26 and elsewhere.

46. *Explanatory Notes upon the New Testament* (1754; Naperville, Ill.: Alec R. Allenson, Inc., 1958 reprint), p. 957.

His Godhead."[47] Edmond Jacob writes, "Holiness is not one divine quality among others, even the chiefest, for it expresses what is characteristic of God and corresponds precisely to his deity."[48] Norman Snaith states that holiness for the Hebrews always indicated the distinguishing nature of God—His essential nature, His "Jehovahness," that which is "most intimately divine."[49]

Th. C. Vriezen writes, "The holiness of God is not only the central idea of the Old Testament faith in God, but also the continuous background to the message of love in the New Testament. In this respect the two are in complete agreement, and here the Christian faith is based on the revelation of God in the Old Testament."[50] And Peter T. Forsyth, whose thought was in so many ways ahead of his time, wrote:

> Everything begins and ends in our Christian theology with the holiness of God. This is the idea we have to get back into our current religious thinking. We have been living for the last two or three generations, our most progressive side has been living, upon the love of God, God's love to us, and it was very necessary that it should be appreciated. Justice had not been done to it. But we have now to take a step further, and we have to saturate our people in the years that are to come, as thoroughly with the idea of God's holiness, as they have been saturated with the idea of God's love.[51]

In his careful study of the concept of holiness, O. R. Jones surveys the biblical terms most often associated with holiness—fear (awe), power, love, wholeness, separatedness, and moral goodness—and notes how all converge at the idea of God. "So close is the kinship [between holiness and God] that one may say that holiness is the very essence of God, so that God is sometimes called 'holiness.'"[52] "God is holiness itself. To say that he is holy is not therefore to describe him but to emphasize that he is the one he is."[53]

47. *Old Testament Theology,* J. A. Paterson, 2 vols. (Edinburgh: T. and T. Clark, 1909), 2:167-77.

48. *Theology of the Old Testament* (New York: Harper and Brothers, 1958), p. 86.

49. *The Distinctive Ideas of the Old Testament* (Philadelphia: Westminster Press, 1946), pp. 100 f.

50. *An Outline of Old Testament Theology* (Boston: Charles T. Branford Co., 1958), p. 151.

51. *The Work of Christ* (London: Hodder and Stoughton, 1910), p. 78.

52. *Concept of Holiness,* p. 144.

53. Ibid., p. 146.

⌐s of persons is thus: "The
‚perates in this way becomes
what like God himself—a holy
‚ holiness is Godliness."[54]
⌐ses the phrase "God is love" (1 John
‚nt speaks of "the Holy One of Israel" (2
K.   ō:41; and frequently in Isaiah, such as 1:4).
This   ‚ly appropriate the designation of the God of
the Bit   ‚ch and by H. Orton Wiley as "the God of holy
love."[55]

IV. THE HOLINESS OF THINGS

Holiness is not only descriptive of what God is; it is also used extensively of both things and people. By extension, holiness is applied to whatever and whoever is separated, set apart, or devoted to Deity. In things and in people, holiness is always derivative. It expresses a relationship with God.

The first use of *q-d-sh* (holy, holiness) is in relation to the Sabbath: "Then God blessed the seventh day and sanctified it, because in it He rested from all His work which God had created and made" (Gen. 2:3, NASB). Thereafter it is frequently applied to seasons, places, and objects: the ground around the burning bush (Exod. 3:5), Mount Sinai (19:23), Aaron's garments and high priestly crown (28:2, 4; 29:6), the gifts of the people (28:38), offerings in the Tabernacle (29:27-28), the altar (v. 37), the Tabernacle itself (30:13), the perfume in the Tabernacle (v. 25), the laver (Lev. 8:11), the fruit of trees (19:24), houses (27:14), fields (vv. 17-19), the tithe (vv. 30, 32), the "holy war" (Deut. 20:1-9), the Temple (2 Chron. 29:5), the ark of the covenant (35:3), the gates, walls, and towers of Jerusalem (Neh. 3:1), special days (8:9-11), times of fasting (Joel 1:14; 2:15), etc.[56]

In the New Testament, *hagios* is applied to Jerusalem (Matt. 4:5), the Temple (24:15; Acts 6:13), the Scripture (Rom. 1:2), the

---

54. Ibid., p. 148.

55. *Christian Theology,* 3 vols. (Kansas City: Nazarene Publishing House, 1940), 1:387.

56. Only typical first references are given. Most of the references could be multiplied many times over.

kiss of salutation (16:16), and the Mount of Transfig
1:18). The Temple sanctifies the gold and the altar sanctifies
(Matt. 23:17-19).

In all these instances, the clear meaning is "separated, set off, or set apart for divine or religious purposes." That which is holy is to be distinguished from the secular or profane. In some sense, it has been devoted or consecrated to God. It must always be treated with respect. It may no longer, therefore, be regarded as other members of the same class are regarded.

These instances are sometimes lumped together and the kind of holiness exemplified is called ceremonial or cultic holiness. No suggestion of moral goodness or righteousness is involved, since moral goodness or righteousness can be referred only to creatures with powers of moral choice. Even so, the sacred is always special and ideas of physical cleanliness and aesthetic beauty are often included.

V. THE HOLINESS OF PERSONS

References to the holiness of persons fall into two major classes. They are difficult to define sharply and therefore difficult to name with precision. One is akin to the holiness of things in that it implies no idea of special moral qualification. It is often known as imputed or positional holiness. It is basically cultic or ceremonial: the priestly concept of holiness. The other class, becoming more important as the Old Testament revelation unfolds and clearly predominant in the New Testament, involves ideas of moral goodness or righteousness: the prophetic concept of holiness.[57]

It must be held firmly in mind that these two streams of meaning are often intertwined. At no stage in the development of biblical theology are they totally separated. However, in anticipation of evidence later to be considered, it may be said that the ceremonial or cultic strand of meaning tends to drop more and more into the background, while the prophetic concept comes more and more to the front until—in the New Testament—the moral and spiritual idea of the holy is preeminent.

---

57. Cf. the discussion in John Wick Bowman, *Prophetic Realism and the Gospel* (Philadelphia: Westminster Press, 1955), pp. 161-63; and Turner, *Vision Which Transforms*, p. 50.

A. Positional Holiness

There are approximately 70 references in the Old Testament to the holiness of people. In 50 of these instances, there is no thought of special moral qualification. The nation as a whole is sanctified or holy (Exod. 19:6). Priests as a class are holy (Lev. 21:1-6). The Nazarites are holy (Num. 6:5, 8). The king and his army may be referred to as holy, and the wars they fight are holy wars (Deut. 20:1-9).

A special instance of this class of reference is found in a few allusions to the temple prostitutes of pagan cults as "holy" (e.g., Deut. 23:17; 1 Kings 14:24; 15:12; 22:46; and 2 Kings 23:7).[58]

People therefore may be described as sanctified or holy in this sense without regard to their moral character. The priests were holy by office but were not necessarily of exemplary character. The nation itself was a holy nation and a holy people although many of the individual persons were idolatrous and disobedient.

"Sanctify" or "make holy" is often used in this sense with finite or human subjects. Moses sanctified the priests and the Tabernacle with its furnishings, and people were often told to sanctify themselves (for example, see Lev. 20:7, RSV, NASB).

Although the New Testament concept of holiness is almost entirely moral, Paul uses the term "sanctified" to describe the unbelieving husband or wife and children of a believer who resides in the home: "For the unbelieving husband has been sanctified through his wife, and the unbelieving wife has been sanctified through her believing husband. Otherwise your children would be unclean, but as it is, they are holy" (1 Cor. 7:14).

B. Moral Righteousness

That the holiness of persons in the Old Testament could have deep moral meaning is a position that will be considered more extensively in the pages that follow. At least 20 references to the holiness of persons in the Old Testament imply qualities of exemplary godliness or piety. The "moralization" of the idea of the holy follows from Israel's concept of the holiness of God and is the great

---

58. *Qadesh* is translated "sodomite" in this context by the KJV, "cult prostitute" (RSV), or "temple prostitute" (NASB), and applies to both male and female prostitutes of the fertility cults. These persons, "set apart" for pagan "worship," were off limits for Israel in an absolute sense.

achievement of the prophetic age from the eighth century B.C. on. The conclusion becomes inescapable that whatever belongs to God must be worthy of God.

Even in a cultic setting, this involved cleansing or purifying by ritual washing or sprinkling that which had been profaned by use or by contact with dirt or death.

The issue becomes more critical in relation to the holiness or sanctification of persons. It is to the eternal credit of the great prophets of the Old Testament that they so defined holiness as to make it virtually synonymous with righteousness, moral rectitude, and goodness. Righteousness in character and conduct becomes almost the equivalent of holiness in the prophetic writings. In a ceremonial context, "Be ye holy, for I am holy" could be understood as a call for ritual cleansing. But Mic. 6:8 puts God's requirement in a totally new light:

> *He has showed you, O man, what is good.*
> *And what does the Lord require of you?*
> *To act justly and to love mercy*
> *and to walk humbly with your God.*

It must always be remembered, however, that from the very beginning of Israel's covenant relationship with Yahweh, the demand upon the people was for righteous living as well as ritual performance. What is known as the "Book of the Covenant" (Exodus 20—23), which opens with the Ten Commandments, is replete with commandments requiring honesty, chastity, truthfulness, and honor in the relationships of the people with each other.

2

Holiness in the
Old Testament

No important biblical doctrine finds its complete expression in the Old Testament. On the other hand, no important biblical doctrine is without Old Testament foundations. We cannot read back into the Old Testament the full meaning of the New Testament. But we should never ignore the Old Testament basis of the Christian faith.

I. GENESIS

The biblical concept of holiness has its earliest expression in the very first book of the Bible. Genesis covers a stage in the religious history of mankind that might fairly be called the patriarchal period as related to the priestly and prophetic periods that follow. The early chapters of Genesis (specifically 1—11) have been subjected to searching critical analysis. But these chapters offer theological data of unequalled importance.[1]

---

1. Note the important article by Bernhard W. Anderson, "From Analysis to Synthesis," *Journal of Biblical Literature*, vol. 97, no. 1 (March, 1978), pp. 23-29. Anderson points out that while the 20th century has been concerned with the genetic development of biblical materials in source and form criticism, "a new generation of biblical scholars has arisen that wants to move beyond this kind of analysis to some kind of synthesis" (p. 25). Anderson comments, "One is compelled to agree that the proper starting-point methodologically is with the text as given, not with the reconstruction of the prehistory of the text which, as [J. P.] Fokkelman observes, is usually 'an unattainable ideal'" (p. 25). "The beginning and end of exegesis is the text itself—not something beyond it" (p. 26).

It is from this portion of the Word of God that we learn of the distinctive nature of the human race, the origins and enduring effects of sin, and the earliest intimations of the God of Abraham, Isaac, and Jacob who acts in redemptive grace towards a rebellious people. George A. F. Knight comments:

> The first chapters of Genesis do not relate a series of early cosmogonic myths now spiritualized, and made to subserve an early history of the origin of the world. These chapters are a theological exposition, in picture language, such as the Hebrews have always excelled in creating, of the reason for the call of Israel out of Egypt at a historical moment occurring within this very flesh and blood world of space and time. . . . It is with the moral purpose of God that the OT is deeply concerned, and with God's relation to that humanity whom he had, indeed, created.[2]

The Genesis account, therefore, belongs not "to the sphere of natural science but to the history of man."[3]

A. Genesis 1—2

The creation accounts of Genesis 1 and 2 lay the foundation for the biblical concept of "the creature of God's saving concern."[4] The term reserved in the Old Testament for the immediate creative act of God (*bara*, create) is used seven times in these chapters: twice in reference to "the heavens and the earth" (Gen. 1:1; 2:4); once in reference to "every living and moving thing" (Gen. 1:21, conscious life); three times in reference to the human species:

> So God created man in his own image,
> in the image of God he created him;
> male and female he created them (Gen. 1:27)

and once in a summary of the whole of creation (Gen. 2:4).

The key word in 1:27 is quite clearly the term "image" *(tselem).* That which most drastically distinguishes human beings from the animal species is the *imago dei,* the "image of God" (Gen. 1:26-27;

---

2. *A Christian Theology of the Old Testament* (Richmond, Va.: John Knox Press, 1959), p. 109. Used by permission.

3. Ludwig Köhler, *Old Testament Theology* (Philadelphia: Westminster Press, 1957), p. 87.

4. Cf. W. T. Purkiser, Richard S. Taylor, and Willard H. Taylor, *God, Man, and Salvation: A Biblical Theology* (Kansas City: Beacon Hill Press of Kansas City, 1977), pp. 251-302.

cf. 9:6). Long debated as to meaning, the reference seems clearly to the distinctive dignity of human beings, standing before God in an "I-Thou" relationship, and representing God in dominion over the remainder of creation (Gen. 1:28).[5] Included are ideas of reason, moral self-consciousness and self-direction (freedom), imagination, and at least a limited creativity. Cuthbert A. Simpson writes:

> The *image* included likeness . . . in spiritual powers—the power of thought, the power of communication, the power of self-transcendence. No doubt these concepts remained to some extent inarticulate in the author's mind; nevertheless they were there. He was trying to state in concrete terms—the only terms with which he, being a Semite, was familiar—what could only be stated, however inadequately, in abstract terms.[6]

In the more detailed account of man's creation in Genesis 2, a key verse occurs: "And the Lord God formed man from the dust of the ground and breathed into his nostrils the breath of life, and man became a living being" (v. 7). Man is seen as a creature of two worlds. He lives at the intersection of the divine and the earthly, the eternal and the temporal. Physically and biologically, he is "dust from the ground." Personally and psychologically, there is in him "the breath of life" breathed into him by the Lord God, so that he is a "living soul" (KJV, NIV).

In the picture language so characteristic of this portion of the Old Testament, human innocence and harmony with God is described. God speaks to Adam and Eve directly (Gen. 1:28-30; 2:16-17; 3:9 ff.). He gives them access to all the trees of the Garden of Eden for food except "the tree of the knowledge of good and evil" (2:9, 17). There is at least the implication of daily fellowship with the Creator (3:8-9).

The image of God is therefore moral (innocence, holiness, communion with the Creator) and natural (intellect, imagination, moral and psychological self-direction, immortality). The idea of the divine image, as William Temple points out, implies both likeness to God and disparity:

> In so far as God and man are spiritual they are of one kind;
> in so far as God and man are rational, they are of one kind. But

---

5. Cf. Norman W. Porteous, IDB, 2:682-85.

6. "Genesis" (Exeg.), *The Interpreter's Bible,* ed. George Arthur Buttrick, et al. (New York: Abingdon Press, 1952), 1:485—hereafter abbreviated IB.

in so far as God creates, redeems and sanctifies while man is created, redeemed and sanctified, they are of two kinds. God is not creature; man is not creator. God is not redeemed sinner; man is not redeemer from sin. At this point the Otherness is complete.[7]

It is this spiritual kinship with God, issuing in a real fellowship with Him, that lies behind the idea of the divine image. Man is never confused with God in the Bible. Scripture never speaks of "the divinity of man." J. N. Schofield remarks that "man is 'theomorphic,' like God, rather than God 'anthropomorphic,' like man. Mankind was made like God to exercise his authority over all created beings."[8]

In view of the confusion that sometimes arises, it is important to state that the resemblance between God and man is not thought of in physical terms. God's self-revelation is channeled through human beings and that revelation is always spiritual. "The essence of the divine revelation was always in the intangible realm of the spirit."[9]

B. The Fall, Genesis 3

The idyllic state of affairs described in Genesis 2 was not to continue. Genesis 3 introduces the widely pervasive biblical theme of human sin and its consequences. The importance of this theme can scarcely be overstated. Hence such statements as: "Genesis 3 is one of the most profound understandings of the human predicament ever penned";[10] and "This chapter is the pivot on which the whole Bible turns."[11]

"The story of the Fall must also be appreciated for its psychological perceptiveness and theological profundity," says Simon J. De Vries. ". . . The Paradise narrative helps us to understand the real nature of sin. Sin is possible only because man has been

---

7. *Nature, Man, and God* (London: Macmillan & Co., 1st ed., 1934), p. 396.

8. *Introducing Old Testament Theology* (Naperville, Ill.: SCM Book Club, 1964), p. 29.

9. H. H. Rowley, *The Faith of Israel: Aspects of Old Testament Thought* (Philadelphia: Westminster Press, 1956), pp. 83-84.

10. Arnold B. Rhodes, "The Message of the Bible," *The Layman's Bible Commentary,* ed. Balmer H. Kelly (Richmond, Va.: John Knox Press, 1959), 1:76—hereafter abbreviated LBC.

11. W. H. Griffith Thomas, *Through the Pentateuch Chapter by Chapter* (Grand Rapids: William B. Eerdmans Publishing Co., 1937), in loc.

created in God's image. He has a freedom of self-assertion which is his divine endowment. Sin comes when man uses this freedom to measure himself against God, trying to be independent of his control."[12]

H. Orton Wiley calls for recognition of the balance between fact and symbolism in Genesis 3:

> Without doubt this historical account of the fall contains a large element of symbolism. Conditions in the paradisiacal history of man were characterized by a degree of uniqueness which was probably more fully understood by our first parents than by us. Such facts as the enclosed garden, the sacramental tree of life, the mystical tree of knowledge, the one positive command representing the whole law, the serpent form of the tempter, the flaming defenses of forfeited Eden—all were emblems possessing deep spiritual significance as well as facts. In defending the historical character of the Mosaic account of the fall, we must not fail to do justice to its rich symbolism.[13]

1. *Sin as Intrusion*

Here sin is seen to be an intrusion in human life and nature. It is no part of human nature as created and as intended to be. This passage, as well as the New Testament affirmation of the Incarnation, directly counters all views of sin as the product of human finiteness or as essentially related to the physical body. Adam and Eve did not become fully human by disobedience to God. If anything, they became less than humanity was meant to be. The concept of the Incarnate Son of God in the New Testament—"holy, blameless, pure" (Heb. 7:26), yet fully human (1 Tim. 2:5)—seconds the teaching of Genesis 3 that sin is no essential part of human experience.

Here also temptation is seen to come through desires which in themselves may be innocent. It has been alleged that persons with pure hearts would be beyond the reach of temptation because sin would find nothing in them to latch on to. That such is not the case is clearly implied in the temptation and fall of persons created without the taint of inner sin. Rather, "Each person is tempted when he is lured and enticed by his own desire." Only when "desire . . . has conceived" (by impregnation with the consent of the will) does it give "birth to sin; and sin when it is full-grown brings forth death" (Jas. 1:14-15, RSV).

---

12. Simon J. De Vries, "The Fall," IDB, 2:236-37.

13. *Christian Theology,* 2:162.

2. *Sin as Choice*

We are given a clue here as to the biblical concept of sin as choice or act. The issue placed before Adam and Eve was clear and unambiguous: "You must not eat from the tree of the knowledge of good and evil, for when you eat of it you will surely die" (Gen. 2:17). All the other trees of the Garden were available. Only one was off limits. Sin in this instance and characteristically throughout Scripture as a whole is not a question of finiteness or of unavoidable failure. It is a question of disobedience, of rebellion against God, of an effort to "be like God" (3:5) and therefore independent of God. As James Orr is reported to have said, "Sin, in the Biblical view, consists in the revolt of the creature's will from its rightful allegiance to the sovereign will of God and the setting up of a false independence, the substitution of a life-for-self for life-for-God."[14]

3. *Sin as Condition*

The act of disobedience, of falsely claimed self-sovereignty, brought estrangement and alienation from God. As they never had done before, Adam and Eve hid themselves from the Presence in the Garden. Still able to hear the voice of God—although now in fear rather than joy—Adam and Eve forfeited the relationship for which they had been created and were driven out of the Garden with its access to the tree of life. Physical death was to follow (Gen. 3:19), but the warning of 2:17, "In the day that you eat from it you shall surely die" (NASB), came to pass in that estrangement from God which Scripture knows as spiritual death (Eph. 2:1, 5; Col. 2:13).

The sin that brought "deprivity" of the holiness in which man was created resulted in depravity for Adam's descendents. It is the New Testament that tells us most specifically of the radical effects of the first sin (specifically, Rom. 5:12-21); yet there is a hint of it in the statement of Gen. 5:3 that Adam "had a son in his own likeness, in his own image." The image was still God's image (v. 1), but it was also Adam's image, without the sanctifying relationship with the Creator, deprived and therefore depraved as a branch cut off

---

14. Quoted without indication of source in A. S. Wilson, *Concerning Perplexities, Paradoxes, and Perils in the Spirit-led Life* (London: Marshall, Morgan, and Scott, 1935), p. 85.

from the vine is corrupt not by the addition of something but by the loss of something (John 15:6).

A full doctrine of what theologians call original sin must depend on other items of biblical evidence which will be considered at some length in the volume on theological foundations. Here it is sufficient to note that Adam's descendents inherited the image of God but an image marred and corrupted as the result of a loss of the relationship with his Creator that Adam had enjoyed before his disobedience.

C. Genesis 4—11

The result was that for Cain, sin (Heb., *chattath*—the first use of a specific term for sin in the Bible) is pictured as "crouching at your door" (Gen. 4:7). The converse of Cain's susceptibility to sin is seen in Enoch (5:22-24). Twice Enoch is said to have "walked with God." "The expression 'walked with God' denotes a devout life, lived in close communion with God."[15] The words "God took him away" are interpreted in Heb. 11:5 as being "removed from this world without experiencing death."[16]

Consideration of the nature and consequences of sin is picked up again in Gen. 6:5. Man's universal evil is attributed to the fact that "every inclination of the thoughts of his heart was only evil all the time." Again in Gen. 8:21, "Every inclination of his heart is evil from childhood."

The term translated "inclination" (NEB, NIV) is *yetser.* It is also translated "bent" (Moffatt) and "intent" (NASB). Its meaning is "to form, frame"; it stands for "purpose or impulse." It comes from a root meaning "to press, squeeze, mould, or determine." It is used in the sense of purpose, mind, or work. Propensity, tendency, impulse direction, movement, or motivation come close to its meaning.

"Imagination" as used for *yetser* in the KJV is apt to be misleading for us. As Lawrence Toombs notes, "The Hebrew word translated 'imagination' has overtones of deliberate planning, and the Yahwist's damning sentence may be paraphrased, 'The designs

---

15. A. C. Grant, "Enoch," in *The International Standard Bible Encyclopedia,* James Orr, ed. (1915; reprint ed., Wilmington, Del.: Associated Publishers and Authors, n.d.), 2:953—hereafter abbreviated ISBE.

16. William Barclay, *The New Testament: A New Translation* (London: Collins, 1969), 2:188.

and schemes made by men in the private deliberations of their own inner lives always and everywhere ran counter to the intention of God.'"[17] In this context, it is in fact the deep-rooted tendency to evil in the human heart.

Although *yetser* is seldom used in the sense of the evil tendency besides in Gen. 6:5 and 8:21 (cf. Deut. 31:21; 1 Chron. 28:9; 29:18; Isa. 26:3, as other instances), it became very important in later Jewish thought as an explanation of the presence of moral evil in God's creation: "Sin is the result of man's fixing his imagination on himself, or on some other person or thing short of God."[18]

It is important to note also that the prohibition of murder issued after the Flood in God's covenant with Noah is based upon the fact that the "image of God" while marred or corrupted is not destroyed:

> Whoever sheds the blood of man,
>   by man shall his blood be shed;
> for in the image of God
>   has God made man (Gen. 9:6).

D. Genesis 12—50

With the call of Abraham (Gen. 12:1-3), the Bible begins a new chapter in the history of human sin and redemption. Abraham, "father of the faithful," is a watershed figure in Old Testament thought. The true God was repeatedly known as "the God of Abraham" or in conjunction with his son and grandson, "the God of Abraham, Isaac, and Jacob." God's call to Abraham was a call to faith: to leave his ancestral home, to go out to a land that God would show him, with the promise of blessing for himself and that in him "all peoples on earth will be blessed" (v. 3).

1. *Abraham as Blameless*

Twenty-four years later, God again appeared to Abraham. This time the injunction was "Walk before me and be blameless" (Gen. 17:1). As was Noah before him (6:9), Abraham is to be "perfect in his generations" (KJV). "In an earlier time, Enoch had illustrated the first part of the commandment ['Walk before me'] by

---

17. *The Old Testament in Christian Preaching* (Philadelphia: Westminster Press, 1961), pp. 91-92.
18. IB, 1:538.

living a life fully obedient and acceptable (Gen. 5:24). Noah also had been designated as **perfect** (see 6:9), meaning that he was a man of one will, a man of integrity. Abram was to be like these men of God."[19]

The Hebrew term translated "perfect, blameless" means "without blemish, complete, full, sincere, sound, whole." George Allen Turner writes:

> All told there are 6 synonyms formed from one Hebrew root (TM) and they are found at least 204 times in the Old Testament. In some fifty-eight of these instances they denote men who are called "perfect," "mature," "wholesome," "sincere," "blameless." The terms connote perfection, completion, uprightness. They emphasize the importance of spiritual wholeness in the man of God.[20]

A second Old Testament word commonly translated "perfect" is *shalem*, "whole, entire, perfect, healthy, full of strength, peace, prosperity." It is often used to describe a "perfect" (KJV), "wholly true" (RSV), "fully committed" heart (1 Kings 8:61; cf. 11:4; 15:3; etc.).

J. G. S. S. Thomson summarizes the total Old Testament evidence, noting that of a total of 230 occurrences of synonyms for perfection, 72 refer to man's character or nature. He writes concerning Gen. 17:1,

> "Perfect" means ethically blameless, and denotes integrity. And the phrase, "walk before me" means "live consciously in my presence." This suggests progress in ethical conduct consistent with a progressive awareness of God's presence. The aspiration is to be well pleasing unto God in whose presence one is constantly walking.[21]

The idea of perfection is found not only in the Old Testament; it also carries over into the New Testament and the Christian doctrine of salvation. It has a long and continuous history in Christian thought. We need, however, the caution of H. W. Perkins:

> *We are discussing, it cannot be too emphatically said, not the production of a perfect man, but union with the perfection of God.* The strong ethical bent of the prophets made them insist on holiness and righteousness as marks of His Perfection. . . .

---

19. George Herbert Livingston, "Genesis," *Beacon Bible Commentary* (Kansas City: Beacon Hill Press of Kansas City, 1969), 1:78—hereafter abbreviated BBC.

20. *Vision Which Transforms*, p. 44.

21. *The Old Testament View of Revelation* (Grand Rapids: William B. Eerdmans Publishing Co., 1960), p. 54.

The perfection towards which man ought to strive was regarded as derivative. It came from walking with God, and could only be retained by a ceaseless communication of His Spirit. It was ethical rather than ceremonial, and in the highest and best, in Deuteronomy and Leviticus and the Testaments, it attained the expression of love towards God and man, on which Jesus has set His seal.[22]

J. Baines Atkinson summarizes what he calls the "three abiding messages" about perfection in the Old Testament:

"The first truth is that perfection is a relative moral condition and not an absolute condition. Gen. 6:9; Isa. 18:5." It is, he says, the perfection of a bud, not that of flower or fruit.

"The second truth is that perfection is a condition of the heart in relation to God. Deut. 18:9-12; Psalms 18:21-23; 101:2; 119:80; 2 Chron. 25:2; Phil. 3:9; 1 Kings 15:3, 14; 1 Chron. 28:9."

"The third truth about perfection in the Old Testament is that the word is sometimes linked with walking. Gen. 17:1; Psa. 15:1-2 (uprightly is *tamim*); 84:11; 2 Kings 20:3; Gen. 6:9. Cf. 1 Jn. 1:7."[23]

2. Job—a Parenthesis

Job belongs to the patriarchal period as far as the religious life is concerned. He is said to be a "blameless [KJV, perfect] and upright" man, who "feared God and shunned evil" (Job 1:1; cf. 1:8; 2:3). While the Book of Job stands in the Old Testament as a classic criticism of the easy orthodoxy that equated righteousness with prosperity, it is also a lesson in piety. It shows that one may be blameless or perfect before God and suffer the loss of property and loved ones; be sorely afflicted physically; be misunderstood and misjudged by others—accused of hypocrisy and sin; be confused in mind, depressed in spirit, sustained only by hope in God—"Though he slay me, yet will I hope in him" (13:15); and have but limited light—"Surely I spoke of things I did not understand, things too wonderful for me to know" (42:3). Turner writes:

Seen in this perspective the Book of Job, in addition to being great poetry concerning the problem of unjust suffering, is a treatise on perfection. In this book one meets the most emphatic claims of perfection and the most categorical denials of its possibility among men. In both prose and poetic sections Job is presented as "pious and upright" (literally, perfect and

---

22. *The Doctrine of Christian or Evangelical Perfection* (London: Epworth Press, 1927), pp. 52-53, italics in the original.

23. *The Beauty of Holiness* (London: Epworth Press, 1953), pp. 63-66.

straight), "God-fearing and removed from evil." This claim, which in the prose sections is admitted with reservations by Satan, is vigorously denied by Job's "friends."[24]

3. *Jacob and Joseph*

As with Abraham, the life of Jacob reveals a two-stage development in the experience of God. Jacob's first recorded encounter with the divine was at Bethel (Gen. 28:10-22). Here, a fugitive from the wrath of his betrayed brother Esau, Jacob met "the Lord, the God of [his] father Abraham and the God of Isaac" (v. 13). Here he received the promise previously given to Abraham (v. 14; 12:3), and here he vowed to serve the Lord as his God and to give a tithe of all God would give him.

Then 20 years later, homeward bound with his family and possessions (Gen. 32:24-32), Jacob wrestled with the angel who actualized for him the presence of God (v. 30; 35:9-13; and Hos. 12:3-4). His name Jacob ("heel-grasper," 25:26; "supplanter"— 27:36, KJV) is changed to Israel—"because you have struggled with God and with men and have overcome" (v. 28).

Joseph (Gen. 37:2-36; 39:1—50:26) has often been regarded as the highest example of a holy life, an embodiment of the truest piety of the patriarchal period. He is one of the very few Old Testament characters about whom no evil is told. His life and conduct bear a remarkable resemblance to that of Jesus, whose life is the ultimate standard of holy living. Joseph was persecuted, betrayed by his own brothers, sold for the price of a slave; yet was triumphant in temptation, forgiving in spirit, providing even for those who had wronged him.

II. EXODUS TO DEUTERONOMY

The Exodus—Leviticus—Numbers sequence of books introduces what we have seen as the "priestly" concept of holiness.[25] This is the "Temple" concept as contrasted with the prophetic or "synagogue" ideal. The priestly idea of holiness is largely positional, cultic or ceremonial. It emphasizes the meaning of holiness as "set apart, separated, dedicated." While ethical and spiritual

---

24. *Vision Which Transforms*, p. 46.

25. E.g., John Wick Bowman, *Prophetic Realism and the Gospel*, pp. 161-63. This in no sense implies a documentary interpretation of Old Testament literature.

ideas are never completely absent, the major stress is on ceremonial cleanness.

A. Exodus

Exodus is in many ways a key book in the Old Testament, comparable to the Gospels in the New Testament.[26] It is "the book of redemption."[27] It opens with the deliverance of the Israelites from Egyptian bondage, an event which became the heart and core of Israel's faith. It relates the establishment of the covenant on Sinai and its supporting Tabernacle cultus. God who is "majestic in holiness, awesome in glory, working wonders" (Exod. 15:11) requires that those He has delivered from death be sanctified (13:2, NASB) and in His covenant makes the people His "treasured possession" out of "all nations . . . a kingdom of priests and a holy nation" (19:5-6; cf. 22:31).

1. *The Exodus*

The event of the Exodus itself is of unparalleled importance in the Old Testament. H. H. Rowley sees in it the unifying core of the entire Bible inasmuch as the New Testament describes a "New Exodus" under Christ our Passover.[28] G. Ernest Wright sees it as the "center of Israel's faith" and a "supreme act of divine love and grace." It becomes the central affirmation in Israel's confessions of faith: the God of Israel is the Lord "who brought you out of Egypt, out of the land of slavery" (Exod. 20:2). "What more was needed to identify or to describe God than that? His complete control over nature and man is adequately implied in the statement; his purposive action in history in fighting the injustice of the strong and making even their sin to serve and praise him is also directly implied; so also is his redemptive love, which saves and uses the weak of the world to accomplish his purpose even among the strong."[29]

---

26. J. Coert Rylaarsdam, "The Book of Exodus: Introduction," IB, 1:846.

27. J. C. Connell, "Exodus," *The New Bible Commentary,* ed. Francis Davidson (Grand Rapids: William B. Eerdmans Publishing Co., 1956), p. 106, hereafter abbreviated NBC.

28. This is the theme of *The Unity of the Bible* (Philadelphia: Westminster Press, 1953).

29. G. Ernest Wright and Reginald H. Fuller, *The Book of the Acts of God* (New York: Doubleday and Co., 1957), p. 77.

The Exodus was brought about as a consequence of the events surrounding the first Passover, from which the annual Jewish festival gets its name. By the shedding and sprinkling of the blood of a lamb, the firstborn of Israel were delivered from the death that overcame the Egyptian households (Exodus 12).

2. *Consecration*

The result was that those who were redeemed were required to be "sanctified": "Sanctify [NIV, consecrate] to Me every firstborn, the first offspring of every womb among the sons of Israel, both of man and beast; it belongs to Me" (Exod. 13:2, NASB). This act of sanctifying was one of separation or consecration: "You are to give over to the Lord the first offspring of every womb. All the firstborn males of your livestock belong to the Lord" (v. 12). As Leo G. Cox writes, "To **sanctify** as used here, and often throughout the OT, has the meaning of consecrating or setting apart for special divine ownership, as compared with the NT meaning, which includes moral purity (Eph. 5:25-27; Heb. 9:13-14). **Sanctify** in this broader OT sense is used of both persons and things."[30]

The sanctification or consecration of the firstborn was the basis for the separation of the tribe of Levi as the priestly tribe of Israel (Num. 3:41). Thus while the nation as a whole was a holy nation (Exod. 19:5-6), the Levites were holy in a special sense as representatives of those whose lives had been redeemed by the blood of the passover lamb.

The concept of holiness in Exodus—Leviticus is taught through the ritual and ceremony of the Old Testament cult.[31] The major idea was not that of the immanence or nearness of God but of His majestic transcendence.[32] Holiness is separation from the secular and profane. It is that which related directly to the worship of God and to maintaining Israel's covenant relationship with God. "The essence of the covenant is the promise of God, backed by the gift of deliverance already given, that Israel will be his special possession and instrument. . . . [a] promise [that] depends on the faithfulness and obedience of Israel."[33]

---

30. "The Book of Exodus," BBC, 1:215.

31. *Cult* is here used not in the prejudicial popular sense but in the technical sense of a prescribed mode of worship.

32. Rylaarsdam, IB, 1:845.

33. Ibid., p. 841.

The Decalogue (Ten Commandments) and the Covenant Code (Exod. 20:1—23:33) illustrate the commingling of the ceremonial and ethical that is characteristic of this period. Both moral and cultic injunctions are given. While there are undoubtedly elements in the law and the covenant which are to be taken collectively, many of the prescriptions given are directly concerned with individual responsibility and action. The Ten Commandments, particularly, stand forever as the nonnegotiable norm of biblical ethics and the divine standard for holy living.

Exod. 31:13 introduces an incidental but impressive point obscured in our English translations. The Lord identifies himself as "the Lord who sanctifies"—"who makes you holy" *(Yahweh meqqaddishkem).*[34] This compound name occurs seven times in the Holiness Code in Leviticus (20:8; 21:8, 15, 23; 22:9, 16, 32) and once in Ezek. 20:12.

B. Leviticus

The Book of Leviticus is baffling to many modern Christian readers. It deals largely with details of worship in Tabernacle and Temple. Much of it pertains to that aspect of Old Testament regulation to which Christ has put an end (Rom. 10:4). Yet it is part of God's revelation and may not be dismissed out of hand as irrelevant. Nathaniel Micklem has pointed out that the main divisions of Leviticus may be summarized under topics always relevant to the Christian: worship (1:1—7:38); the ministry (8:1—10:20); the dedication of national life—laws of purification (11:1—15:33); the atonement (16:1-34); and the Holiness Code (17:1—26:46).[35] "Leviticus is thus a manual of worship."[36]

The laws of sacrifice themselves are given to "distinguish between the holy and the profane, between the unclean and the clean" (10:10). That cleansing is necessary for acceptance with a holy God is an age-long lesson the Church must never forget.

The object of the cult is itself to constitute a "holy people." What is called the Holiness Code constitutes the largest single division in the Book of Leviticus (17:1—26:46). This important

---

34. Cf. John H. J. Barker, *This Is the Will of God* (London: Epworth Press, 1956), p. 21; and Nathaniel Micklem, IB, 2:86.

35. IB, 2:9.

36. BBC, 1:320.

section is a mixture of cultic and ethical regulations. Micklem comments:

> At first sight the Holiness Code appears to consist of a jumble of heterogeneous elements. Thus it treats of the blood of slain beasts, of sexual ethics, of general morality, of regulations about haircutting, of rules connected with fruit trees, of wizards, and the duty owed to parents, of the ecclesiastical calendar, of oil for lamps, and blasphemy, of sabbaths, and the year of jubilee, and the treatment of servants, of idolatry, of divine promises and threats. But all these different elements adhere in the conception of a holy people in a holy land, the servants of a holy God: **Consecrate yourselves therefore, and be holy; for I am the Lord your God** (20:7).[37]

The motivation to holiness constantly held before the people is the holiness of God (Lev. 11:44; 19:2; 20:26; 21:8; cf. 1 Pet. 1:15-16). "Speak to the entire assembly of Israel and say to them: 'Be holy because I, the Lord your God, am holy'" (19:2). "'You shall consecrate [sanctify, KJV] yourselves therefore and be holy, for I am the Lord your God. And you shall keep My statutes and practice them; I am the Lord who sanctifies you'" (20:7-8, NASB). "'You are to be holy to me, because I, the Lord, am holy, and I have set you apart from the nations to be my own'" (v. 26). Here the thought is mainly that of separation, a distinctive relationship with God, a ceremonial holiness. But the number of moral and ethical principles included in the Holiness Code makes it impossible to exclude the deeper ideas of righteousness that later in Scripture came to be almost exclusively characteristic of holiness. That Peter could use 19:2 as the basis for holiness "in all you do" (1 Pet. 1:15) foreshadows the moral purity so essential to the full biblical idea of holiness in persons.

J. Baines Atkinson quotes the late chief rabbi, Dr. Hertz, on Leviticus 19:

> Holiness is thus not so much an abstract or a mystic idea, as a regulative principle in the everyday lives of men and women. The words "ye shall be holy" are the keynote of the whole chapter. . . . Holiness is thus attained, not by flight from the world, nor by monk-like renunciation of human relationships of family and station, but by the spirit in which we fulfill the obligations of life in its simplest and commonest details; in

---

37. IB, 2:87. Cf. Thomas, *Through the Pentateuch,* p. 108: "The keynote of the book is 'holiness,' in its primary meaning of separation, which includes separation *from* evil and separation *to* God."

this way—by doing justly, loving mercy, and walking humbly with our God—is everyday life transfigured.[38]

Another Jewish commentator, S. R. Hirsch, reflecting on the words "For I am holy," is quoted as saying:

> This constitutes the basis of your duty to sanctify yourselves, as well as the guarantee of your capacity to attain sanctification of life. Holiness is the very essence of the Divine Being; and in breathing His Spirit into you, He made you the partaker of His Divine nature, and endowed you with the power to attain to holiness. "Because I am holy, you shall be holy, and you can be holy."

Atkinson adds, "You could almost think Wesley was speaking there."[39]

C. Deuteronomy

In Deuteronomy we find the beginnings of a truly prophetic emphasis in regard to man's relationship to God in general and holiness in particular. There is a transition here to an increasing emphasis on the heart and its love and loyalty as necessary for the validity of the cultic sacrifices. "Here more than any other book in the Pentateuch, God declares His love for His people (7:13; 10:15; 23:5) and His desire for theirs (6:5; 30:6)."[40]

G. Ernest Wright points out that despite its name ("the second law") Deuteronomy is not primarily a book of regulations for the outer life. "It is a preaching, a proclamation and exposition of the faith of the nation, which includes the law as the expression of the will of God which must be obeyed, but which in itself is not primarily a law. It is a gospel of the redeeming God who has saved a people from slavery and has bound them to himself in a covenant."[41]

1. God's Special Possession

Israel's response to God's guidance is to be based on the fact that God has separated her from all other people to be His special possession: "For you are a people holy to the Lord your God. The Lord your God has chosen you out of all the peoples on the face of

---

38. *Beauty of Holiness,* p. 95.
39. Ibid.
40. BBC, 1:507.
41. IB, 2:312.

the earth to be his people, his treasured possession" (7:6). **"Holy,"** says G. Ernest Wright, "is used here in a derivative sense. Properly, holiness is a special attribute of God which distinguishes him as God from everything in creation. However, God chooses to confer holiness on special objects and people who are separated, yet related to him in a way that others are not."[42] "A people for His own possession" translates a word (*segullah;* KJV, peculiar) that "has applied to a possession which belonged particularly to an individual, as his very own, distinguished from the general family inheritance."[43]

The same thought is echoed in 14:2: "For you are a people holy to the Lord your God. Out of all the peoples on the face of the earth, the Lord has chosen you to be his treasured possession" (cf. v. 21 and 26:19). Although Israel's special status could not be earned, it could be forfeited. It must be maintained by obedience and communion with God: "The Lord will establish you as his holy people, as he promised you on oath, if you keep the commands of the Lord your God and walk in his ways" (28:9).

2. *Love in Deuteronomy*

Deuteronomy gives the famous Shema (from the Hebrew of the first word, "Hear") traditionally recited twice a day by devout Jews: "Hear, O Israel: The Lord our God, the Lord is one. Love the Lord your God with all your heart and with all your soul and with all your strength" (6:4-5). Jesus cited these words as the first and great commandment, adding mind to heart and soul (implied in the Hebrew) and joining as the second commandment a quotation from Lev. 19:18, "Love your neighbor as yourself" (Mark 12:29-31).

Jack Ford and Alex Deasley point out that "the essence of holiness is love." "The *Shema,*" they say, "sums up the supreme duty of man in such terms. God loves His people and seeks their love. He desires them to serve Him with joy. He will make possible this love by removing all that hinders it, so that we may love the Lord with all our hearts (30:6)."[44]

Wright claims that by use of the term "love," Deuteronomy avoids the legalism of obedience based on necessity and duty. Love

---

42. Ibid., p. 380.
43. NBC, p. 206.
44. BBC, 1:508.

becomes the root of all obedience. Deuteronomy is the first to use love as the primary attitude people should have toward God. "Our relationship to God is thus expressed by the most intimate and warm of all human emotions." One must not sentimentalize Deuteronomy here, however. "Man cannot love God as he loves another human being. Love of God involves a holy fear or reverence (v. 13), and it expresses itself in that devoted and single-minded loyalty which issues in wholehearted and obedient service. The love of God without obedience is not love (cf. 1 John 4:7-21)."[45]

The key importance of this Deuteronomic concept of love will be seen in the emphasis on love in the New Testament. One of John Wesley's most characteristic definitions of holiness was "loving God with all the heart, soul, mind, and strength; and one's neighbor as oneself" and Dr. Mildred Wynkoop justly remarks that "love is the essential inner character of holiness, and holiness does not exist apart from love. That is how close they are, and in a certain sense they can be said to be the same thing. At least Wesley consistently defined holiness, as well as perfection, as love."[46]

3. *Circumcision of the Heart*

Another emphasis in Deuteronomy closely related to that of love is the concept of "circumcision of the heart": "Circumcise your hearts . . . and do not be stiff-necked any longer" (10:16); "The Lord your God will circumcise your hearts and the hearts of your descendants, so that you may love him with all your heart and with all your soul, and live" (30:6). Echoed by Jeremiah—

> *Circumcise yourselves to the Lord,*
> *circumcise your hearts* (4:4)—

this thought is picked up by Paul and applied to the Christian life: "A man is a Jew if he is one inwardly; and circumcision is circumcision of the heart, by the Spirit, not by the written code" (Rom. 2:29); "It is we who are the circumcision, we who worship by the Spirit of God, who glory in Christ Jesus, and who put no confidence in the flesh" (Phil. 3:3); and "You have been given fullness in Christ, who is the head over every power and authority. In him

---

45. IB, 2:373.

46. *A Theology of Love* (Kansas City: Beacon Hill Press of Kansas City, 1972), p. 24.

you were also circumcised, in the putting off of the sinful nature, not with a circumcision done by the hands of men but with the circumcision done by Christ, having been buried with him in baptism and raised with him through your faith in the power of God, who raised him from the dead" (Col. 2:10-12).

The contrary condition is "the uncircumcised heart" (Lev. 26:41; Jer. 9:26). "Uncircumcised lips" (Exod. 6:12, 30, NASB, marg.) and the "uncircumcised ear" (Jer. 6:10, marg.) are also mentioned. "To circumcise" is thus a metaphor used to describe the removal of something regarded as detrimental or a hindrance—"the sign of an internal change, effected by God."[47] In the full New Testament context, what is removed is "the body of the flesh" (NASB) or "the sinful nature" (Col. 2:11)—one of Paul's many descriptions of original sin.

III. The Historical Books

Joshua continues where Deuteronomy leaves off in a recital of Israel's long-delayed possession of the Promised Land. The stress in Joshua, says Hugh J. Blair, is three-pronged: God's faithfulness, God's holiness, and God's salvation. God's holiness is seen in His judgment on the gross sinfulness of the original inhabitants of Canaan, and in His insistence that the instruments of that judgment be holy. "Again and again it is insisted that this is a holy war, and that Israel will succeed in the task committed to her only as every evil thing is put away from her."[48]

Josh. 3:5 uses "sanctify" (KJV) in relation to the preparation of the people for entrance into Canaan, a term which in this context is properly translated "consecrate" (NASB, NIV) or "hallow" (NEB):

---

47. Marten H. Woudstra, "Circumcision," *Baker's Dictionary of Theology*, ed. Everett F. Harrison (Grand Rapids: Baker Book House, 1960), pp. 127-28; hereafter cited BDT. One of John Wesley's early sermons, from which he quoted at the beginning of his *Plain Account of Christian Perfection* (Kansas City: Beacon Hill Press of Kansas City, reprint 1966), p. 12, was on "The Circumcision of the Heart." He said, "It is that habitual disposition of soul which, in the sacred writings is termed holiness; and which directly implies the being cleansed from sin, 'from all filthiness both of flesh and spirit,' and, by consequence, the being endued with those virtues which were in Christ Jesus; the being so 'renewed in the image of our mind,' as to be "perfect as our Father in heaven is perfect.'" Cf. the chapter on "Circumcision of the Heart" in Laurence W. Wood, *Pentecostal Grace* (Wilmore, Ky.: Francis Asbury Publishing Company, Inc., 1980), pp. 137-68.

48. NBC, p. 226.

"Consecrate yourselves, for tomorrow the Lord will do amazing things among you."

It is interesting that at least twice the New Testament uses Israel's crossing into Canaan—particularly in relation to the prior defeat at Kadesh-barnea (Num. 13:1—14:45)—as typical of the Christian's higher life (Hebrews 3—4; Jude 5). "Kadesh," it has been noted, is the English form of the Hebrew *qadesh*—"holiness," "consecration."

One must always move with caution in reading New Testament truth into Old Testament history. But there is at least illustrative value in the analogy between the deliverance of Israel from Egyptian bondage and the Christian experience of justification on the one hand; and the command to take possession of the Promised Land in relation to God's call to holiness on the other hand. Griffith Thomas quotes the lines:

> *They came to the gates of Canaan,*
> *But they never entered in!*
> *They came to the very threshold,*
> *But they perished in their sin.*
>
> *On the morrow they would have entered,*
> *But God had shut the gate;*
> *They wept, they rashly ventured,*
> *But alas! it was too late.*
>
> *And so we are ever coming*
> *To the place where two ways part;*
> *One leads to the land of promise,*
> *And one to a hardened heart.* [49]

That possession of Canaan was not without its battles, victories, and defeats could also illustrate the fact that an experience of Christian holiness is not necessarily a life of unruffled tranquillity. Nor is it a finished conquest at the time of first entrance. "When Joshua was old and well advanced in years, the Lord said to him, 'You are very old, and there are still very large areas of land to be taken over'" (Josh. 13:1).

---

49. *Through the Pentateuch,* ad loc. A most effective discussion of the total biblical meaning of the Exodus-Conquest motif in relation to the Resurrection of Christ and His exaltation and pouring out of the Holy Spirit is given in Wood, *Pentecostal Grace,* pp. 25-95, 113-24.

The Book of Judges is a recital of the way God's purposes were defeated in the life of His people in Canaan by:

(1) Presumption and self-confidence: "When Israel became strong, they pressed the Canaanites into forced labor but never drove them out completely" (1:28).

(2) The inattention and carelessness of a new generation: "Another generation grew up, who knew neither the Lord nor what he had done for Israel" (2:10).

(3) Relativity and lawlessness in conduct: "In those days Israel had no king; everyone did as he saw fit" (17:6).

Yet even here the action and power of the Spirit of God is seen in a beautiful phrase in the Hebrew, used two other times (1 Chron. 12:18; 2 Chron. 24:20), "So the Spirit of the Lord clothed himself with Gideon" (Judg. 6:34, lit.; NASB marg.).

The books of Samuel and Kings tell of the transition from theocracy to monarchy, and trace the varying fortunes of the kingdom through to the Babylonian Exile. The rise of the prophetic order in Israel is described. Relevant to our understanding of the meaning of holiness is the description of the moral and religious character of the kings of Judah and Israel as having hearts that were or were not perfect *(shalem)* with or before the Lord (1 Kings 8:61; 11:4; 15:3; 2 Kings 20:3; 1 Chron. 12:38; 28:9; 29:9, 19; 2 Chron. 15:7; 16:9; 19:9; 25:2). Especially instructive is the allusion to King Asa where a distinction is made between Asa's imperfect performance and his perfect heart (1 Kings 15:14).

IV. The Psalms and Proverbs

The poetic and wisdom literature also contribute to our understanding of holiness.

A. The Psalms

The Psalms incorporate both priestly and prophetic elements of holiness but reflect predominantly the prophetic emphasis on the moral and spiritual aspect.[50] The Book of Psalms gives us our clearest insight into the true nature of piety in the Old Testament. It describes the type of character possible to those who walk with

---

50. See the balanced discussion of the "cultic element" in the Psalms in Helmer Ringgren, *Faith of the Psalmists* (Philadelphia: Fortress Press, 1963), pp. 1-19. Worship in the Temple was the vehicle to nourish the faith and piety of the people.

God. That the Book of Psalms has been the hymnbook not only of the Old Testament but of New Testament people as well is a testimony to its spiritual depth. The comment of A. F. Kirkpatrick is still appropriate:

> The Psalms represent the inward and spiritual side of the religion of Israel. They are the manifold expression of the intense devotion of pious souls to God, of the feeling of trust and hope and love which reach a climax in such Psalms as 23, 42, 43, 63, 84. They are the many-toned voice of prayer in the widest sense, as the soul's address to God in confession, petition, intercession, meditation, thanksgiving, praise both in public and private. They offer the most complete proof, if proof were needed, how utterly false is the notion that the religion of Israel was a formal system of external rites and ceremonies.[51]

The Psalms are pervaded with a deep feeling for the holiness of God and with reverent awe for His house and His "holy hill." Throughout is a pervasive sense of yieldedness, openness, utter dependence on God, and loyal commitment in obedience. There is a deep conviction of the horror of sin, of loss of fellowship with God. There is confidence in God's love and good will, and trust in the face of opposition and adversity.

Marked also is the prayerfulness of the Psalmists—bringing all of life, inner and outer, under the scrutiny of God. Love and longing for God, trust in Him, the joy of His presence, and delight in communion with the Lord are all manifest. Strange to modern ears is the Psalmist's delight in the law of the Lord (1:2; 119, 36 times, plus many synonyms). The law of the Lord is no harsh and restrictive legislation imposed on man from without. As Ringgren notes:

> The Hebrew word for "law" means "instruction" or "showing the way." In other words, the law reveals God's will and shows man the way he is to walk in obedience before his God. But the law is not regarded here as a list of difficult duties or as a heavy burden. On the contrary, it is a gracious illumination for man's welfare, an instruction in God's will for which the psalmist feels profound gratitude. He loves God's law and finds his joy in it.[52]

---

51. "The Book of Psalms," in *The Cambridge Bible for Schools and Colleges* (Cambridge: University Press, 1894), 1:lxvii; cf. Ringgren, *Faith of the Psalmists*, p. xviii.

52. *Faith of the Psalmists*, p. 111.

1. *Psalm 15*

The Psalms give many insights into the nature of God's holiness and His requirements for His followers. Psalm 15 is described as "a liturgy specifying the moral qualities required for admission" to God's holy hill,[53] the Temple. It demands integrity, righteousness, and truth. It prohibits slander, doing evil to the neighbor, or taking up a reproach against a friend. Only such may "live on your holy hill" (v. 1) who despise the reprobate but honor those who fear God, the one who "keeps his oath/even when it hurts" (v. 4), who does not loan with usury and who does not take bribes. "He who does these things/will never be shaken" (v. 5).

2. *Psalm 24*

Psalm 24 combines ideas of "clean hands and a pure heart" (v. 4), a thought picked up in the New Testament (Jas. 4:8, NASB—"Cleanse your hands, you sinners; and purify your hearts, you double-minded"):

> *Who may ascend the hill of the Lord?*
> *Who may stand in his holy place?*
> *He who has clean hands and a pure heart,*
> *who does not lift up his soul to an idol*
> *or swear by what is false* (vv. 3-4).

"The biblical writer uses *bar* (pure) in a moral sense," says Mitchell Dahood,[54] in contrast with a legal or ceremonial usage. The idea of a heart that is pure is frequently found in the New Testament (Matt. 5:8; Acts 15:8-9; 1 Tim. 1:5; et al.). For the Old Testament *(lebab)* as for *kardia* in the New, "heart" means the whole subjective inner life—not just feelings or purposes.

3. *Psalm 29*

Psalm 29 is the psalm read at the festival of Pentecost, memorable in the New Testament as the occasion for the outpouring of the Holy Spirit upon the waiting disciples of Jesus (Acts 2). Although variously translated, v. 2 calls on the people of God to worship the Lord "in the splendor of his holiness," "in holy array,"

---

53. Mitchell Dahood, "Psalms I," *The Anchor Bible,* ed. William Foxwell Albright and David Noel Freedman (Garden City, N.Y.: Doubleday & Co., 1966), 16:83; hereafter abbreviated AB.

54. Ibid., p. 151.

"in the majesty of holiness" (NASB and marg.), or "in the beauty of holiness" (KJV).

4. *Psalm 37*

Ps. 37:37 alludes to the "perfect" (KJV; Heb., *tam*) man, placing "upright" in the position of a synonym:

> *Consider the blameless, observe the upright;*
> *there is a future for the man of peace.*

Psalm 37 is one of three psalms (49; 73) that struggle with the problem of the prosperity of the wicked in relation to the adversities that often beset the righteous. The answer is found in the fact that both are temporary: death ends the rejoicing of the wicked, but the blameless ("perfect, whole, complete") person of peace has a future in the purpose of God (vv. 38-40).

5. *Psalm 51*

Psalm 51 is one of the most penetrating passages in the Old Testament in relation to human sin and salvation. Classified as a penitential psalm, it involves a clear recognition of the twofold nature of human sin: acts of transgression which call for forgiveness, and a deeper reality that requires cleansing. The psalm is not a studied theological treatise. It is the impassioned cry of a deeply troubled heart. There is no careful analysis of the difference between sinful acts and the sinful nature, between the need for pardon and the call for purity. Yet there is a natural movement from the cry for pardon, through insight into the deeper problem, on to prayer for purity and the promise of praise and service. G. Campbell Morgan writes:

> The penitent soul cries for forgiveness on the basis of confession. Suddenly the intensity of conviction deepens as the act of sin is traced back to its reason in the pollution of the nature. This leads to a deeper cry. As the first was for pardon, the second is for purity, for cleansing of heart, and renewal of spirit. The prayer goes on to seek for the things which follow such cleansing, maintenance of fellowship, and consciousness of joy. Looking on in hope, the song anticipates that service of thanksgiving and praise which will issue from such pardon and purity.[55]

---

55. *An Exposition of the Whole Bible* (Westwood, N.J.: Fleming H. Revell Co., 1954), pp. 239-40.

The Psalmist mourns his transgressions (vv. 1, 3), his sins and iniquities (v. 9). "I have sinned," he says, "and done what is evil in Thy sight" (v. 4, NASB). But the problem goes deeper than sinful deeds. He cries:

> *Wash away all my iniquity*
>   *and cleanse me from my sin* (v. 2).

> *Behold, I was brought forth in iniquity,*
> *And in sin my mother conceived me.*
> *Behold, Thou dost desire truth in the innermost being,*
> *And in the hidden part Thou wilt make me know wisdom*
>   (vv. 5-6, NASB).

The nature of the cure for this deeper problem of inner sin is clearly identified:

> *Wash away . . . and cleanse me* (v. 2).

> *Cleanse me with hyssop,*[56] *and I will be clean;*
>   *wash me, and I will be whiter than snow* (v. 7).

> *Create in me a pure heart, O God,*
>   *and renew a steadfast spirit within me.*
> *Do not cast me from your presence*
>   *or take your Holy Spirit from me.*
> *Restore to me the joy of your salvation*
>   *and grant me a willing spirit, to sustain me.*

> *Then I will teach transgressors your ways,*
>   *and sinners will turn back to you* (vv. 10-13).

Lawrence E. Toombs writes about the strong word translated "wash" in v. 7:

> The Hebrew language has two words for "wash." The first is applied to washing the body, kitchen utensils, and, in general, any object that can be dipped in water or have water poured over it. The second is almost a specific word for washing garments by beating them with a stick or pounding them on a flat rock submerged in water. The Psalmist deliberately chooses the second word, rejecting by implication the metaphor of the warm shower and the mild soap pleasantly rinsing

---

56. The reference to hyssop is an allusion to Lev. 14:4 where hyssop was used to sprinkle the blood that symbolized the cleansing of a leper from his defilement.

away the dirt while the bather luxuriates. He knows that sin is so deeply entrenched in his nature that God may literally have to beat it out of him.[57]

Such a cleansing, the Psalmist asserts, will assure God's presence and the continued abiding of His Holy Spirit (v. 11). This is one of three times (cf. Isa. 63:10-11) where the Old Testament uses the exact title "Holy Spirit" in reference to the Spirit of God or Spirit of the Lord. "Though the expression [Holy Spirit] is infrequent in the OT; its substance is common."[58]

The joy of salvation and the sustaining of "a willing spirit" will result (v. 12), God's ways will be taught to transgressors, and sinners will be converted (v. 13)—results paralleled in the Gospel of John in reference to the coming of the Holy Spirit in His fullness upon the disciples (John 14—17).

6. *Psalms 73; 93; 110*

Psalm 73 has already been cited in reference to the problem of the wicked who prosper and the righteous who suffer. It opens with a summary statement to which it returns at the conclusion (v. 28):

> *Surely God is good to Israel,*
> *to those who are pure in heart* (v. 1).

The pure in heart are blessed with the vision of the Lord (Matt. 5:8; Heb. 12:14) and with a sense of the goodness of God, although temporarily their piety may seem to have been in vain (v. 13).

A constant sense of the holiness of God's house (in context, the Temple) pervades the Psalms and comes clear in 93:5:

> *Your statutes stand firm;*
> *holiness adorns your house*
> *for endless days, O Lord.*

The Temple and the hill on which it was located are holy in that they are separated from the secular and profane. So must be the people who worship there.

Psalm 110, certainly one of the most outstanding Messianic passages in the Old Testament, is quoted a total of 21 times in the

---

57. *Old Testament in Christian Preaching,* p. 178. Used by permission.
58. TDNT, 1:103.

New Testament in reference to Christ and His kingdom, most notably by Jesus himself. A feature of life in the Kingdom is willing obedience on the part of God's people in view of His holiness:

> *Thy people will volunteer freely in the day of Thy power;*
> *In holy array, from the womb of the dawn,*
> *Thy youth are to Thee as the dew* (v. 3, NASB).

Commentators differ on the subject of the phrase "in holy array," but it seems best to refer it to God as the Subject.[59] Consecration is always the act of a freely surrendered will. Reluctant service, while better than none at all, will never satisfy the requirements of divine holiness.

7. "Saints" in the Psalms

The Psalms are also replete with references to the "saints." Two Old Testament words lie behind this translation. One is *chasid,* from *chesed,* "covenant love and loyalty," "kind, pious, godly"— translated "godly ones" in the NASB. It is used in the Psalms in this sense 16 times. The "saints" or "godly ones" are said to sing praise to the Lord (30:4), to love Him (31:23), to share the fellowship of waiting on God's name (52:9, KJV), to sing for joy (132:9, 16), etc. They are not forsaken (37:28), are gathered before the Lord (50:5), are blessed with peace (85:8), are preserved (97:10), and their death is precious in His sight (116:15), etc.

The other term translated "saints" (holy ones, NASB) is *qadosh,* "those set apart, separate, holy." The Psalmists use it five times, twice in relation to the "assembly" or "council" of the saints (89:5, 7). They are described as "the glorious ones in whom is all my delight" (16:3). They are to fear the Lord, "for those who fear him lack nothing" (34:9). Psalm 106, one of the great historical psalms, refers to Aaron as *qadosh,* "the holy one of the Lord" (v. 16, NASB), "who was consecrated to the Lord."[60]

Thus it seems clear that while the entire body of the covenant people may be described as "holy," there are some out of the whole group who are in a particular way "godly" or "holy." Their godliness or holiness is not merely a matter of ritual separation or covenant uniqueness. It is related to their personal piety in the

---

59. Cf. Marvin H. Pope, IDB, 2:528-29.
60. Ringgren, *Faith of the Psalmists,* p. 38.

worship of God and in loyalty to Him. This is a note that becomes more insistent with the literature of the prophetic period.

B. Proverbs

The Book of Proverbs is a major source in understanding the ethics of the Old Testament. It shares with the wisdom literature as a whole the conviction that existence is fundamentally rational and moral.[61] Personal conduct, not religious experience, is its major theme. Yet the style of life the Proverbs teach is motivated by "the fear of the Lord" (1:7; 9:10) and represents ideals of honesty, integrity, truthfulness, humility, prudence, sexual purity, liberality, self-control, industry, compassion, justice, and peaceableness.[62]

For all its concern with conduct, Proverbs is amazingly sensitive to the key place of "the heart" as the motive-spring of life, "the seat and symbol of intelligence and will":[63]

> Above all else, guard your heart,
> for it is the wellspring of life (4:23).

The crooked or perverse heart (KJV, "froward"—from *iqqesh*, "distorted, crooked, false") is the source of evil in life (6:14; 11:20; 12:8 [*avah*, "crooked," "perverse," "wicked"]; 17:20). Such a heart "devises wicked schemes" (6:18); is "of little value" (10:20); is deceitful (12:20); and is prone to backsliding (14:14, KJV).

On the other hand, the heart may be understanding (2:2; 8:5), wise (2:10; 10:8; 11:29; etc.), tranquil (14:30); righteous (15:28); clean (20:9); pure (22:11)—and

> The crucible for silver and the furnace for gold,
> but the Lord tests the heart (17:3).

That the heart is the control room of life is a point Jesus also made in Matt. 15:18-20 and Mark 7:20-23.

---

61. Cf. J. C. Rylaarsdam, *Revelation in Jewish Wisdom Literature* (Chicago: University of Chicago Press, 1946), p. 14.

62. R. B. Y. Scott, AB, 18:22; cf. Purkiser, Taylor, and Taylor, *God, Man, and Salvation*, pp. 112-14.

63. Scott, AB, 18:52.

V. THE PROPHETS

In the prophetic literature we find the essential norms of Old Testament theology. Prophets and priests have often been contrasted and considered to be in fundamental opposition. A truer view sees in the prophetic emphasis not a repudiation of the Temple cult, but a deepening and spiritualizing of its meaning. It was not against ritual as such that the prophets spoke. It was against ritual without righteousness, the degeneration of ritual into empty formalism. The Old Testament prophets came to a deep understanding of holiness both as it relates to God and as it relates to human beings. The very fact that since their time holiness invariably suggests goodness, personal integrity, and moral rectitude is an unspoken tribute to the insights of the Old Testament prophets.

The idea of a norm of character was never fully absent from the ideal of holiness as applied to persons. It becomes distinctive in the thought of the prophets. Hermann Schultz wrote concerning this period in the development of Old Testament theology:

> A proper relation to Jehovah was considered to depend absolutely on moral integrity. The will of God was expressed in the grand fundamental requirements of morality . . . a daily life of justice, goodness, and truth. . . . In the eyes of God, sacred forms have absolutely no value, except as expressions of faith, humility, and obedience. Such is the burden of the prophetic messages from Amos and Hosea down to the Exile.[64]

In similar vein, Harold H. Rowley writes: "In Israel it was perceived in germ in the beginning, and with increasing clearness as time passed, that what God is they who worship him should become. Thus the religion of Israel is ethical in its essence, and not merely in its demands."[65] Similarly, Walter Eichrodt says, "The man who belongs to God must possess a particular kind of nature, which by comprising at once outward and inward, ritual and moral purity will correspond to the nature of the holy God."[66]

A. Isaiah

Isaiah stands first among the major prophets not only in time but in eminence as well. With good reason he has been called "the

64. *Old Testament Theology,* 2:53-54.
65. *Faith of Israel,* p. 59.
66. *Theology of the Old Testament* (Philadelphia: Westminster Press, 1961), 1:137.

evangelical prophet" and the book that bears his name described as "the gospel according to Isaiah."

Deeply conscious of the sinfulness of his people, Isaiah never lost the note of redemption and hope. He speaks the word of promise as an oracle of God:

> *I will turn my hand against you;*
> *I will thoroughly purge away your dross*
> *and remove your impurities* (1:25).

1. *Isaiah 6*

The prophet's account of his specific commission in 6:1-8 is a crucial passage for understanding the holiness both of God and of persons. As Procksch notes, "The concept of holiness is central to the whole theology of Isaiah. The trisagion of his initial vision (Is. 6:3) remained normative for his picture of God."[67] We have previously considered this passage in relation to the holiness of God (chap. 1). We look at it now in relation to holiness as conferred on man.

Isaiah had begun his prophetic ministry some time before the death of King Uzziah (1:1). But in the year the king died, the prophet experienced a vision of God "seated on a throne, high and exalted, and the train of his robe filled the temple" (6:1). God is high above the earthly, the profane, and the sinful (His transcendence), but also so near one could almost reach out and touch Him (His immanence).

The keynote in the experience is sounded in the seraphim cry, "Holy, Holy, Holy, is the Lord of hosts" (v. 3, NASB). The prophet's reaction was not to a sense of his finiteness in the presence of the Infinite. It was a sense of his sinfulness in the presence of holiness. The vision of the Lord brought a demand for personal cleansing. Ludwig Köhler writes: "Here holiness is the opposite of sinfulness. God is holy because He does not tolerate sin, He uncovers it, He rebukes it, refuses to connive at it, punishes it or atoning for it forgives it. Sin separates a person from the Holy God."[68] Isaiah's cry was: "Woe to me! . . . I am ruined! For I am a man of unclean lips, and I live among a people of unclean lips, and my eyes have seen the King, the Lord Almighty" (6:5).

---

67. TDNT, 1:93.
68. *Old Testament Theology,* p. 53.

Isaiah's confession here is not essentially a confession of rebellion, of active and conscious disobedience against God. That problem had been settled when he became a prophet. His problem here was not what he had done but what he was: unclean by nature when measured in light of the holiness of God. As Richard C. Trench writes:

> He who uttered this cry was one who had kept himself from his iniquity, holding the mystery of the faith in a pure conscience; and yet in that terrible light he saw and avowed himself as a man undone, saw stains in himself which he had not imagined before, saw his own sin and his people's sin, till that mighty cry of anguish was wrung from him. Yet that moment, with all its dreadfulness, was a passage into a true life.[69]

In view of his prophetic office, the prophet's concern about his lips was a proper one. "Unclean" *(tame)* does not necessarily mean blasphemous or morally corrupt. It is basically a ceremonial term and means "unhallowed," "unconsecrated," or "unsanctified." When touched with the heavenly coal (v. 7), Isaiah's lips became his greatest asset. Jesus said, "Out of the overflow of the heart the mouth speaks" (Matt. 12:34; Luke 6:45). The cleansing of the lips symbolizes the purging of the heart: "Your iniquity is taken away, and your sin is forgiven" (v. 7, NASB; better, as KJV, "purged"; the term used literally means "covered, atoned for").[70]

John 12:41 relates Isaiah's vision to Christ: "He saw Jesus' glory and spoke about him." Jewish tradition regarded the throne of God which Isaiah saw as behind the veil or curtain in the holy of holies in the Temple. None but the high priest, and he but once a year, was permitted into the holy of holies. It was screened off from the view of others, priests and people alike.

But when Christ Jesus died, "the curtain of the temple was torn in two from top to bottom" (Matt. 27:51). In this the writer to the Hebrews sees a deep spiritual meaning: "Since therefore, brethren, we have confidence to enter the holy place by the blood of Jesus, by a new and living way which He inaugurated for us through the veil, that is, His flesh, and since we have a great priest over the house of God, let us draw near with a sincere heart in full assurance of faith, having our hearts sprinkled clean from an evil conscience and our bodies washed with pure water" (10:19-22,

69. Quoted by Albert F. Harper, *Holiness and High Country* (Kansas City: Beacon Hill Press of Kansas City, 1964), p. 287.

70. Cf. Ross E. Price, BBC, 4:51, note.

NASB). Isaiah's Temple experience therefore stands as a significant prototype of the realization of God's holiness in the New Testament.

When the prophet's lips were touched, his ears were opened and he "heard the voice of the Lord saying, 'Whom shall I send? And who will go for us?'" His reply was immediate, "Here am I. Send me!" He did not so much as stop to ask, "Where?" The message Isaiah was given to proclaim is cited often in the New Testament (Matt. 13:14-15; Mark 4:12; Luke 8:10; Acts 28:26-27; Rom. 11:8) and is probably best understood in the version reflected in the Septuagint: "Go and tell this people":

> *You will be ever hearing, but never understanding;*
> *you will be ever seeing, but never perceiving;*
> *This people's heart has become calloused;*
> *they hardly hear with their ears,*
> *and they have closed their eyes* (vv. 9-10; cf. Acts 28:26-27).

2. Isaiah and the Holiness of God

That holiness is the theme of Isaiah's theology is abundantly verified throughout. His distinctive title for the true God, "the Holy (One) of Israel" (1:4; 5:19, 24; 10:20; 12:6; passim—a total of 30 times), has already been mentioned.[71] This holy God is to be "sanctified" by His people in their recognition of and praise for His holiness (5:16; 8:13; 29:23), and His name is also to be hallowed (29:23). He is thrice holy (6:3). His arm, the manifestation of His power, is holy (52:10); His name is holy (57:15); His Spirit is holy (63:10-11).

All that is distinctively related to God is holy: His city, Jerusalem (48:2; 52:1); Mount Zion (27:13; 56:7; 57:13; etc.); His habitation (63:15); His courts (62:9); His "place" (57:15); His house (64:11); and His day, the Sabbath (58:13). Even the plunder from Tyre, set apart for the use of God's people, is designated *qodesh.*

Similarly God's people are holy. They are to sanctify themselves (66:17, NASB). Their remnant (4:3) is to be "the holy seed" (6:13). The preexile nation is known as "thy holy people" (63:18, NASB; "the people of thy holiness," KJV). The very return from exile is seen as typical of the Messianic age in which human life is

---

71. See chap. 1, III, A.

viewed as a reclaimed desert, full of life and joy (35:1-7), through which it is said:

> *And a highway will be there;*
> *it will be called the Way of Holiness.*
> *The unclean will not journey on it;*
> *it will be for those who walk in that Way;*
> *wicked fools will not go about on it.*
> *[the simple will not stray from it, marg.]*
>
> *No lion will be there,*
> *nor will any ferocious beast get up on it;*
> *they will not be found there.*
> *But only the redeemed will walk there,*
> *and the ransomed of the Lord will return.*
> *They will enter Zion with singing;*
> *everlasting joy will crown their heads.*
> *Gladness and joy will overtake them,*
> *and sorrow and sighing will flee away (35:8-10).*

Bishop J. Paul Taylor makes an appropriate application of the metaphor "way (or highway) of holiness" in Christian experience:

Believers are not sanctified wholly simply for security in the next world, but also for service in this world. Full salvation is not a dead-end street, stopping at the door of the sanctified man's home. It is not a house where he lives, but a highway where he travels, the highway of holiness crossing mountains and leveling them, crossing valleys and filling them, crossing deserts and making them rejoice and blossom as the rose, penetrating wilderness to transform the habitation of dragons into a habitation of God, a place where waters break out to quench the thirst of dying men.[72]

Those who travel this highway will be called "The Holy People, The Redeemed of the Lord" (62:12).

3. *Isaiah and the Age of the Spirit*

Isaiah sees in the tragedy at Kadesh-barnea a spurning of God's Holy Spirit. Those who had known the kindnesses and praises of the Lord; who had witnessed His great goodness and compassion; who had been known as His people; to whom He was

---

72. *Holiness the Finished Foundation* (Winona Lake, Ind.: Light and Life Press, 1963), p. 105.

the Savior, afflicted in their affliction and saving them by the angel
of His presence; those who were redeemed in love and mercy,
"lifted" and "carried . . . all the days of old" (63:7-9) are described
in the words:

> *Yet they rebelled*
> *and grieved his Holy Spirit.*
> *So he turned and became their enemy*
> *and he himself fought against them.*
>
> *Then his people recalled the days of old,*
> *the days of Moses and his people—*
> *where is he who brought them through the sea,*
> *with the shepherd of his flock?*
> *Where is he who set*
> *his Holy Spirit among them . . . ?* (vv. 10-11).

Here, as in Ps. 51:11, the Spirit is designated by what becomes
the characteristic term of the New Testament, the "Holy Spirit." For
in Isaiah we pick up a new note. The coming age of deliverance is
to be characteristically the "age of the Spirit."

The Spirit of God, the Spirit of the Lord, "his Spirit," and "my
Spirit" often appear on the pages of the Old Testament. The Spirit
of God moves over the surface of the waters while the earth is
formless and void, shrouded in darkness (Gen. 1:2). God's Spirit
will not always strive with, contend with, or rule in man (6:3).
Joseph's wisdom is attributed by Pharaoh to "the spirit of God"
(41:38). Bezalel was "filled . . . with the Spirit of God in wisdom, in
understanding, in knowledge, and in all kinds of craftsmanship"
(Exod. 31:3, NASB) to accomplish the work involved in building
the Tabernacle in the wilderness.

The Spirit of God comes upon Balaam (Num. 24:2) and resides
in Joshua (27:18). The "Spirit of the Lord" comes upon Othniel
(Judg. 3:10), Gideon (6:34), Jephthah (11:29), Samson (13:25; 14:6,
19; 15:14), Saul (1 Sam. 10:6, 10; and departs from him, 16:14), and
comes upon David (16:13). The Spirit of God was "upon" Saul's
messengers and Saul himself (19:20, 23). The Spirit of the Lord
"spoke" by David (2 Sam. 23:2) and by Micaiah (1 Kings 22:24).
Obadiah is afraid Elijah will be carried away by the Spirit of the
Lord (18:12); and at the end of his prophetic career Elijah is
thought to have been "picked . . . up" by the Spirit and removed to
some remote spot (2 Kings 2:16). The Spirit of God "came upon"

Jahaziel (2 Chron. 20:14) and Zechariah, the son of Jehoiada (24:20). Job finds the Spirit of God as his breath, the Source of life (Job 27:3—"breath" is literally "spirit"), as does Elihu (33:4).

The Psalmist prays that God's "Holy Spirit" be not taken from him (Ps. 51:11) and sees in the Spirit the power that creates life for the animal world (104:24-30). The rebelliousness of Israel at Meribah was rebellion against God's Spirit (106:33). The Spirit of the Lord is equated with His presence (139:7) and leads His people "on level ground" (143:10).

While elements of moral and spiritual efficacy peep through in these many references to the Spirit of God or Spirit of the Lord, in the main they have to do with the Spirit as God's active agency in nature, and His function in enduing chosen people with wisdom or physical might.

It is with Isaiah that the work of the Spirit becomes more distinctively ethical and spiritually redemptive. The Spirit is intimately connected with the coming age of deliverance. That there is a prophecy in Isaiah of the return of the exiles from Babylonia may well be admitted. At the same time, there is in view a new and Messianic age. . . .

> *A shoot will come up from the stump of Jesse;*
> *from his roots a Branch will bear fruit.*
> *The Spirit of the Lord will rest on him—*
> *the Spirit of wisdom and of understanding,*
> *the Spirit of counsel and of power,*
> *the Spirit of knowledge and of the fear of the Lord* (11:1-2).

In what has come to be known as the first of the "Servant Songs" of Isaiah, the Servant is introduced as Bearer of the Spirit:

> *Behold, My Servant, whom I uphold;*
> *My chosen one in whom My soul delights.*
> *I have put My Spirit upon Him;*
> *He will bring forth justice to the nations* (42:1, NASB).

Isa. 61:1-2 is the source of the prophecy Jesus appropriated to himself in His synagogue address (Luke 4:18-19):

> *The Spirit of the Sovereign Lord is on me,*
> *because the Lord has anointed me*
> *to preach good news to the poor* (v. 1).

In a passage that in short range refers to Cyrus but in long range to Christ (48:12-16), the speaker says:

"From the first announcement I have not spoken in secret;
at the time it happens I am there."

And now the Sovereign Lord has sent me,
with his Spirit (v. 16).

Not only will the Spirit rest upon the Deliverer, He will be poured forth upon the people. The desolation will continue

Until the Spirit is poured out upon us from on high,
And the wilderness becomes a fertile field
And the fertile field is considered as a forest.
Then justice will dwell in the wilderness,
And righteousness will abide in the fertile field.
And the work of righteousness will be peace,
And the service of righteousness, quietness and confidence
forever (32:15-17, NASB).

The promise is repeated in 44:3:

For I will pour water on the thirsty land,
and streams on the dry ground;
I will pour out my Spirit on your offspring,
and my blessing on your descendants.

The "pouring" of the Spirit (Joel 2:28; Acts 2:17) is indicative of abundance, and the promise to the descendents is cited by Peter on the Day of Pentecost in Acts 2:39. Again in Isa. 59:21: "'As for me, this is my covenant with them,' says the Lord. 'My Spirit, who is on you, and my words that I have put in your mouth will not depart from your mouth, or from the mouths of your children, or from the mouths of their descendants from this time on and forever,' says the Lord."

B. Jeremiah

Jeremiah lived through the tragic days of Judah's final collapse and the beginnings of the Babylonian exile. He saw more clearly than any other of his day that the nation as a nation was doomed by its idolatry and waywardness of heart. But he shared the faith of Amos and Hosea that God would yet redeem and restore His people. The old covenant had failed; but God would make a new covenant with His people.

There is pathos in the past tense:

> *Israel was holy to the Lord,*
>   *the firstfruits of his harvest; . . .*
>
> *"My people have committed two sins:*
> *They have forsaken me,*
>   *the spring of living water,*
> *and have dug their own cisterns,*
>   *broken cisterns that cannot hold water"* (2:3, 13).

Jeremiah saw clearly that the problem of sin is not one of circumstances or external influences. It is the problem of a fallen, depraved nature: "The heart is deceitful above all things / and beyond cure. / Who can understand it?" (17:9).

But there is hope of a new day in which God will work within His people to fulfill His righteousness:

> "Behold, days are coming," declares the Lord, "when I will make a new covenant with the house of Israel and with the house of Judah, not like the covenant which I made with their fathers in the day I took them by the hand to bring them out of the land of Egypt, My covenant which they broke, although I was a husband to them," declares the Lord. "But this is the covenant which I will make with the house of Israel after those days," declares the Lord, "I will put My law within them, and on their heart I will write it; and I will be their God, and they shall be My people" *(31:31-33, NASB).*

It is worthy of note that the writer to the Hebrews applies this promise to the atoning death of Christ by which "He has perfected for all time those who are sanctified" (Heb. 10:14, NASB; cf. vv. 15-16).

C. Ezekiel

Ezekiel, Jeremiah's contemporary living among the exiles in Babylonia, envisions the coming new age as a time of cleansing from all uncleanness:

> "I will show the holiness of my great name, which has been profaned among the nations, the name you have profaned among them. Then the nations will know that I am the Lord, declares the Sovereign Lord, when I show myself holy through you before their eyes. . . . I will sprinkle clean water on you, and you will be clean; I will cleanse you from all your

impurities and from all your idols. I will give you a new heart
and put a new spirit in you; I will remove from you your heart
of stone and give you a heart of flesh. And I will put my Spirit
in you and move you to follow my decrees and be careful to
keep my laws" *(36:23, 25-27)*.

It has been pointed out that John Wesley made chief reliance
on this one Old Testament text in his *Plain Account of Christian
Perfection* in support of the doctrine of entire sanctification. It is not
the only verse from the Old Testament he quoted, but the one he
quoted most frequently.

J. Kenneth Grider writes concerning v. 23, "All the attributes of
God, metaphysical and moral, are subsumed under His holiness.
That is what He is—Holiness. God's **great name** (23) is here used
as a synonym of His **holy** name (22)."[73]

D. Joel

The promise of the coming age of the Spirit is repeated again
by Joel in a famous passage quoted by Peter as having been fulfilled at Pentecost:

> *And afterward,*
> *I will pour out my Spirit on all people.*
> *Your sons and daughters will prophesy,*
> *your old men will dream dreams,*
> *your young men will see visions.*
> *Even on my servants, both men and women,*
> *I will pour out my Spirit in those days*
> (2:28-29; cf. Acts 2:16-18).

E. Zechariah

The last section of Zechariah is one of the high Christological
passages in the Old Testament. It continues the promise of the
Spirit featured in Isaiah, Ezekiel, and Joel: "And I will pour out on
the house of David and on the inhabitants of Jerusalem, the Spirit
of grace and of supplication, so that they will look on Me whom
they have pierced; and they will mourn for Him, as one mourns for
an only son, and they will weep bitterly over Him, like the bitter
weeping over a first-born" (12:10, NASB).

---

73. BBC, 4:599.

The oracle of Zechariah 12 is continued in c. 13: "On that day a fountain will be opened to the house of David and the inhabitants of Jerusalem, to cleanse them from sin and impurity" (v. 1). G. N. M. Collins writes: "This verse 'exhibits the two grand doctrines of the gospel—justification and sanctification' (Henderson). The grace of the Spirit of Christ is needed for the latter, as the virtue of the blood of Christ is needed for the former."[74] "Justification means the putting away of our sin, the rectification of a wrong relationship with God, so that by faith we are restored to the favor of a holy and just God. Sanctification in the broadest sense means the entire moral renewal of our fallen natures, beginning with 'the washing of regeneration, and renewing of the Holy Ghost' (Titus 3:5) and being made complete by the baptism with the Holy Spirit and fire (Matt. 3:11; Acts 1:4-5; 15:8-9)."[75]

A change of figure from fountain to fire is found in 13:9, where the remnant ("the third part") will be refined as silver or gold:

> *And I will bring the third part through the fire,*
> *Refine them as silver is refined,*
> *And test them as gold is tested.*
> *They will call on My name,*
> *And I will answer them;*
> *I will say, "They are My people,"*
> *And they will say, "The Lord is my God"* (NASB).

In a passage high in imagery, the coming age is described as an age of widespread holiness: "In that day there will be inscribed on the bells of the horses, 'HOLY TO THE LORD.' And the cooking pots in the Lord's house will be like the bowls before the altar. And every cooking pot in Jerusalem and in Judah will be holy to the Lord of hosts . . ." (14:20-21, NASB). As Collins notes:

> In the closing verses of the prophecy we are given a picture of Jerusalem wholly consecrated to Jehovah—a picture in which the holy city is the symbol of the Christian Church regnant in the world. The distinction as between secular and sacred is done away, for everyone and everything is now consecrated to the Lord's purposes. The *bells*, or plates, of the horses bear the same inscription as the mitre of the High Priest;

---

74. NBC, p. 760.
75. BBC, 5:395.

the pots and common vessels of the Lord's house shall be holy as the *bowls before the altar;* all shall be consecrated to holy purposes.[76]

F. Malachi

The Old Testament closes with the same forward-looking note so familiar through the prophetic writings. Malachi gives God's oracle of hope in which Messiah shall refine and purify His people: "'See, I will send my messenger, who will prepare the way before me. Then suddenly the Lord you are seeking will come to his temple; the messenger of the covenant, whom you desire, will come,' says the Lord Almighty.

"But who can endure the day of his coming? Who can stand when he appears? For he will be like a refiner's fire or a launderer's soap. He will sit as a refiner and purifier of silver; he will purify the Levites and refine them like gold and silver. Then the Lord will have men who will bring offerings in righteousness" (3:1-3). As William M. Greathouse says of Malachi, "The little book which comes from his hand witnesses to a forceful and vigorous preacher who pled for sincerity in worship and holiness of life."[77]

Before leaving the Old Testament, a backward look is in order. What is holiness in the Old Testament? It is first of all the inherent, essential nature of the one true God. In the ultimate sense, He alone is holy. Yet by the same token, everything and everyone brought into relationship with Him shares in some way in that holiness. It is cut off from the profane and unhallowed. It is set apart as a special possession of the Lord.

Such separation or setting apart as this is both a human and a divine work. "To sanctify" is a verb used often of human agents: "Sanctify to Me every first-born" (Exod. 13:2, NASB; and 19:22; 28:41; Josh. 3:5 where *qadesh* is translated "consecrate"). But it is likewise used with God as the Agent: "I am the Lord who sanctifies you" (Exod. 31:13, NASB; Lev. 20:8; 21:15; etc.). While the Old Testament has another phrase commonly translated "consecrate" (literally, "to fill the hand"), "to sanctify" when used of human agents means what we should now call consecration.

As related to persons, holiness in the Old Testament appears

---

76. NBC, p. 763.
77. BBC, 5:407.

under three major concepts: patriarchal, priestly, and prophetic. The patriarchal concept of holiness, exemplified in Genesis and Job, is a blameless walk with God (e.g., Enoch, Gen. 5:22, 24; Noah, 6:9; Abraham, 17:1; Job, 1:1, 8; 2:3). The priestly or Temple concept, applying to both things and people, emphasizes the cultic or ceremonial holiness whose major meaning is to be set apart, dedicated, separated, or regarded as sacred.

It should be said again that the priestly concept of holiness does not exclude the moral element. This is clearly seen in Leviticus 19, the heart of the priestly Holiness Code. Here, along with the ceremonial (vv. 5-8, 19, 21-28, 30) are injunctions that are clearly ethical (vv. 15, 17-18, 20, 29, 33-36)—both alike expressions of the meaning of the injunction, "Be holy because I, the Lord your God, am holy" (v. 2).

The prophetic or synagogue concept of holiness represents the growing moralization of the idea of the holy. Its clearest expression is seen in the experience of Isaiah (Isa. 6:1-8).

It is through the prophetic emphasis that holiness comes to include moral righteousness or goodness in character and conduct. Peter T. Forsyth writes:

> The very history of the word holiness in the Old Testament displays the gradual transcendence of the idea of separation by that of sanctity. It traverses a path in which the quantitative idea of *tabu* changes to the qualitative idea of active and absolute purity. The religious grows ethical, that it may become not only more religious but the one religion for the conscience and for the world. The one God can only be the holy God.[78]

And Bowman adds: "The New Testament, finally, takes up only the prophetic side of the definition of the term and perpetuates it. All Christians are to be 'saints' (holy ones—Rom. 1:7), that is, ethically holy, separated, consecrated to God's service (Mark 6:20; John 17:11; Rev. 3:7), that they may have fellowship with a holy God (Acts 9:13; Rom. 1:7; Heb. 6:10; Rev. 5:8)."[79]

To that New Testament development we now turn.

---

78. *Positive Preaching and the Modern Mind* (New York: George H. Doran Co., 1907), p. 310.

79. *Prophetic Realism and the Gospel*, p. 163. Note the slightly different contrast between priestly and prophetic concepts offered in Turner, *Vision Which Transforms*, p. 50.

3

Holiness in the Gospels

The New Testament opens with four documents of a kind absolutely unique. They are traditionally called Gospels. In a narrower sense they comprise a fourfold Gospel: each is titled "The Gospel According to Matthew; or Mark; or Luke; or John."

It has often been argued that the Gospels are not biographies, and in an ordinary sense of the word such is true. The total reported activity of Jesus includes only what could be compressed into a month's time.[1] Of a life span totalling approximately 12,000 days and an active ministry of more than 1,270 days, all the Gospel narratives together tell of events which happened on only 34 different days. Out of 879 verses in John, 237 pertain to one day of Jesus' life.[2] Fully one-third of the Gospels is given to the last week in the earthly life of Jesus.

Yet the point must not be pushed too far. While the Gospels are, in modern New Testament terminology, *kerygma*—the proclamation of the good news of Christ to the world—they are proclamation centered in a life. Evangelistic in nature—the literary deposit of a preaching Church—they are a recognition of the fact that the vital element in evangelism is the plain story of what happened in the ministry of Jesus.

---

1. Everett F. Harrison, "Historical Problems in the Fourth Gospel," *Bibliotheca Sacra*, vol. 116, no. 463 (July, 1959), p. 206.
2. Batsell Barrett Baxter, *I Believe Because . . . : A Study of the Evidence Supporting Christian Faith* (Grand Rapids: Baker Book House, 1971), p. 179.

There is selectivity in the choice of Gospel materials (John 21:25). But the purpose of that selectivity is centered in a Person: "Jesus did many other miraculous signs in the presence of his disciples, which are not recorded in this book. But these are written that you may believe that Jesus is the Christ, the Son of God, and that by believing you may have life in his name" (John 20:30-31). L. Harold DeWolf writes in an eloquent paragraph:

> In the midst of the world's tyranny, oppression and fear a wonderful story once began and spread like wildfire from village to village and from nation to nation. Those who told it called it "the good news" and they were so full of its wonder and gladness that even the sternest commands and hardest punishments of emperors could not stop the telling of it. So revolutionary was their message and its power that guardians of the old order said to one another, "They are turning the world upside down." So they were. By the influence of their faith slaves were freed, cruel oppressors were brought down from their thrones, the poor were assisted, the ill were healed, little children were made to laugh and sing as never before and the timid were enabled to face death with triumphant serenity and even with fierce joy.[3]

I. THE CHARACTER OF JESUS

Holiness in the Gospels centers chiefly in the picture given of the character of Jesus. Two inescapable facts emerge: Jesus of Nazareth was completely of the nature of God—the Eternal Word made flesh, dwelling among men (John 1:1, 14); and Christ Jesus was totally human in everything that humanity was meant to be and may become by the grace of God. Jesus is, in a way quite unintended by Protagoras who first used a similar phrase, "the Man who is the measure of all things."

Much has been made of an alleged disparity between the "Jesus of history" and the "Christ of faith." W. D. Davies, however, says correctly: "It would seem to me essential that there should be no incongruity between the Jesus of History and the Christ of Faith. The problem of their congruity cannot be silenced or shelved. Should they be incongruous, while a Theology of the Word might be possible, a Theology of the Word made flesh would

---

3. *A Theology of the Living Church,* rev. ed. (New York: Harper and Brothers, 1960), p. 17. Used by permission. Cf. Orlo Strunk, Jr., *The Choice Called Atheism* (Nashville: Abingdon Press, 1968), p. 138.

hardly be so, and it is to such a theology that the New Testament commits us."[4] Or as Jesse B. Weatherspoon writes, "If we begin with history we call him 'Jesus Christ the Lord'; if we begin with theology we call him 'the Lord Jesus Christ.' The 'Christ of faith' is the 'Jesus of history.'"[5]

That Jesus Christ is Lord is the central faith of the New Testament. That Lordship affirms His deity. As Balmer H. Kelly writes:

> Basic to the Gospels, and in fact to the entire New Testament, is the proclamation that Jesus, and he alone, is the Lord of life. To him is due all loyalty and all honor. The Gospels themselves are the expression of the one central faith of the Church, in that they locate in a place, Palestine, and in a definite time, during the procuratorship of Pontius Pilate, One who stands so fully in the place of honor and worship normally reserved for God alone, that there can be no question of his equality with God and of the absolute claims of his Kingdom.[6]

But that Lordship also has direct bearing on the Christian life. As William Barclay says:

> To call Jesus Lord is to affirm that he is our *absolute owner,* and to confess that we must give him our *absolute obedience.* To call Jesus Lord is to affirm that he is our *absolute master,* and to confess that we must give him *absolute submission.* To call Jesus Lord is to affirm that he is our *absolute king,* and to confess that we must give him *absolute loyalty.* To call Jesus Lord is to affirm his *absolute deity,* and to confess that we must give him *absolute reverence.*[7]

No delineation of holiness is higher than Christlikeness. None sets before the believer a more comprehensive ideal. Jesus was a Person of unequalled magnetism. His love, understanding, humor, humility, compassion, courage, and forgiveness have made a mark on the collective consciousness of mankind that is inerasable. The highest and noblest in human conduct or character is described as Christlike.

Jesus combined gentleness and firmness, decisiveness and forbearance. There was nothing about Him that bordered on self-pity,

---

4. "A Quest to Be Resumed in New Testament Studies," *New Directions in Biblical Thought,* ed. Martin E. Marty (New York: Association Press, 1960), p. 72.

5. *Sent Forth to Preach: Studies in Apostolic Preaching* (New York: Harper and Brothers, 1954), p. 97.

6. LBC, 1:62.

7. *The Apostles' Creed for Everyman* (New York: Harper and Row, Publishers, 1967), pp. 68-69.

vindictiveness, or craving for fame.[8] His personality and His teaching radiate the pure love of God—a love that is joyful, serene, patient, kind, good, faithful, gentle, and self-controlled (Gal. 5:22-23).

At the same time, Jesus was subject to the full range of human emotions. He knew the burden of grief (John 11:35). He knew what it was to be troubled in spirit (12:27). His experience of anger (Matt. 21:13; Mark 3:5) shows us that there is a dimension of human anger that is without sin (Eph. 4:26), although the line may not be easy for us to discern (Col. 3:8). The element of sin enters anger when it is out of control, when it is used to hurt others, and when it is allowed to linger in the heart (e.g., "Do not let the sun go down while you are still angry" [Eph. 4:26]).

No other prototype could have been in mind when Paul wrote his unparalleled "Hymn to Love" than the image of Christ Jesus: "Love is patient, love is kind. It does not envy, it does not boast, it is not proud. It is not rude, it is not self-seeking, it is not easily angered, it keeps no record of wrongs. Love does not delight in evil but rejoices with the truth. It always protects, always trusts, always hopes, always perseveres" (1 Cor. 13:4-7).

The character of Jesus as presented in the Gospels is constantly held before His followers as the ideal after which they seek. The purpose of the ministry of the Church is "the equipping of the saints for the work of service, to the building up of the body of Christ; until we all attain to the unity of the faith, and of the knowledge of the Son of God, to a mature man, to the measure of the stature which belongs to the fulness of Christ" (Eph. 4:11-13, NASB).

The mind in us is to be the mind of Christ: "Your attitude should be the same as that of Christ Jesus" (Phil. 2:5). "We have the mind of Christ" (1 Cor. 2:16). "To this you were called, because Christ suffered for you, leaving you an example, that you should follow in his steps.

> *He committed no sin,*
> *and no deceit was found in his mouth.*

---

8. Cf. Everett F. Harrison, *A Short Life of Christ* (Grand Rapids: William B. Eerdmans Publishing Co., 1968), pp. 257-64.

When they hurled their insults at him, he did not retaliate; when he suffered, he made no threats. Instead, he entrusted himself to him who judges justly" (1 Pet. 2:21-23). "Your life is now hidden with Christ in God" (Col. 3:3).

Jesus is thus both the ideal beyond and the norm within the believer. If justification is Christ *for* us with the Father, sanctification is Christ *in* us by the Spirit. In performance, "attaining to the whole measure of the fullness of Christ" (Eph. 4:13) is a lifetime ideal, ever before us. In motivation, Christ in us is the dynamic that cleanses and molds His image within. As Herbert H. Farmer wrote: "It is the calling and privilege of the Christian disciple . . . to have increasingly in all his dealings with persons what it is not possible for the unreconciled man to have, namely, the mind of Christ. He is called to be sanctified through the Spirit in the fellowship of the church."[9]

Christ is so human He can reach us, and so divine He can redeem us. As Athanasius said, "He became what we are that He might make us what He is."[10] "To the two questions: What does God offer to man? and What does God require of man? the New Testament returns one answer: the Life of Christ."[11]

> *O Lord and Master of us all,*
> *Whate'er our name or sign,*
> *We own Thy sway, we hear Thy call,*
> *We test our lives by Thine.*

II. The Synoptic Gospels

E. C. Blackman states that in the first three Gospels:

Man's chief requisite is not warning against sinful actions so much as purification of heart where the overt sins are motivated (Matt. 5:21-32; 6:22-23; 7:17-18; 12:34-35). Jesus understood his mission to be to cleanse men from that inward uncleanness which vitiates their life, issues in wrong deeds to their fellow men, and makes them unfit for fellowship with God. To this purpose he devoted his life, even to the ultimate

---

9. Quoted by G. E. Thomas, *A Pocket Book of Discipleship* (Nashville: The Upper Room, 1960), p. 91.

10. Quoted by Gerald Kennedy, *The Preacher and the New English Bible* (New York: Oxford University Press, 1972), p. 74.

11. T. W. Manson, quoted by Harrison, *Short Life of Christ*, p. 11.

sacrifice of death, believing that God would make this sacrifice potent for the emancipation and sanctification man needs (Matt. 26:28; Mark 10:45; 14:21-24).[12]

A. Matthew

The Gospel According to Matthew is the Gospel of the Messiah. There is an inner logic in the arrangement of the four Gospels in the New Testament. Matthew forms the nexus with the Old Testament. As A. M. Hunter observes:

> It was a true instinct that put the Gospel according to St. Matthew first in the New Testament. This Gospel with its repeated insistence that Christ came to fulfil the olden prophecies, serves to remind us that "it is one purpose of God which is being fulfilled throughout both testaments, one People of God, the story of which is being told from Abel to the Apostolic Age." . . . He is hammering out one main thesis—that Christianity is not an accident but a consummation of God's saving purpose for His People begun in the Old Testament dispensation.[13]

1. *The Two Baptisms, Matt. 3:11-12*

Matthew opens his account of the ministry of Jesus with a description of the preaching of the forerunner John the Baptist. John's introduction of Jesus is expressed in terms paralleled in the other three Gospels (Mark 1:8; Luke 3:16-17; John 1:33) and echoed twice in Acts (1:5; 11:16): "I baptize you with water for repentance. But after me will come one who is more powerful than I, whose sandals I am not fit to carry. He will baptize you with the Holy Spirit and with fire. His winnowing fork is in his hand, and he will clear his threshing floor, gathering the wheat into his barn and burning up the chaff with unquenchable fire" (Matt. 3:11-12).

The full significance of these words and their meaning for Christian life can be seen only in connection with the events of the Day of Pentecost. It is sufficient here to point out that John's words introduce a relationship of comparison and contrast between his baptism and that which Jesus is to administer. Both are described as acts of baptism with the inescapable connotation of event or occurrence at a given point of time. They are contrasted as water with fire, and as repentance and "forgiveness of sins" (Mark 1:4) is

---

12. IDB, 4:211.

13. *Introducing the New Testament* (London: SCM Press, 1951), p. 55.

with the Holy Spirit. The contrast is not between John's water baptism and water baptism in the name of Christ as had often been assumed. It is the contrast between a baptism with water and a baptism with the Holy Spirit as fire.

The consequence of Christ's baptism with the Spirit will be a cleansing (RSV, NASB) of the threshing floor, gathering the wheat into the barn, and burning up the chaff with unquenchable fire. There is an eschatological interpretation of these words which relates them to the final Judgment. However, the usual eschatological contrast is not between wheat and chaff but between wheat and tares (Matt. 13:24-43). Perhaps to be preferred is an existential interpretation which sees in the chaff a separable but valueless part of the kernel of wheat which is to be "burned up" by the sin-consuming fire of the Holy Spirit. As William Barclay writes, "The drabness of life, and the inadequacy of life, and the futility of life, and the earth-boundedness of life, which characterize so many of us, all come from the failure to submit to that baptism of the Spirit which Christ alone can give."[14]

Arnold E. Airhart writes:

> Only the chaff is burned, and this only in order that the wheat—the genuine values in personality—may be garnered and set to use. There is potential in our personalities which only God can discern. There are possibilities of grace, dormant talents, buried treasure, within believers' lives, but largely useless because as yet encased in the chaff of an unsanctified nature. The baptism with the Holy Spirit will provide the basis to bring to realization the personality possibilities known to the Spirit, but otherwise forever lost.[15]

The time element suggested by the baptism metaphor in relation to the Holy Spirit's work must not be ignored. Baptism is never partial, a long-drawn-out process never completed. While a study of the relationship between the baptism with the Holy Spirit and entire sanctification must wait until we come to the Book of Acts, the words of J. Paul Taylor are appropriate here:

> It is tragic beyond telling when, by any theory embraced, one is induced to postpone the hour of complete deliverance, for the crux of the matter is not clocks and calendars, but carnality. The same carnal nature that leads the sinner to postpone

14. *The Promise of the Spirit* (Philadelphia: Westminster Press, 1960), p. 25.
15. "The Baptism with the Holy Spirit," *Preacher's Magazine,* vol. 38, no. 5 (May, 1963), p. 14.

forgiveness leads the believer to postpone cleansing. If the sinner could be forgiven a few sins at a time, he would not be so rebellious. (Perhaps this accounts in part for the appeal of Romanism.) And if believers could be sanctified a little at a time, they would not object, for some of sinful self would remain always. But we are not forgiven by fractions nor sanctified by sections. It is all or nothing in both cases, therefore it is instantaneous in both cases.[16]

2. The Pure in Heart, Matt. 5:8

Matthew gives the most complete account of the Sermon on the Mount in cc. 5—7 (cf. Luke 6). Opening the Sermon are the Beatitudes, the nine colors of the spectrum of true Christian light and life. Of special interest in this context is the sixth beatitude: "Blessed are the pure in heart, / for they will see God" (5:8).

The entire Sermon on the Mount has sometimes been relegated to a future Kingdom Age, including the possibility of being "pure in heart." But all the other qualities named in the Beatitudes are aspects of life here and now: the poor in spirit, those who mourn, those who hunger and thirst after righteousness, the persecuted. It would be totally arbitrary to deny the possibility of heart purity in light of Christ's present tense: "Blessed *are* the pure in heart."

Ralph Earle writes, "Heart purity is the end and summation of the previous beatitudes. The possibility of such inner rectitude is clearly implied; but it is also apparent both from Scripture and universal experience that no one is natively pure (Jer. 17:9); hearts can be pure only by being purified. Nor will human culture purge the depths of corruption; there must be a work of divine grace."[17]

The biblical concept of a pure heart roots in the Old Testament (e.g., Ps. 24:4; 51:10). It finds explicit statement in the New Testament (Acts 15:8-9; 1 Tim. 1:5; 2 Tim. 2:22; Jas. 4:8; 1 Pet. 1:22, KJV). Modern psychology and psychiatry have made us aware of areas of human personality variously called subconscious, unconscious, or marginally conscious. Much of this has bearing on what is meant by heart purity. The caution of J. Baines Atkinson is appropriate here:

> We are vehemently warned by writers today that we cannot bear witness that all sin has been completely removed from

---

16. *Holiness the Finished Foundation,* p. 99.
17. BBC, 6:70.

the heart, because we cannot really know what is in the heart. We readily accept the warning, and will say that we have asked God to do what He means by cleansing the heart from all sin, and we believe He has done it, and we leave it there without further definition. My testimony, and God's testimony, is not primarily to my state, but to God's redeeming work.[18]

All that is included in "pure in heart" can be determined only when the entire biblical concept of sanctification is before us. The heart in Scripture is "the innermost spring of individual life, the ultimate source of all its physical, intellectual, emotional, and volitional energies, and consequently the part of man through which he normally achieves contact with the divine."[19]

Soren Kierkegaard's phrase is well known: "To be pure in heart is to will one thing."[20] J. B. Phillips paraphrases, "utterly sincere." R. V. G. Tasker says, "*The pure in heart* are the single-minded, who are free from the tyranny of a divided self, and who do not try to serve God and the world at the same time. From such it is impossible that God should hide Himself."[21] William Barclay renders it:

O THE BLISS OF THE MAN WHOSE MOTIVES ARE ABSOLUTELY PURE, FOR THAT MAN WILL SOME DAY BE ABLE TO SEE GOD![22]

Not faultless but blameless is the connotation.

In addition to biblical affirmations of *heart* purity, there are other references to the purifying or cleansing of the person (1 Tim. 5:22; Titus 2:14; 1 John 1:7; 3:3).

3. *Christian Perfection, Matt. 5:48*

The use of terms in the Old Testament ordinarily translated "perfect" *(tam, tamim, shalem)* has already been noted. There the proper meaning is "whole, entire, sound, upright, or blameless." The major New Testament word is *teleios*. It is encountered first in

---

18. *Beauty of Holiness,* p. 114; cf. Turner, *Vision Which Transforms,* pp. 273, 288.

19. IDB, 2:549.

20. This is the title of his book published in 1938 by Harper and Bros., New York and London, translated from the Danish by Douglas V. Steere.

21. "The Gospel According to St. Matthew," in *The Tyndale New Testament Commentaries* (Grand Rapids: William B. Eerdmans Publishing Co., 1961), 1:62; hereafter cited as TNTC.

22. "The Gospel of Matthew," *The Daily Study Bible* (Edinburgh: Saint Andrew Press, 1962), 1:102. Hereafter cited DSB.

the Sermon on the Mount, "Therefore you are to be perfect, as your heavenly Father is perfect" (Matt. 5:48, NASB). The parallel in Luke 6:36 is "Be merciful, just as your Father is merciful." In neither instance is it suggested that the human should equal the divine. The likeness is in a sense qualitative, the disparity is quantitative.

The perfection of Matt. 5:48 is evangelical perfection, not absolute perfection. *Teleios* means "full-grown, mature, having reached the appointed end *(telos)* of its development."[23] William Barclay writes:

> It has nothing to do with what we might call abstract, philosophical, metaphysical perfection. . . . A thing is perfect if it fully realizes the purpose for which it was planned, and designed, and made. . . . *Teleios* is the adjective formed from the noun *telos*. *Telos* means an *end,* a *purpose,* an *aim,* a *goal.* A thing is *teleios* if it realizes the purpose for which it was planned; a man is perfect if he realizes the purpose for which he was created and sent into the world.[24]

The context clarifies the area in which perfection is to be realized. It is in relation to the impartial love of others that embraces even one's enemies (vv. 42-47). As Leo G. Cox notes:

> Jesus said we are to be as perfect as our Heavenly Father. I think it significant that He used the term "Father." He knew we could not be as God in His absolute attributes. God knows all things, and never errs in judgment. He can do all things, so never fails in accomplishment. Jesus was not meaning this kind of perfection.
> But He said, "as your Father." The fatherhood of God means He is forgiving, kind, loving, and forbearing. He turns the other cheek, goes the second mile, is good to evil men as to the good ones. It is clear from the context of this verse that Jesus is talking about love, especially love for those who wrong us. In this aspect we are to be as perfect as our Father.[25]

"Christian perfection" was a term commonly used by John Wesley, a term he was always explaining and defending.[26] Two familiar excerpts here from the *Plain Account of Christian Perfection*

---

23. J. Y. Campbell, IDB, 3:730.

24. *Gospel of Matthew,* 1:176.

25. *Further Insights into Holiness,* ed. Kenneth Geiger (Kansas City: Beacon Hill Press, 1963), p. 181.

26. Cf. Wesley's normative account of his concept of entire sanctification titled *A Plain Account of Christian Perfection* (Kansas City: Beacon Hill Press of Kansas City, 1966), reprint of 1872 edition. The final revision of this work was made in 1777 when Mr. Wesley was 74 years of age.

will help establish Mr. Wesley's point of view, a position to which we shall return later. Similar passages are found throughout his other writings. Wesley is talking about evangelical perfection, not absolute perfection. It is dynamic rather than static: the perfection of a bud or a baby, rather than the perfection of a painting or statue:

> The best of men still need Christ in His priestly office, to atone for their omissions, their shortcomings (as some improperly speak), their mistakes in judgment and practice, and their defects of various kinds. . . . I believe there is no such perfection in this life as excludes these involuntary transgressions which I apprehend to be naturally consequent on the ignorance and mistakes inseparable from mortality. Therefore *sinless perfection* is a phrase I never use, lest I should seem to contradict myself. I believe a person filled with the love of God is still liable to these involuntary transgressions.[27]

> Look at it [Christian perfection] again; survey it on every side, and that with the closest attention. In one view, it is purity of intention, dedicating all the life to God. It is the giving God all our heart; it is one desire and design ruling all our tempers. It is the devoting, not a part, but all, our soul, body, and substance, to God. In another view, it is all the mind which was in Christ, enabling us to walk as Christ walked. It is the circumcision of the heart from all filthiness, all inward as well as outward pollution. It is a renewal of the heart in the whole image of God, the full likeness of Him that created it. In yet another, it is the loving God with all our heart, and our neighbor as ourselves. Now, take it in which of these views you please (for there is no material difference), and this is the whole and sole perfection, as a train of writings prove to a demonstration, which I have believed and taught for these forty years, from the year 1725 to the year 1765.[28]

A more recent statement, directly related to Matt. 5:48, is that of R. Gregor Smith:

> To be perfect means, therefore, to be whole or sound or true; and to be perfect as the Heavenly Father is perfect (Matt. 5:48, the main NT reference) means to be wholly turned, with the whole will and being, to God, as he is turned to us. This is a response of obedience and of effort carried out *in faith*. It is the call to purify our heart and to will one thing. The command falls within a religious situation, not simply a moral situation of improving our conduct by ever more strenuous efforts or the like. . . .

---

27. Ibid., pp. 53-54.
28. Ibid., pp. 117-18.

"Be perfect" is the command of God, springing from his own life, which can strike from our hearts only one response, that of faith. Our obedience in faith is not the beginning of some vague progress on a shadowy moral way, but is the acceptance of grace, which is always whole, complete, perfect; and in the strength of this encounter our life is lived. "Perfect" is something belonging to God and coming to us by our contact with God, not as a possession but as a gift. All that God has, and is, is perfect: it is never partial or unfulfilled. Our relation to him determines our share in this kind of wholeness.[29]

The quotations above all indicate the need to qualify our use of "perfect" or "perfection" with an adjective such as "Christian" or "evangelical" or "perfect love." "The closer definition of Christian perfection is almost invariably stated in the New Testament in terms of love."[30] Harold William Perkins makes this point:

This gift may be called Christian Perfection, seeing that it is to be received by one who follows and believes in Jesus the Christ. Or it may be spoken of as Evangelical Perfection inasmuch as it is set before us as a part, and the crowning part of the Evangel. In other words, we assume first that God is able and willing to communicate His own perfection to man, and then that He has actually done so in an historic person.[31]

Biblical perfection is not faultlessness but blamelessness.[32] It is perfection of heart, not of "head" or "hand." It relates to intention, not intelligence; to love, not life; to purity, not performance. It has to do with deliverance from sin, not from ignorance, mistakes, infirmities, temptations, or the constant necessity for watchfulness and prayer.[33]

B. Mark

If Matthew is the Gospel of the Messiah, Mark is the Gospel of the Mighty Conqueror. As Ralph Earle notes: "For the Romans Mark presents Jesus as the mighty Conqueror. He shows Him conquering nature, demons, disease, and death. . . . Mark gives a

---

29. *A Theological Word Book of the Bible* (London: SCM Press, 1950), p. 167.

30. *Encyclopedia of Religion and Ethics*, ed. James Hastings (New York: Charles Scribner's Sons, 1951), 9:729; hereafter cited ERE.

31. *Doctrine of Christian or Evangelical Perfection*, p. 15.

32. R. H. Coats, "Holiness," ERE, 6:745.

33. Cf. James R. Bishop, *The Spirit of Christ in Human Relationships* (Bangarapet, Mysore State, India: South India Bible Institute, 1964), p. 2.

forceful, vivid, graphic, powerful picture of the earthly ministry of Jesus Christ."[34]

1. *The Source of Sin, Mark 7:18-23*

Mark gives special emphasis to a statement of Jesus which Matthew also cites (Matt. 15:15-20). Christ identifies the heart as the source of moral corruption in human life. He denies the defilement from outer sources that was the concern of ceremonial or cultic holiness. The source of evil is within: the depravity of a carnal heart. Jesus said to His disciples, "'Don't you see that nothing that enters a man from the outside can make him "unclean"? For it doesn't go into his heart but into his stomach, and then out of his body.' (In saying this, Jesus declared all foods 'clean.')

"He went on: 'What comes out of a man is what makes him "unclean." For from within, out of men's hearts, come evil thoughts, sexual immorality, theft, murder, adultery, greed, malice, deceit, lewdness, envy, slander, arrogance and folly. All these evils come from inside and make a man "unclean"'" (Mark 7:18-23).

The extent to which the redemption provided in Christ cleanses the evil of the heart that is "more deceitful than all else / And is desperately sick" (Jer. 17:9, NASB) will continue to unfold. While his own answer is ambivalent, Reinhold Niebuhr fairly states the issue: "The question is whether the grace of Christ is primarily a power of righteousness which so heals the sinful heart that henceforth it is able to fulfill the law of love; or whether it is primarily the assurance of divine mercy for a persistent sinfulness which man never overcomes completely."[35]

William Barclay comments:

> In effect, Jesus was saying that *things* cannot be either unclean or clean in any real religious sense of the term. Only *persons* can be really defiled; and what defiles a person is his own actions, which are the product of his own heart. This was new doctrine and shatteringly new doctrine. The Jew had, and still has, a whole system of *things* which are clean and unclean. With one sweeping pronouncement Jesus declared the whole thing irrelevant, and declared that uncleanness has nothing to

---

34. "The Gospel According to Mark," *The Evangelical Commentary on the Bible,* ed. George A. Turner, et al. (Grand Rapids: Zondervan Publishing House, 1957), p. 22; hereafter cited EC.

35. *Christianity and Power Politics* (New York: Charles Scribner's Sons, 1952), p. 18. Atkinson, *Beauty of Holiness,* p. 77, called my attention to the statement.

do with what a man takes into his body, and everything to do with what comes out of his heart.[36]

2. *Total Love, Mark 12:28-34*

Both Matthew (22:34-40) and Luke (10:25-28) give the story of Christ's encounter with the questioning scribe detailed in Mark 12:28-34:

> One of the teachers of the law came and heard them debating. Noticing that Jesus had given them a good answer, he asked him, "Of all the commandments, which is the most important?"
>
> "The most important one," answered Jesus, "is this: 'Hear, O Israel, the Lord our God, the Lord is one. Love the Lord your God with all your heart and with all your soul and with all your mind and with all your strength.' The second is this: 'Love your neighbor as yourself.' There is no commandment greater than these."
>
> "Well said, teacher," the man replied. "You are right in saying that God is one and there is no other but him. To love him with all your heart, with all your understanding and with all your strength, and to love your neighbor as yourself is more important than all burnt offerings and sacrifices."
>
> When Jesus saw that he had answered wisely, he said to him, "You are not far from the kingdom of God."

Both "first" and "second" commandments are quotations from the Old Testament (Deut. 6:4-5 and Lev. 19:18). But no one had put the two together before to make one supreme summary of all "the Law and the Prophets" (Matt. 22:40). Jesus makes the "law" of love the supreme law of the Kingdom. The kingdom of God and His righteousness are to be the supreme goal of all His followers (Matt. 6:33), and love is the motivating principle of the Kingdom.

The order here—love for God first and love for neighbor second—is right and essential. We cannot love our neighbors as ourselves until we love God more than ourselves. But the New Testament ethic is insistent throughout that love for neighbor is the touchstone and evidence of love for God. Much of evangelical Christianity has been long on love for God and short on love for neighbor. Both must be dominant and both must characterize the holiness ethic.

A. Elwood Sanner writes, "The commandment calls for a complete response of man's whole being. This is the perfect love of

---

36. "The Gospel of Mark," DSB, pp. 175-76.

Christian perfection."[37] Love is demanding, but it is also rewarding. A pure love for God safeguards all human loves. Oswald Chambers writes:

> "Thou shalt love the Lord thy God with all thy heart"—the sovereign preference of our personality for God. Can I say before God, "For in all the world there is none but Thee, my God, there is none but Thee"? Is it true? is there a woman there? is there a man there? is there a child there? is there a friend there? "Thou shalt love the Lord thy God with all thy heart." Do you say, "But that is so stern"? The reason it is stern is that when once God's mighty grace gets my heart wholly absorbed in Him, every other love of my life is safe; but if my love to God is not dominant, my love may prove to be lust. Nearly all the cruelty in the world springs from not understanding this. Lust in its highest and lowest form simply means I seek for a creature to give me what God alone can give, and I become cruel and vindictive and jealous and spiteful to the one from whom I demand what God alone can give.[38]

C. Luke

Luke is the Gospel for the Greeks, as Matthew is the Gospel for the Jews and Mark the Gospel for the Romans. Renan hailed it as "the most beautiful book in the world."[39] Consonant with Luke's authorship of Acts and his close association with the apostle Paul, the Gospel puts particular emphasis on the Holy Spirit (e.g., 1:15, 35, 41, 67; to a total of 11 times) and on joy (e.g., 1:14, 44; 2:10; 6:23; to a total of 10 times).

1. *Holiness and Righteousness, Luke 1:73-75*

Luke cites the prophecy of Zacharias, father of John the Baptist, as envisioning the accomplishment of redemption (1:68) and fulfillment of God's holy covenant (v. 72):

> *the oath he swore to our father Abraham:*
> *to rescue us from the hand of our enemies,*
> *and to enable us to serve him without fear*
> *in holiness and righteousness before him all our days*
>   *(1:73-75).*

---

37. BBC, 6:376.

38. *If Thou Wilt Be Perfect* . . . (reprint ed., London: Simpkin Marshall, 1949), pp. 89-90.

39. Hunter, *Introducing the New Testament,* p. 206.

The conjunction of holiness and righteousness is significant. The time is for "all our days"; not a future, heavenly state. John Wesley comments on this passage: "Here is the substance of the great promise, that we shall be always holy, always happy; that being delivered from Satan and sin, from every uneasy and unholy temper, we shall joyfully love and serve God, in every thought, word, and work."[40] As Charles Childers writes:

> God's promises and the fulfillment of those promises in the redeeming work of Christ include personal holiness and righteousness for His children. In these two terms we have the Godward and manward aspects of the Christian life. To serve God in holiness is to serve with an inward nature conformed to God's nature and will; to serve Him in righteousness is to serve in uprightness in all human and earthly relationships. Acceptable devotion to God includes not only religious fervor but sound ethics.
>
> The possibility of such inward and outward rectitude constitutes the core of the gospel. Anything less is unthinkable, being contradictory to both the character and the commands of God. Also the love of God is not consistent with a plan of salvation which would leave man below the plane of personal freedom from both the acts and the principle of sin. **All the days of our lives.** Here is the answer to any quibble over the divine timetable for holy living. These are not only future heavenly blessings in store for God's people, but privileges which we may enjoy now. Nor does this inward grace need to be spasmodic; it is intended to be an established mode of life.[41]

2. *Prayer and Purity, Luke 11:2*

Karl Barth calls attention to a significant textual variation in Luke's version of the Lord's (or "Disciples'") Prayer (11:2):

> A variant reading in the Lucan text of the Lord's prayer (Codex Bezae) adds [to the petition, Thy kingdom come] the words: "That thy Holy Spirit may come upon us and purify us." Even though only the accepted texts of Matthew and Luke are authentic, this variant is interesting and provides a fitting commentary on the text. If we pray for the coming of God's Kingdom we are also praying that the Holy Spirit may enter into us.[42]

3. *The Father's Gift, Luke 11:13*

Luke conveys Christ's promise concerning the Father's gift of

---

40. *Explanatory Notes, New Testament,* p. 206.
41. BBC, 6:443.
42. *Prayer and Preaching* (Naperville, Ill.: SCM Book Club, 1964), p. 40.

the Spirit: "If you then, though you are evil, know how to give good gifts to your children, how much more will your Father in heaven give the Holy Spirit to those who ask him!" (11:13). This is one of seven times prior to the Passion Week when Jesus is quoted as having spoken of the Holy Spirit (Matt. 10:20; 22:43; [parallel, Mark 12:36]; Mark 3:29; Luke 4:18; John 3:5-6; 6:63; 7:37-39). Matthew's parallel quotes the promise as "give good gifts to those who ask" (7:11). For Luke, the Holy Spirit is the gift of a Father to His children, a gift conditioned on their asking. Childers comments:

> Here we see that the Holy Spirit is given in answer to prayer and that the Father is anxious to give Him to us. He is the best of all "good things," and the wise Christian will ask for Him before and in preference to all else. We need the Holy Spirit in His sanctifying fullness, and we need Him as our abiding Paraclete or Advocate. This discourse in Luke comes later in Jesus' ministry and nearer to Pentecost than does the Sermon on the Mount, in which the passage cited in Matthew appears. Therefore Jesus can be more specific in His references to the needs of His disciples.[43]

4. The Promise of the Father, Luke 24:49

Luke also gives the risen Lord's assurance to His disciples: "I am going to send you what my Father has promised; but stay in the city until you have been clothed with power from on high" (24:49). The "promise of my Father" (many trans.) is echoed in Acts 1:4-5 and related to John's statement about Christ's baptism with the Spirit in contrast to his own baptism with water. That these words have primary reference to the coming Pentecost as a historic event is certainly true. At the same time, there may well be an existential application pointing to every disciple's need for the qualifying fullness of the Spirit.

III. THE GOSPEL OF JOHN

John writes the Gospel of the Son of God. He writes for the entire Christian community whether Jew, Roman, or Greek. His Gospel is framed within two of the greatest declarations in the New Testament of the unqualified deity of Jesus Christ (1:1 and 20:28). A. J. Macleod writes, "The keynotes of the Gospel are life,

---

43. BBC, 6:509.

light and love. Christ comes to give a fuller, more abundant life to men. He is the light that was in the world, in conflict with its darkness, and the source of man's true life. The sacrifice of His life for the world was the expression of God's love to men."[44]

Dwight E. Stevenson contributes a significant insight into the character of the Fourth Gospel:

> In the Fourth Gospel the reader meets Jesus in Palestine during three years of an active and very human ministry. In the same pages he also meets the Christ of all peoples, humanity's Eternal Contemporary. Here he finds historical facts which pass into timeless symbols and symbols of eternity which root in definite historical fact. It is a book that can be read at two levels: by the outsider meeting Jesus as a historical personage for the first time, or by the committed Christian who is being led into a deeper communion with his living Lord.[45]

A. Before the Last Supper

John the Baptist's introduction of Jesus as the "Lamb of God" is related to His taking away "the sin of the world" (1:29). Raymond E. Brown sees in the singular ("the sin") a contrast with the plural of 1 John 3:5 which has "take away sins." He says, "The plural refers to sinful acts while the singular refers to a sinful condition."[46]

1. *The Baptizer with the Spirit, John 1:33-34*

John's version of the promise of a second baptism (with the Holy Spirit, Matt. 3:11; Mark 1:8; Luke 3:16) makes explicit what is implied in the Synoptic Gospels. Christ Jesus is the One who administers the baptism with the Holy Spirit. John the Baptist says, "I would not have known him, except that the one who sent me to baptize with water told me, 'The man on whom you see the Spirit come down and remain is he who will baptize with the Holy Spirit.' I have seen and I testify that this is the Son of God" (1:33-34). The baptism with the Spirit is in a special way Christ's baptism ministered by the Father in His name.

John's baptism is a "baptism with water only, which cannot purify the people of God. It can only make known the universal

---

44. NBC, p. 866.

45. *Preaching on the Books of the New Testament* (New York: Harper and Brothers, 1956), p. 49.

46. AB, 29:56.

need of sanctification. The baptism of John can only direct men to Christ."[47] William Barclay writes:

> . . . Jesus' baptism was *a baptism of the Spirit.* . . . When the Spirit takes possession of a man certain things happen.
> (i) His life is *illumined.* There comes to him the knowledge of God. The will of God becomes clear. He knows what God's purpose is, what life means, where duty lies. Some of God's wisdom and light has come into him.
> (ii) His life is *strengthened.* Knowledge without power is a haunting and frustrating thing. But the Spirit gives us, not only knowledge to know the right, but also strength and power to do the right. The Spirit gives us a triumphant adequacy to cope with life.
> (iii) His life is *purified.* Christ's baptism with the Spirit was to be a baptism of *fire* (Matthew 3:11; Luke 3:16). The dross of evil things, the alloy of the lower things, the base admixture is cleansed and burned away, until a man is clean and pure.[48]

2. *Rivers of Living Water,* John 7:37-39

John gives a significant promise made by Jesus on the occasion of the Feast of Lights: "On the last and greatest day of the Feast, Jesus stood and said in a loud voice, 'If a man is thirsty, let him come to me and drink. Whoever believes in me, as the Scripture has said, streams of living water will flow from within him'" (7:37-38).

John's comment is, "By this he meant the Spirit, whom those who believed in him were later to receive. Up to that time the Spirit had not been given, since Jesus had not yet been glorified" (v. 39). That the Holy Spirit was in the world and active from Creation is well attested in Scripture. Yet there was a dimension of His presence and His working which could only come after the Cross and the Resurrection. Barclay uses an appropriate analogy:

> Nuclear energy has always existed; it is built into the very structure of the world, but it only became available to man in the twentieth century. So what we are to think is that the Spirit has always existed in all his grace and power, but that the work of Jesus opened the flood gates and the Spirit in all his splendour became fully available to men. . . . Just as the life and death of Jesus opened to men the love of God, so the resurrection and the ever-continuing life of Jesus open to men the grace and the power of the Spirit. The incarnate Jesus brings us the

---

47. Edwin Clement Hoskyns, *The Fourth Gospel,* ed. Francis Noel Davey (London: Faber and Faber, 1947), p. 169.
48. "The Gospel of John," DSB, 1:68.

love of God; the Risen Christ makes available for us the power of the eternal Spirit.[49]

V. Raymond Edman sees in the abundance suggested by "rivers of living water" not the impartation of the Spirit at the new birth (John 3:3-8) but in a subsequent gift of the Spirit to those already believers:

> The deep dealing of God with His children varies in detail but the general pattern seems much alike for individual cases. Into each life there arises an awareness of failure, a falling short of all that one should be in the Lord; then there is a definite meeting with the risen Saviour in utter surrender of heart, which is indeed death to self. There follows an appropriation by faith of His resurrection life through the abiding presence of the Holy Spirit. As a result there is realized an overflow of life likened by the Lord Jesus to "rivers of water."[50]

B. The Last Supper Discourses

In the Last Supper Discourses of John 13—17 we have the most fundamental teaching of Scripture concerning the Holy Spirit and His place in the Christian life. Here is the best antidote to the common tendency to regard the relationship "to the Holy Spirit in terms of a doctrine to be believed rather than a [Person and] power to be experienced."[51] "In the New Testament the Spirit of Christ is not something to be cultivated but someone to be received."[52] Lycurgus M. Starkey, Jr., writes:

> Without the Holy Spirit, Christianity degenerates into a futile humanistic striving after goodness, the "bootstrap" religion about which there has been justified complaint. The Christian life calls us to obey God rather than men; to love our friends and enemies across all the barriers of human prejudice; to be forgiving and kind; to turn the other cheek and bear the animosity of others with patience; to be co-operative rather than competitive; to accept the woes of life with courage. Without the Holy Spirit such a life is impossible. Indeed without the triune God available and present within, the church as a witnessing fellowship that finds its oneness in Christ and brings all of society under submission to God's reign is quite impossible.

---

49. *Apostles' Creed for Everyman*, p. 243. Used by permission.

50. *They Found the Secret* (Grand Rapids: Zondervan Publishing House, 1960), p. 17.

51. Weatherspoon, *Sent Forth to Preach*, p. 49.

52. Thomas H. Keir, *The Word in Worship* (London: Oxford University Press, 1962), p. 44.

All things are possible, however, when God is present and active, working through the Holy Spirit in the mind and experience of the church.[53]

1. *The Paraclete Sayings*

The core of Christ's teaching concerning the Holy Spirit in the Last Supper Discourses is found in the five "Paraclete Sayings" (14:15-17, 26-27; 15:26-27; 16:7-11, 13-14). "Paraclete" comes from the Greek term *Paraklētos* variously translated "Comforter" (KJV), "Counselor" (RSV, NIV), or "Helper" (NASB, Barclay). In 14:26, the *Paraklētos* is specifically identified with the Holy Spirit. The difficulty in translating this term is a testimony to its richness and diversity in meaning. It literally means "one called alongside." W. E. Vine says it means "called to one's side, i.e., to one's aid [and] is primarily a verbal adjective [suggesting] the capability or adaptability for giving aid. It was used in a court of justice to denote a legal assistant, counsel for the defence, an advocate; then, generally, one who pleads another's cause, an intercessor, advocate, as in 1 John 2:1, of the Lord Jesus. In the widest sense, it signifies a succourer, comforter."[54] Barclay writes:

> The Greeks used the word in a wide variety of ways. A *parakletos* might be a person *called in* to give witness in a law court in someone's favor; he might be an advocate *called in* to plead someone's cause when someone was under a charge that would issue in serious penalty; he might be an expert *called in* to give advice in some difficult situation. He might be a person *called in* when, for example, a company of soldiers were depressed and dispirited to put new courage into their minds and hearts. Always a *parakletos* is *someone called in to help* when the person who calls him is in trouble or distress or doubt or bewilderment. . . . The Holy Spirit comes to us and takes away our inadequacies and enables us to cope with life. The Holy Spirit substitutes victorious for defeated living.[55]

Paraklētos is "used as a proper name . . . to designate an intelligent agent, not an abstract quality or influence."[56] The Paraclete

---

53. *The Work of the Holy Spirit: A Study in Wesleyan Theology* (New York: Abingdon Press, 1962), pp. 8-9. Used by permission.

54. *An Expository Dictionary of New Testament Words* (London: Oliphants, 1940), 1:208; hereafter cited EDNTW.

55. *Gospel of John,* DSB, 2:194-95.

56. Thomas N. Ralston, *Elements of Divinity,* p. 41; quoted in T. M. Anderson, comp., *Our Holy Faith: Studies in Wesleyan Theology* (Kansas City: Beacon Hill Press of Kansas City, 1965), p. 102.

sayings provide substantial New Testament evidence for the personality of the Holy Spirit. Samuel J. Mikolaski writes:

> Two strands of New Testament evidence are noteworthy. First, there are those passages where the personal pronoun is distinctly used of the Holy Spirit, i.e., the "he" passages (e.g., Mark 3:20-30; Luke 12:12; John 14:26; 15:26; 16:7-15; Acts 8:29; 10:19-20; 13:2; 15:28; 16:6, 7; 20:28; Rom. 5:5). Second, there are other passages, i.e., the "it" passages, that may allow of a personal reading but do not demand it (e.g., Matt. 1:18; 4:1; 12:28; Luke 1:15; John 3:9; Acts 1:8; Rom. 8:26-27). . . . One can account for the "it" passages in terms of the "he" passages, but it is simply impossible to account for the "he" passages in terms of the "it" passages.[57]

a. Another Comforter, John 14:15-18. The first Paraclete Saying is in some ways the most significant of the five. Jesus said, "If you love me, you will obey what I command. And I will ask the Father, and he will give you another Counselor to be with you forever— the Spirit of truth. The world cannot accept him, because it neither sees him nor knows him. But you know him, for he lives with you and will be in you. I will not leave you as orphans; I will come to you" (14:15-18).

It is to be noted that the promise is given to those who love Christ and keep His commandments. The conjunction of love and obedience is constant throughout the New Testament, and particularly in John's writings (vv. 21, 23-24; 15:10, 13-14, etc.). Obedience without love is legalism; love without obedience is sentimentalism. Neither qualifies as true discipleship.

While the Helper (NASB) is to be the Father's gift in answer to the prayer of Jesus, He is known by the disciples and is with them.

There is a sense in which these words are predictive of the specific event of Pentecost to follow by 50 days. But there is a broader sense in which they are applicable to all believers. When Jesus did pray, as He said He would (John 17), He said, "My prayer is not for them alone. I pray also for those who will believe in me through their message" (17:20). When the promise was first fulfilled, Peter broadened its scope to include all Christ's disciples in every age: "The promise is for you and your children and for all

---

57. Samuel J. Mikolaski, *The Triune God,* "Fundamentals of the Faith," essay no. 4 (Washington, D.C.: Christianity Today, 1966), p. 17; copyrighted 1966 and used by permission.

who are far off—for all whom the Lord our God will call" (Acts 2:39).

He whom they have known and who has been with them will come in a new way to be "in" them. That the terms "with" and "in" are not to be interpreted spatially as equivalent to "outside" and "inside" is seen in v. 23 where the fulfilled promise makes real the presence of Father and Son "with" the disciples. What is in view is a new, settled, abiding relationship. R. B. Rackham says,

> The change lies in the relation of the Holy Spirit to the human spirit. This relation was made quite new. Previously the Holy Spirit had acted on men from without; as the prophet Ezekiel describes it, "the hand of the Lord was upon me." But now the Holy Spirit acts from within. He is in man. Before Pentecost his manifestations had been transient and exceptional: Now his presence in man's heart is an "abiding" one and regular.[58]

Further, "the world cannot receive" (NASB) Him. There is an impartation of the Spirit to the world in conviction (16:8-9) and in the new birth (3:3-8; Rom. 5:9). But there is a "receiving" of the Spirit possible only to those who know Him and have Him and who love Christ and keep His commandments. To identify the birth of the Spirit with the baptism or fullness of the Spirit is either to question Jesus' testimony concerning His disciples, or the relevance of the Gospels for Christian life today. "The Holy Spirit gate-crashes no man's heart; He waits to be received."[59] To "receive Him" in this deeper and special sense is the privilege of those who know Him in the new birth and are therefore "not of the world" (John 17:14, 16; cf. vv. 6, 9)

b. The Teacher, John 14:26-27. The second Paraclete Saying stresses the Holy Spirit's position as "teacher" and "reminder" of what Jesus had taught, and His gift of peace: "But the Counselor, the Holy Spirit, whom the Father will send in my name, will teach you all things and will remind you of everything I have said to you. Peace I leave with you; my peace I give you. I do not give to you as the world gives. Do not let your hearts be troubled and do not be afraid" (14:26-27).

---

58. *The Acts of the Apostles,* p. 14; quoted by Weatherspoon, *Sent Forth to Preach,* pp. 40-41.

59. Barclay, *Gospel of John,* DSB, 2:195. See Wood, *Pentecostal Grace,* pp. 15-17, for evidence that "receiving the Spirit" as here used relates to the baptism with or fullness of the Spirit.

That these words had special application to the apostolic group immediately cannot be doubted. They were the ones through whom the teachings of Jesus would be preserved and communicated to the world. Yet there is a broader promise here in the illumination the Holy Spirit gives to the disciples of the Lord Jesus in every age. His instruction is correlated with the teachings of Jesus. He glorifies Christ (16:14). "All our conclusions must be tested against the things which Jesus said."[60] Barclay says it well:

> To the end of the day the Christian must be a learner, for to the end of the day the Holy Spirit will be leading him deeper and deeper into the truth of God. There is never any time in life when the Christian can say that he knows the whole truth. There is never any excuse in the Christian faith for the shut mind. The Christian who feels that he has nothing more to learn is the Christian who has not even begun to understand what the doctrine of the Holy Spirit means.[61]

The Holy Spirit conveys Christ's gift of peace to His people (Gal. 5:22). The word translated "leave" can have the meaning "to bequeath." In a beautiful comment, Matthew Henry somewhere remarks that when Jesus went back to heaven, He left His soul to the Father, His body to Joseph of Arimathea, His garments to the gambling soldiers, His mother to the apostle John. But to His disciples, Jesus left a bequest not of silver or gold but of worth far beyond anything the world could give. He left His peace.

Peace in the Bible means more than absence of turmoil. It "means everything which makes for our highest good."[62] Raymond E. Brown notes a play here on the traditional Hebrew salutation *Shalom* (peace) which carries the thought of wholeness, soundness, health, and well-being.[63] "The peace which Jesus offers us is the peace . . . which no experience in life can ever take from us. It is the peace which no sorrow, no danger, no suffering can make less. It is the peace which is independent of outward circumstances."[64]

c. The Witness, John 15:26-27. The third Paraclete Saying further expresses the Spirit's relationship to Jesus: "When the Counselor comes, whom I will sent to you from the Father, the Spirit of

---

60. Ibid., 2:199.
61. Ibid., pp. 198-99.
62. Ibid., p. 199.
63. AB, 29A:651.
64. Barclay, *Gospel of John*, DSB, 2:199.

truth who goes out from the Father, he will testify about me; but you also must testify, for you have been with me from the beginning" (15:26-27). The Holy Spirit bears witness to Christ, giving inward persuasion that what Jesus taught is true. And in the power of the Spirit, the disciples also bear witness to Christ (Acts 5:32).

d. Convicting the World, John 16:7-11. The fourth Paraclete Saying describes the function of the Spirit in convicting the world and preparing the unbelieving heart to receive the Savior. "I tell you the truth: It is for your good that I am going away. Unless I go away, the Counselor will not come to you; but if I go, I will send him to you. When he comes, he will convict the world of guilt in regard to sin and righteousness and judgment: in regard to sin, because men do not believe in me; in regard to righteousness, because I am going to the Father, where you can see me no longer; and in regard to judgment, because the prince of this world now stands condemned" (16:7-11).

Although the world cannot "receive" the Holy Spirit as the disciples can, the Spirit exercises a ministry to the world that is one of "conviction" (literally, "proving wrong").[65] This may be a witness to the disciples about the world, and a witness to the world about itself. The conviction of the Spirit has three objects: sin, defined as essentially unbelief; righteousness as exemplified in Christ and demonstrated by His resurrection and ascension; and judgment, because Satan and the kingdom of darkness received definitive judgment at the Cross and in the empty tomb.

e. Revealing Christ, John 16:12-15. The final Paraclete Saying returns to the Spirit's ministry in revealing Christ more adequately. The coming of the Holy Spirit is not to supply Christ's absence, but to make real His presence. "I have much more to say to you, more than you can now bear. But when he, the Spirit of truth, comes, he will guide you into all truth. He will not speak on his own; he will speak only what he hears, and he will tell you what is yet to come. He will bring glory to me by taking from what is mine and making it known to you. All that belongs to the Father is mine. That is why I said the Spirit will take from what is mine and make it known to you" (16:12-15). To "bring glory to" is to honor, magnify, adorn

---

65. Brown, AB, 29A:705.

with lustre, clothe with splendor, or cause the dignity and worth of to be known.[66]

Andrew Murray comments: "The great gift of the Father, through whom He obtained salvation and brought it near to us, is the Son. On the other hand, the great gift of the Son, whom He sends to us from the Father to apply to us an inner and effectual salvation, is the Holy Spirit. As the Son reveals and glorifies the Father, so the Spirit reveals and glorifies the Son."[67]

We have already noted the dispensational or historical application of words such as these. They had a direct application to the work of the apostolic group in communicating to their own and all future generations the words and teachings of Jesus. But they also have an existential application. The work of the Holy Spirit did not stop with the death of the apostles.[68] It continues in humble and teachable believers to the end of time. Barclay writes:

> Revelation is taking of the things of Jesus, and the revealing of their significance to us. The greatness of Jesus is His inexhaustibleness. No man has ever grasped all that Jesus came to say. No man has fully worked out all the significance of the teaching of Jesus. No man knows all that it means for life and for belief, for the individual and for the world, for society and for the nation. Revelation is a continual opening out of the meaning and the significance of Jesus Christ.[69]

2. The High Priestly Prayer

The Last Supper session ended with what has come to be known as Christ's "High Priestly Prayer."[70] It is a prayer for himself (17:1-5); for His disciples (vv. 6-19); and for all believers (vv. 20-26). It is easily one of the most majestic passages in Scripture, and takes us right into the heart of Christ's parting concern for the work He had come to do and the people who would carry it on. "Jesus still speaks in the context of the Last Supper; but from the

---

66. EDNTW, 2:152-53. "It is not for an instant that the disciples are to have the Spirit *instead* of the Son. But to have the Spirit *is* to have the Son."—Moberly, quoted by Samuel Chadwick, *The Way to Pentecost* (Kansas City: Beacon Hill Press, n.d.), p. 59.

67. *The New Life: Words of God for Young Disciples of Christ,* trans. from the Dutch by J. P. Lilley (1903: reprint ed., slightly abr., Minneapolis: Bethany Fellowship, 1965), p. 107.

68. This present work is, of course, not revelation in the sense of an inspired truth, but interpretation.

69. *Gospel of John,* DSB, 2:229.

70. First by David Chytraus, 1531-1600—so Brown, AB, 29A:747.

tone of what He says and from the tenses of the verbs, one feels that Jesus has crossed the threshold from time to eternity and is already on the way to the Father or, at least, halfway between this world and the Father's presence."[71]

The major concerns of Jesus are clearly seen. He prays that those who had been given to Him might be kept and sanctified, that they might all be one, that the world might believe, and that all His own should share His glory in the presence of the Father.

Though spoken before Pentecost and the full inauguration of the age of the Spirit, Jesus gives a striking testimony to the spiritual state of His disciples. Three major points are mentioned:

(1) The disciples had received and been obedient to God's Word. "I have revealed you to those whom you gave me out of the world. They were yours; you gave them to me and they have obeyed your word. . . . For I gave them the words you gave me and they accepted them" (vv. 6, 8).

(2) Christ had been glorified in them. "Glory has come to me through them" (v. 10). Barclay comments: "It is the patient whom he has cured who brings honour to the doctor; it is the scholar whom he has taught who brings honour to the teacher; it is the athlete whom he has trained who brings honour to his trainer. It is the men whom Jesus has rescued and redeemed and made good who bring honour to him. The bad man who has been made good, the man who has been strengthened to live the Christian life, is the honour of Jesus."[72]

(3) They were not of the world "even as" He was not of the world. This point had been made in 14:17. It is repeated with emphasis here: "I pray for them. I am not praying for the world, but for those you have given me, for they are yours" (v. 9); "I have given them your word and the world has hated them, for they are not of the world any more than I am of the world" (v. 14); "They are not of the world, even as I am not of it" (v. 16).

Here is the basis of the distinction between being "in the world" and "of the world." The disciples were in and were to remain in the world: "I will remain in the world no longer, but they are still in the world, and I am coming to you. Holy Father, protect them by the power of your name—the name you gave me—so that

---

71. Ibid.
72. *Gospel of John*, DSB, 2:250.

they may be one as we are one" (v. 11); "My prayer is not that you take them out of the world but that you protect them from the evil one" (v. 15). Christianity is not isolation from the world, but insulation from the corruption of a worldly spirit.

The prayer of Jesus is, "Sanctify them by the truth; your word is truth. As you sent me into the world, I have sent them into the world. For them I sanctify myself, that they too may be truly sanctified" (vv. 17-19). The word translated "sanctify" is *hagiazein* from the adjective *hagios,* usually translated "holy." Jesus is recorded as having used it prior to this only three times: in regard to the Temple and the gold in it (Matt. 23:17); the altar and the gift on it (Matt. 23:19); and in John 10:36 of himself as sanctified by the Father and sent into the world.

The usage here illustrates a feature of *hagiazein* already noted in its Old Testament counterpart *qadesh:* to sanctify carries a two-fold meaning. It means to set apart or consecrate to divine use; and, in the case of persons, to make free from sin or moral pollution. Now one and again the other may be uppermost, but both are essential parts of any complete biblical definition of the term. In point of time, the idea of consecration is first. But the moralization of the idea of sanctity that occurred through the Old Testament period and is carried on into the New Testament makes the idea of cleansing essential to the full biblical scope of sanctification.

What is true of *qadesh* is even more apparent in the lexicon definitions of *hagiazein.* Thomas Sheldon Green gives as its essential meaning, "to separate, consecrate; cleanse, purify, sanctify; regard or reverence as holy."[73] The verb form is an aorist imperative. It means "consecrate, dedicate, sanctify, treat as holy, reverence, purify."[74] "The fact that the verb is an aorist imperative clearly indicates that the sanctification of the disciples was to be a crisis experience. It 'cannot possibly mean an incomplete process but a definite act of sanctification.' (H. Orton Wiley, *The Epistle to the Hebrews,* p. 326)."[75] Richard S. Taylor writes:

73. *A Greek-English Lexicon of the New Testament,* rev. ed. (New York: The Macmillan Co., 1890), pp. 1-2.

74. William F. Arndt and F. Wilbur Gingrich, *A Greek-English Lexicon of the New Testament and Other Early Christian Literature* (Chicago: University of Chicago Press, 1957), pp. 8-9.

75. Joseph H. Mayfield, BBC, 7:193.

The prayer that the Father would "sanctify" the disciples is voiced in the aorist tense. While this tense does not of itself prove an instantaneous work, it proves a definite and *completed* work, and cannot be construed to imply a gradual sanctifying which is never completed; therefore the fulfillment by a crisis experience such as at Pentecost is strongly implied. But in v. 19 an even stronger tense is used: ". . . they may be sanctified" is in the perfect tense, clearly expressing our Lord's intention that they shall be brought into a *state* of sanctification, definitely accomplished and continuously maintained.[76]

Jesus used the term "sanctify" both of His disciples and of himself. The difference in the two uses shows clearly in v. 19: "For them I sanctify myself, that they too may be truly sanctified." Here the self-sanctification of the Savior carries the meaning of consecration, setting himself apart to the atoning sacrifice of the Cross. He whom the Father had already consecrated (John 10:36) consecrates or sanctifies himself.

But Jesus consecrates himself in order that something may be done in and for His disciples: "that they too may be truly sanctified." Here the verb is in the passive voice. In this sense, sanctification is nothing the disciples can do for themselves. It is something that must be done for them by the Father (v. 17) as a consequence of the self-dedication of Christ to the atoning and cleansing Cross.

Henry Alford, while stressing a gradual work, yet notes: "In *them* it was strictly *sanctification*, the *making holy*: but (2) in HIM it was that pure and entire self-consecration by His submission to the Father's holy will, the entire possession of His sinless humanity with the living and speaking Truth of God, which should be at the same time the efficient cause of their sanctification and their Pattern."[77]

The agency of the truth and the Word in the sanctification of the disciples also suggests that something more is in view than their self-dedication. As the Word of God is instrumental in regeneration (1 Pet. 1:23), so is it instrumental in sanctification. It is

---

76. *Life in the Spirit* (Kansas City: Beacon Hill Press of Kansas City, 1966), p. 82, fn. 1. Cf. Robert W. Lyon, "The Baptism of the Spirit—Continued," *Wesleyan Theological Journal* (hereafter cited *WTJ*), vol. 15, no. 2 (Fall, 1980), pp. 70 ff., for a different understanding.

77. *The Greek New Testament*, with revisions by Everett F. Harrison, 4 vols. (Chicago: Moody Press, 1958), 1:880.

through the Word that light comes (1 John 1:7). The Word is not passive but powerful (Heb. 4:12). Expressed in the gospel and united with faith, it is "the power of God for the salvation of everyone" (Rom. 1:16).

The results anticipated in Christ's prayer also suggest more to sanctification than a human act of consecration. Jesus prays for His disciples "so that they may have the full measure of [His] joy within them" (v. 13). He prays "not that you take them out of the world but that you protect them from the evil one" (v. 15). He prays for the unity of His people—the true ecumenicity: "That all of them may be one, Father, just as you are in me and I am in you. . . . that they may be one as we are one: I in them and you in me. May they be brought to complete unity" (vv. 21-23). Jesus prays that "the world may believe that you have sent me . . . to let the world know that you sent me and have loved them even as you have loved me" (vv. 21, 23). A final result is eschatological: "Father, I want those you have given me to be with me where I am, and to see my glory, the glory you have given me because you loved me before the creation of the world" (v. 24).

3. *"Receive the Holy Spirit," John 20:21-23*

In John 20, the appearance of the risen Christ to His disciples is related. After His greeting, Jesus said, "Peace be with you! As the Father has sent me, I am sending you." Then He "breathed on them" and said, "Receive the Holy Spirit. If you forgive anyone his sins, they are forgiven; if you do not forgive them, they are not forgiven" (vv. 21-23).

That Christ here fully conveyed the gift of the Spirit can scarcely be intended, for He had said, "Unless I go away, the Counselor will not come to you; but if I go, I will send him to you" (16:7). Here are both an impartation of the Spirit and an anticipation of Pentecost. Samuel Chadwick writes:

> They [the apostles] had already received the gift of the Spirit for salvation. In the Upper Room on the first day of the Resurrection the Risen Lord had breathed on them and said: "Receive ye the Holy Ghost." Pentecost was a second gift, which verified and completed the first in an infilling Presence and an overflowing power. It is the fullness that makes the difference.[78]

---

78. *The Way to Pentecost* (Kansas City: Beacon Hill Press, n.d.), p. 117.

Nor is a priestly rite of absolution in view in v. 23. Rather, preaching in the power of the Holy Spirit makes plain the conditions for the forgiveness of sins and makes possible faith for its acceptance. As A. J. Macleod notes, "The power bestowed is one of authoritatively declaring forgiveness on the basis of the sin-bearing death of Christ. His authority was intrinsically theirs because of the Spirit's presence in their lives. Authority is not given only to those specially ordained, but the whole Church has an authority derived from the presence of the Spirit in her life and from the teaching of her Head."[79]

---

79. NBC, p. 895.

4

Holiness in the
Book of Acts

The Acts of the Apostles lies right at the heart of the New Testament and has been called by Adolf Harnack its "pivot book." It has been suggested that the book might more properly be titled "The Acts of the Holy Spirit," for it contains almost 60 references to the Spirit in its 28 chapters.[1] F. F. Bruce writes:

> On the theological side, the dominating theme of Acts is the work of the Holy Spirit. . . . The Holy Spirit controls the whole work; He guides the messengers, such as Philip in chapter viii and Peter in chapter x; He directs the Antiochene church to set Barnabas and Saul apart for the work to which He Himself has called them (xiii.2); He guides them from place to place, forbidding them to preach in Asia or enter Bithynia, but giving them clear indications that they must cross into Europe (xvi.6-10). . . . He is the primary witness to the truth of the gospel (v. 32).[2]

I. The Baptism with the Spirit and Sanctification

The interpreter of the theology of Acts is confronted immediately with a basic conflict in hermeneutics (the principles of biblical interpretation) between a salvation-history view and a dispensational emphasis. Renewed attention has been given to Acts in terms of its relation to Christian experience. Scholars from

---

1. Barclay, *Apostles' Creed for Everyman,* p. 251.
2. NBC, pp. 899-900.

different theological backgrounds have turned to Acts again, some quite frankly in reaction to the Pentecostal and charismatic emphasis of the 20th century.[3]

John R. W. Stott among others has argued that Acts is history and experience and that neither can be used as theology.[4] That Acts is history and experience may readily be conceded. That it therefore has no theological significance is by no means a necessary conclusion. Biblical theologians are all but unanimous in the conviction that much of the theology of Scripture is embedded in history. History is "His story." God speaks through His mighty acts in salvation history from Genesis to Revelation.

Much of the debate centers specifically on the meaning of Spirit baptism in the Gospels and in Acts. We have already noted the references in the Gospels to Christ as the One who baptizes with the Holy Spirit (Matt. 3:11-12; Mark 1:7-8; Luke 3:15-18; John 1:32-34). Each of these references is in the context of the ministry of John the Baptist.

Jesus himself used the same terminology in Acts 1:5, "For John baptized with water, but in a few days you will be baptized with the Holy Spirit." The phraseology occurs the last time in 11:16 as Peter reports to the Jerusalem church on the results of his visit to the household of Cornelius: "Then I remembered what the Lord had said, 'John baptized with water, but you will be baptized with the Holy Spirit.'"[5]

This means that in effect explicit references to Spirit baptism

---

3. E.g., Frederick D. Bruner, *A Theology of the Holy Spirit* (Grand Rapids: William B. Eerdmans Publishing Co., 1970); James D. G. Dunn, *Baptism in the Holy Spirit* (Philadelphia: Westminster Press, 1970); Merrill F. Unger, *The Baptism and Gifts of the Holy Spirit* (Chicago: Moody Press, 1974); Michael Green, *I Believe in the Holy Spirit* (Grand Rapids: William B. Eerdmans Publishing Co., 1975).

4. *The Baptism and Fullness of the Spirit* (Downers Grove, Ill.: InterVarsity Press, 1964). Cf. the critique by George Allen Turner, "An Evaluation of John R. W. Stott's and Frederick Bruner's Interpretations of the Baptism of the Holy Spirit," WTJ, 8:45-51 (1973).

5. First Cor. 12:13 is often cited as a Pauline reference to Spirit baptism. However, it occurs in a setting emphasizing the unity of the Church and is best translated by the NEB, "For indeed we were all brought into one body by baptism, in the one Spirit, whether we are Jews or Greeks, whether slaves or free men, and that one Holy Spirit was poured out for all of us to drink." The baptism is water baptism, in connection with which the Holy Spirit brings believers into the one body. That the Spirit is not the medium with or in which the believer is baptized would seem evident from the allusion to drinking. One does not drink baptismal water.

drop out of the New Testament at Pentecost.[6] When the promise of Jesus was fulfilled, the description is, "All of them were *filled with the Holy Spirit*" (Acts 2:4, italics added). "Full of" or "filled with" then becomes the normal way of describing the spiritual enduement of believers (4:8, 31; 6:3, 5; 7:55; 9:17; 11:24; 13:9; Eph. 5:18). The Holy Spirit is said to be "poured out" upon (2:33; 10:45), "received" (2:38; 8:17), "given" (8:18; 15:8), or He "comes on" persons (10:44; 19:6).

No very ready explanation for this change of terminology can be found unless it be that "baptism" tends to emphasize the epochal or momentary aspect of the Spirit's work, while "fullness" tends to emphasize the ongoing or continuing ministry of the Spirit. There is, of course, no necessary contradiction between "baptism" language and "fullness" language. Both fit the normal Christian experience. There is no maintained condition of fullness without an initial filling. And the initial experience would have little enduring meaning without the ongoing fullness.

A. Major Positions

The major issue revolves largely around the question as to the point at which, if any, Spirit baptism relates to present-day Christian experience. Although the issue is not a new one, it has recently come into new prominence. The purpose of Luke in writing the Acts is, to be sure, not primarily to give an *ordo salutis*, an order of salvation. His concern is an apologetic one, a defense of Christianity against the suspicion of insurrection against the Roman Empire.[7] But where he touches evidence relative to the order of salvation, Luke's report is accurate, trustworthy, and meaningful.

Four major positions may be noted:

(1) Spirit baptism is said to be collective and dispensational with no direct application to personal Christian experience. Pentecost is viewed as the inauguration of a distinctively Christian experience that has little or no relation to biblical faith preceding it. The baptism with or in the Spirit is viewed as corporate rather than individual. It is the Church that is baptized with the Holy Spirit

---

6. Although some exegetes identify the one baptism of Eph. 4:5 and baptism in such references as Rom. 6:3-4 and Col. 2:12 with Spirit baptism.

7. Cf. F. F. Bruce, "The Book of Acts," *The New International Commentary on the New Testament* (Grand Rapids: William B. Eerdmans Publishing Co., 1974), pp. 17-24. Hereafter cited NICNT.

once for all, and individual believers are incorporated into the Body which was constituted and baptized with the Spirit at Pentecost. The baptism with the Spirit would be considered as churchly and corporate, relating to the entire Body of Christ, and not individual or personal at all. It is a once-for-all event that occurred at Pentecost and never since.

While there are many variations, this would seen in general to be the Reformed position. As nearly as Keswick may be said to have an official position, such would also represent the view of this historic conference on the "higher life." A. S. Wilson notes a report in the London *Christian* of 1923 written by F. B. Meyer:

> A conference was held some years ago by the leaders of the Keswick movement, which I well remember, to decide whether or not we should refer to the Pentecostal gift as a *baptism*. After a careful consideration of the matter, it was finally decided that it would be wiser to confine the phrase to the outstanding events of Acts II and X, while reserving "filled" or "anointed" for the experience of individual believers. There was no thought of binding anyone, on the platform or off, to abandon the use of the phrase; but, on the whole, the position was taken that the Spirit had been given to the Church during the present dispensation, and given once for all; so that each member of the Body of Christ may claim his or her share in His gracious anointing. "Ye have an unction from the Holy One."[8]

(2) A second view grows out of the first and is closely related. It is the idea that Spirit baptism is accomplished individually at conversion or regeneration, whether or not subsequently followed by an experience of fullness. This would seem to describe the position of John Wesley, at least prior to his discussions with John Fletcher in and following 1770—although he may in fact mean to be saying what we have described as the third view. The degree to which Wesley accepted Fletcher's identification of Christian perfection with the baptism with the Spirit in his sixth check to antinomianism is still a moot point.[9] In his *Explanatory Notes upon the*

---

8. *Concerning Perplexities*, p. 82.

9. Cf. "The Last Check to Antinomianism," *The Works of the Rev. John Fletcher*, 4 vols. (New York: Phillips and Hunt, 1883), 2:628-33; and the article by Timothy L. Smith, "The Doctrine of the Sanctifying Spirit in John Wesley and John Fletcher," *Preacher's Magazine*, vol. 55, no. 1 (September, October, November, 1979), pp. 16-17, 54-58; and "How John Fletcher Became the Theologian of Wesleyan Perfectionism, 1770-1776," WTJ, vol. 15, no. 1 (Spring, 1980), pp. 68-87. Also, J. Kenneth Grider, "Spirit-baptism the Means of Entire Sanctification," WTJ, vol. 14, no. 2 (Fall, 1979), pp. 31-50, and the rejoinder by Robert W. Lyon, "The Baptism of the Spirit—

New Testament, Wesley comments on the promise of Jesus in Acts
1:5 ("Ye shall be baptized with the Holy Ghost" [KJV]), "And so are
all true believers, to the end of the world." Scholars have long
recognized that Wesley did not consistently relate Spirit baptism
with Christian perfection or entire sanctification.[10]

This would also seem in general to describe the positions of
John R. W. Stott, Frederick D. Bruner, Michael Green, and James
D. G. Dunn—in the latter case without emphasis on a subsequent
filling.[11]

(3) A third view considers Spirit baptism to embrace the entire scope of individual Christian experience, initially in regeneration but not fully accomplished until there is a cleansing of the
moral nature. This would be a reasonable construction to place on
the comment of Adam Clarke in reference to Acts 1:5, "Christ
baptizes with the Holy Ghost, for the destruction of sin, the illumination of the mind, and the consolation of the heart . . . for as
this promise most evidently refers to the communication of the
Holy Spirit on the following pentecost . . . to *illuminate, regenerate,
refine,* and *purify* the heart."[12] Such could be called a holistic view
and is held by some present-day Wesleyan scholars.[13]

(4) The fourth view identifies the baptism with the Holy
Spirit as a spiritual epoch occurring in the individual Christian life

---

Continued," WTJ, vol. 15, no. 2 (Fall, 1980), pp. 70-79. Lyon calls for consideration
of Luke's purpose in writing Acts, e.g., the spread of the gospel beyond its Pal-
estinian birthplace. However, the critical issue is the nature of that gospel: not a
truncated, partial message without a real and complete sanctification. There is no
reason to suppose that Luke does not share the vision of John and Paul that holiness
is not an exception but the normality of Christian experience. Only such an understanding of the order of salvation would properly account for Luke's careful detailing of the sequence of events in the experiences of the Samaritans, Saul of
Tarsus, Cornelius, and the disciples in Ephesus.

10. Cf. Herbert McGonigle, "Pneumatological Nomenclature in Early Methodism," WTJ, 8:61-72 (1973); Leo G. Cox, *John Wesley's Concept of Perfection* (Kansas
City: Beacon Hill Press, 1964), p. 122; Turner, *Vision Which Transforms,* p. 149; and
Alex R. G. Deasley, "Entire Sanctification and the Baptism with the Holy Spirit:
Perspectives on the Biblical View of the Relationship," WTJ, vol. 14, no. 1 (Spring,
1979), pp. 27-28. John A. Knight comments that Wesley often uses the phrase "true
believers" when he means those who have received the fullness of the Spirit, who
are enjoying "Christian perfection" (Letter, Knight to Purkiser, July 6, 1981).

11. Cf. the bibliographical data in notes 3 and 4 above.

12. *Commentary,* 6 vol. (reprint ed., New York: Abingdon-Cokesbury Press,
n.d.), 5:683.

13. Cf. Deasley, "Perspectives," pp. 39-40.

after conversion or regeneration. This is a view which many representatives of Keswick would hold despite the caution of Meyer
cited above. It is the view commonly advocated in Pentecostalism.
As expressed by John Fletcher, Charles G. Finney, Asa Mahan,
Phoebe Palmer (with, of course, many individual variations), and
almost all the leading advocates of entire sanctification through
the later 19th and 20th centuries, it has become virtually standard
in the modern holiness movement.[14]

B. Principles of Interpretation

The leading data dealing with the possible identification of
the baptism with the Holy Spirit and entire sanctification come
from a consideration of the instances recorded in the Book of Acts
in which the Spirit was poured out upon or came upon individuals
or groups. It has been claimed that each of these instances is
related to the initiation or induction of the persons concerned into
the Christian life and is therefore to be identified with conversion
or regeneration. On the other hand, it is maintained that in no
instance is the Holy Spirit said to have been "given" or "poured out
upon" those for whom there is not at least some evidence of prior
spiritual life.

In part, at least, the debate relates to the hermeneutic involved
and to certain assumptions which are at least marginal in the
minds of the exegetes. Using the term in a broad and imprecise
sense, a dispensational approach to Acts leads to the contention
that there could be no truly Christian experience prior to Pentecost
since the work of the Holy Spirit is essential to Christian experi-

---

14. Cf. the studies by Donald W. Dayton, "Asa Mahan and the Development
of American Holiness Theology," WTJ, 9:60-69 (1974), and "The Doctrine of the
Baptism of the Holy Spirit: Its Emergence and Significance," WTJ, 13:114-26 (1978);
Vinson Synan, *The Holiness-Pentecostal Movement in the United States* (Grand Rapids: William B. Eerdmans Publishing Co., 1971), pp. 13-54. "[Entire sanctification]
is wrought by the baptism with the Holy Spirit . . . This experience is also known
by various terms representing its different phases, such as 'Christian perfection,'
'perfect love,' 'heart purity,' 'the baptism with the Holy Spirit,' 'the fullness of the
blessing,' and 'Christian holiness'" (Article X, *Manual* of the Church of the Nazarene
[Kansas City: Nazarene Publishing House, 1980], p. 31); "Entire sanctification is
effected by the Baptism of the Holy Spirit which cleanses the heart of the child of
God from all inbred sin through faith in Jesus Christ" (Articles of Religion, Consti-
tution, *The Discipline of the Wesleyan Church,* Marion, Ind.: The Wesleyan Publishing
House, 1976, p. 24).

ence and the Holy Spirit was not "given" until Jesus was glorified and until the age of the Spirit began.

That the work of the Holy Spirit is essential to Christian experience would be conceded by all. That the Spirit became active in human experience only after Pentecost is not all that sure. Here dispensationalism seems to put unwarranted limitations on the sovereignty of the Spirit and moves in a direction counter to such passages as Ps. 51:11; Isa. 63:10; Luke 11:13; John 3:5-8; 14:17; 20:21-22.

Pentecost has its own importance as we shall shortly see. But its importance is that of fulfillment, not as a sign of radical discontinuity. In a new way and to a new degree the grace and power of the Holy Spirit became available to the people of God. But that very newness had been anticipated in the Old Testament and in the Gospels (Isa. 32:14-17; 44:1-5; Ezek. 36:22-28; Joel 2:28-32; Zech. 12:10-14; Luke 11:13; John 14:15-17; 15:26-27; 16:5-15)—a point Peter makes in his Pentecost sermon (Acts 2:16-36).

As dispensationalism stresses the discontinuities in each new step in God's unfolding plan of redemption, salvation history emphasizes the continuities. It finds in the Old Testament itself models of godliness, and it views the whole of Scripture as the record of God's progressive covenant of grace. The progression is such as to warrant the designation "old" for that portion of the covenant pointing to and leading up to Christ, and "new" for that portion expressing the full unfolding of the divine plan. But the old covenant itself was an integral part of salvation history. Scripture, from Genesis to Revelation, is informed with the same continuity of saving purpose. Admittedly, H. Orton Wiley at times used dispensational language. But his limitation should be heeded:

> Pentecost marks a new dispensation of grace—that of the Holy Spirit. This new economy, however, must not be understood as in any sense superseding the work of Christ, but as ministering to and completing it. The New Testament does not sanction the thought of an economy of the Spirit apart from that of the Father and the Son except in this sense—that it is the revelation of the Person and work of the Holy Spirit, and therefore the final revelation of the Holy Trinity. . . . As the Son revealed the Father, so the Spirit reveals the Son and glorifies Him.[15]

---

15. *Christian Theology,* 2:310-11.

It is not without significance that when Paul would illustrate his great doctrine of justification by faith, the models he chose were Abraham and David (Rom. 4:1-25; Gal. 3:6-9). It is at least possible that in the transitional period covered by the New Testament those who walked with God in obedient faith might pass directly from their status under the old covenant into the full blessing of the new.

Much of the discussion of the spiritual status of the disciples in Acts 2, the Samaritans, Cornelius, and the Ephesian disciples of Acts 19 is clouded by the assumption that the outpouring of the Holy Spirit related in each case was the first impartation of the Spirit any of these persons had. But there is little scriptural warrant for confining the work of the Spirit to these particular epochal moments. The evidence seems to indicate that the Holy Spirit works as often unobtrusively as He does with sound of mighty rushing wind or tongue of flame. Here the insight of Richard S. Taylor is incisive and vitally important:

> There is a threefold reception of the Spirit: (1) He is "received" incognito and non-volitionally in awakening and conviction; (2) He is received as the unidentified Agent of our new birth, when we consciously receive Christ as Savior; (3) He is received consciously and volitionally as a Person in His own right, by the regenerate child of God, to indwell and rule completely as Christ's Other Self.[16]

C. Other Considerations

There are some indirect indications of a possible identification of the baptism with the Holy Spirit as the means by which entire sanctification occurs.

(1) There is a basic coincidence or intersection of meaning in "sanctify" and "baptize." Each has an area of meaning distinct from the other. But each has an area of meaning identical with the other. "To sanctify" is typically defined as "to make sacred or holy; to free from sin; to purify." "To baptize" is typically defined as "to administer the sacrament of baptism to; to purify or purge spiritually; to

---

16. In Myron F. Boyd and Merne A. Harris, eds., *Projecting Our Heritage* (Kansas City: Beacon Hill Press of Kansas City, 1969), p. 61 fn. See also Wood, *Pentecostal Grace*, p. 259, where it is pointed out that the new elements in Pentecost do not mean "that the regenerating grace of God was inoperative before Pentecost."

dedicate; to christen."[17] The overlap in meaning occurs at the point of purifying or cleansing.

Something of this is at least suggested by the New Testament use of the term "Holy" in relation to the Spirit. Paul S. Rees writes, "Professor D. W. Dillistone, in the midst of a careful survey of the biblical data, makes the suggestion that in these two words— adjective and noun—we have a profound double symbol: 'Holy . . . the symbol of an intense purity' and 'Spirit . . . the symbol of a boundless grace.'"[18]

In John 3:25-26 in the ministry of John the Baptist, purifying (albeit in a ritual sense) is identified with baptizing. It does little honor to the Holy Spirit to suppose that He would baptize or fill the human heart without cleansing that heart of all the remains of sin.

(2) Both the baptism with the Holy Spirit and entire sanctification are wrought by the same Agent, the Holy Spirit. This is obvious in the very phrase "baptism with [or in] the Holy Spirit." Virtually all schools of thought recognize that the Holy Spirit is the Agent in sanctification. Both Paul and Peter use the phrase "sanctification of the Spirit" (2 Thess. 2:13; 1 Pet. 1:2, both KJV). Paul speaks of his ministry as working to the end "that the Gentiles might become an offering acceptable to God, sanctified by the Holy Spirit" (Rom. 15:16).

(3) There is what appears to be a more positive identification in Acts 15:8-9. Admittedly, the experience of Cornelius has some ambiguities for the modern interpreter.[19] But when Peter reported the "Gentile Pentecost" to his fellow Jewish Christians in Jerusalem some 15 years after the event had occurred, he said, "God, who knows the heart, showed that he accepted them by giving the Holy Spirit to them, just as he did to us. He made no distinction between us and them, for he purified their hearts by faith." Wesley said of Cornelius before Peter's visit, "It is certain, in the Christian sense, Cornelius was then an unbeliever. He had not then faith in Christ." Yet one of Wesley's frequent descriptions of Christian perfection is a "heart purified by faith."[20]

---

17. Grolier, *New Webster International Dictionary*, 1:78.

18. *Don't Sleep Through the Revolution* (Waco, Tex.: Word Books, 1969), p. 128.

19. See below, section E.

20. *Explanatory Notes, New Testament*, p. 432; cf. *Plain Account*, pp. 26, 28, 40, 80-81; *Sermons on Several Occasions*, 2 vols. (New York: Lane and Scott, 1852), 1:366.

(4) It is important to recognize that both in Scripture and theology different terms are used to identify or describe the same experience. The initial redemptive encounter whereby a person becomes a Christian is variously known as conversion, the new birth, regeneration, justification, salvation, adoption, a new creation, becoming children of God. It is also called "initial sanctification" and "the birth of the Spirit."

In a similar way, the subsequent epoch or crisis in the individual spiritual life is known as holiness, entire sanctification, the fullness of the Spirit, evangelical or Christian perfection, perfect love, heart purity, the rest of faith, the spiritual man, full salvation, circumcision of the heart, the fullness of the blessing of Christ, and the baptism with the Spirit.

Different terms in many instances reflect different aspects cf each of the Spirit's inner ministries. By no means can each term be said to indicate a different work of grace.

While a significant amount of evidence would seem to incline toward identification of the New Testament baptism with the Spirit and entire sanctification, it may still be admitted that the case is not finally closed. The term "baptism" in the New Testament is used at times with a broad meaning, and such could conceivably be the case when used in relation to the Spirit's work.

II. KEY PASSAGES IN ACTS

There are seven key passages in the Book of Acts relating to holiness when holiness is understood as the result of the baptism or fullness of the Holy Spirit in its total meaning.

A. Christ's Preascension Promises, Acts 1:4-8

Jesus commanded His disciples to "wait for the gift my Father promised, which you have heard me speak about" (v. 4). The "promise of the Father" (KJV) goes back into the Old Testament:

> *Till the Spirit is poured upon us from on high,*
> *and the desert becomes a fertile field,*
> *and the fertile field seems like a forest* (Isa. 32:15).

> *I will pour out my Spirit on your offspring,*
> *and my blessing on your descendants* (44:3).

"I will sprinkle clean water on you, and you will be clean; I will cleanse you from all your impurities and from all your idols. I will give you a new heart and put a new spirit in you; I will remove from you your heart of stone and give you a heart of flesh. And I will put my Spirit in you and move you to follow my decrees and be careful to keep my laws" (Ezek. 36:25-27).

> *And afterward,*
> *I will pour out my Spirit on all people.*
> *Your sons and daughters will prophesy,*
> *your old men will dream dreams,*
> *your young men will see visions.*
> *Even on my servants, both men and women,*
> *I will pour out my Spirit in those days* (Joel 2:28-29).

"And I will pour out on the house of David and the inhabitants of Jerusalem a spirit of grace and supplication" (Zech. 12:10).

That the disciples had heard the substance of these promises from Jesus himself is the tenor of John 14:16-17, 26; 15:26; 16:7.[21]

Jesus identified the coming of the Holy Spirit as the fulfillment of John's comparison and contrast of water baptism and the baptism with the Spirit as fire: "For John baptized with water, but in a few days you will be baptized with the Holy Spirit" (v. 5). This is typically Christ's baptism: "Exalted to the right hand of God, he has received from the Father the promised Holy Spirit and has poured out what you now see and hear" (2:33).

The purpose of the coming of the Spirit is not to restore the old kingdom to Israel but to establish the new Kingdom. Opinions differ as to the meaning of Christ's words in the Gospels: "I tell you the truth, some who are standing here will not taste death before they see the Son of Man coming in his kingdom" (Matt. 16:28), or as Mark reports the saying, "Some who are standing here will not taste death before they see the kingdom of God come with power" (Mark 9:1; cf. Luke's similar phraseology, "before they see the kingdom of God"—9:27). Some would refer these words to the Transfiguration which occurred a week later. It is more probable and the terminology more natural if they refer to the coming of the Holy Spirit, almost a year later.

---

21. Bruce, *Book of Acts,* p. 36.

The coming of the Holy Spirit will empower the disciples' witness: "But you will receive power when the Holy Spirit comes on you; and you will be my witnesses in Jerusalem, and in all Judea and Samaria, and to the ends of the earth" (v. 8). The power is not only "power to witness"; it is power to "*be* my witnesses." The witness of the lip must be backed by the witness of character and life.

B. Pentecost, Acts 2:1-4, 37-39

A second major passage is the account of Pentecost and its extension to "all who are far off . . . whom the Lord our God will call" (v. 39). That the Day of Pentecost had profound historical meaning is clear on the surface. It was the beginning of a new age, the inauguration of the "age of the Spirit," and the full establishment of the Christian Church. It was also the official and public proclamation of Jesus as Christ and Lord. "Pentecost was God's seal upon the Messiahship of Jesus, and the fulfilling of His promise to Israel."[22]

The coming of the Holy Spirit was inescapable evidence of the exaltation of Jesus at the right hand of God: "Exalted to the right hand of God, he has received from the Father the promised Holy Spirit and has poured out what you now see and hear" (Acts 2:33). Further, Peter says, "Therefore let all Israel be assured of this: God has made this Jesus, whom you crucified, both Lord and Christ" (v. 36). In this context there could be little doubt about the meaning of "Lord" *(Kurios)*. It was the term in the Greek Old Testament used to translate *Yahweh,* God's own personal name. William M. Greathouse comments:

> At His baptism Jesus had been *identified* as Messiah; by His resurrection and enthronement He was *installed* as Messiah. As the glorified Christ He was "designated the Son of God in power" (Rom. 1:4, RSV; cf. 2 Cor. 3:17-18). At His baptism He was revealed as the *Bearer* of the Spirit; on the day of Pentecost, he becomes the *Baptizer* with the Spirit (John 1:33; Acts 2:32-33).[23]

Historically Pentecost has two vitally important sides. It was the inauguration and proclamation of the Church as the Body of

---

22. Chadwick, *Way to Pentecost,* p. 20.

23. "The Baptism with the Holy Spirit" (Unpublished paper, 1979), p. 7. Many of the ideas in the next several pages have been drawn from Dr. Greathouse's paper.

Christ and the perpetuation of His incarnation in the world. And it was the institution of the new covenant with its promise of inward renewal and cleansing for the people of God, the fulfillment of what was implicit in the old covenant.

1. *The Inauguration of the Church*

H. Orton Wiley writes:

> Pentecost was the birthday of the Christian Church. As Israel redeemed from Egypt was formed into a church-state by the giving of the law at Sinai; so also from individuals redeemed by Christ our Passover, the Holy Spirit formed the Church at Pentecost. This was accomplished by the giving of a new law, written upon the hearts and within the minds of the redeemed.[24]

The Holy Spirit is therefore not only the bond which unites the individual to Christ; He is also the bond which unites the members of the Body to each other and to their living Head. "The Spirit is the life of the body, and since His inauguration at Pentecost [the Holy Spirit] has His 'See' or seat within the Church."[25]

Wiley further points out that the Church in its corporate life is a kingdom of the Incarnation as well as a kingdom of the Spirit. "The Church is not merely an independent creation of the Spirit, but an enlargement of the incarnate life of Christ."[26]

2. *The Establishment of the New Covenant*

It is in connection with the enactment of the new covenant that Pentecost relates most nearly to the theme of this study. Old Testament prophets had promised a coming of the Spirit of the Lord that would be the hallmark of the Messianic age. The gift of the Spirit was to be universal and permanent. He was to rest upon the Servant-Messiah (Isa. 11:1-2; 42:1-4), and then upon the entire people of God (32:14-17; 44:3; Joel 2:28-29).

The effect of this coming of the Spirit was to be profoundly moral and spiritual. He would establish and impart justice, righteousness, peace, quietness, confidence (Isa. 32:16-17), blessing

---

24. *Christian Theology,* 2:329. That the Church existed in embryonic form before Pentecost is not denied. Scholars differ in terminology, and some prefer "inauguration" to "birthday." Cf. John Lawson, *Introduction to Christian Doctrine* (Wilmore, Ky.: Francis Asbury Publishing Co., n.d.), pp. 135-37, for a strong statement of the continuity of the Church under both old and new covenants.

25. Ibid., p. 330.

26. Ibid., pp. 330-31.

(44:3), and inner renewal, banishing guilt and sanctifying the nature (Ezek. 36:25-27). Although Jeremiah does not explain the role of the Spirit in the immediate context, there is little doubt that the new covenant of which he spoke (Jer. 31:31-34), written in the mind and heart, is the same spiritual heritage of which Joel sang in the famous prophecy quoted by Peter at Pentecost (Joel 2:28-29; Acts 2:16-21).

In the words of the Nicene Creed, the Holy Spirit is "the Lord and Giver of Life." He is "'the Spirit of holiness,' who in the New Birth initiates the holiness which as cleansing is perfected in entire sanctification (2 Cor. 7:1) and which viewed positively is the progressive restoration of our image of God, by 'the Lord who is the Spirit' (2 Cor. 3:18, RSV)."[27]

Pentecost is the actualization of the promises of Jesus in the "Paraclete Sayings" of John 14—16[28] and the initial fulfillment of the closely related prayer of John 17: "Sanctify them by the truth; your word is truth. . . . For them I sanctify myself, that they too may be truly sanctified" (vv. 17-19).

The Holy Spirit, resident in the world since creation (Gen. 1:2), now becomes President in the Church. The baptism with which Messiah was to baptize His people (cf. Matt. 3:11 and elsewhere) is a baptism with the Spirit. At Pentecost, He who had always been present in the world comes in a new relationship. He who was the regenerating life of Christ's disciples became their sanctifying Lord. As Greathouse notes:

> The Spirit who came at Pentecost (and who comes to us who believe in Christ), however, is pre-eminently the sanctifying Spirit whose distinctive work in the eschaton is to purify the hearts of believers and perfect them in God's love, thus fulfilling the promise of the new covenant (Ezek. 36:25-27; Jer. 31:31-34). "He shall baptize you with the Holy Spirit and fire," John the Baptist announced (Mt. 3:11; Lk. 3:16). John here echoes Malachi's pledge that the Messenger of the Covenant should "purify the sons of Levi, and purge them as gold and silver" so that they might "offer unto the Lord an offering in righteousness" (Mal. 3:1-3).[29]

---

27. Greathouse, "Baptism with the Spirit," p. 8.
28. Bruce, *Book of Acts*, p. 36.
29. Greathouse, "Baptism with the Spirit," p. 11.

3. *Inaugural Signs*

The significance of Pentecost is further attested by the great historic signs that accompanied the outpouring of the Spirit. There is every evidence that these were "inaugural" signs, marking a new stage in God's full revelation and never again to be repeated in this way.

(1) "A sound like the blowing of a violent wind . . . came from heaven and filled the whole house where they were sitting" (2:2). The suggestion here is that of power, symbolizing the power promised (1:8) and later exemplified. This was a collective manifestation: It "filled the whole house."

(2) "What seemed to be tongues of fire that separated and came to rest on each of them" (2:3). The suggestion here is that of purity. Fire in Scripture is a major symbol of God's manifest presence, and of the cleansing and purging that Presence effects. It was an individual, personal manifestion: It "came to rest on each of them."

(3) They "began to speak in other tongues [marg., languages] as the Spirit enabled them" (2:4). The suggestion here is that of productivity—Spirit-endowed abilities that result in the building of the Body of Christ. From its occurrence at strategic points in the Book of Acts when the gospel was moving out into previously untouched areas (e.g., Cornelius, the Roman proselyte, in Acts 10:46; and the Ephesian disciples, converted out of raw paganism, in Acts 19:6), it is evident that this gift of languages represents the universal preaching of the gospel.

Few miracles in Scripture have been more debated than the language phenomenon described in Acts 2 (and repeated in 10:46 and 19:6). It has been claimed that the miracle was one of hearing rather than speaking. Certainly it was a miracle of *communication* —there was no "interpretation" and the words were understood— and Luke appears to be claiming that the disciples spoke languages they had not learned but which were intelligible to those present from the variety of geographical areas listed in vv. 9-10.

Beyond the necessity of historical record, Luke three times makes the point that the languages spoken were understood. The "crowd came together in bewilderment, because each one heard them speaking in his own language" (v. 6). Their amazement was not that they were hearing "unknown tongues." "Utterly amazed, they asked: 'Are not all these men who are speaking Galileans?

Then how is it that each of us hears them in his own native language?'" (v. 8). "We hear them declaring the wonders of God in our own tongues!" (v. 11).

There is virtually no basis for equating Pentecost with the phenomenon of glossolalia, either in its modern expression or as some have thought to be implied by the reference to a gift of languages in 1 Corinthians 12 and its problematic expression in 1 Corinthians 14. While scholarship is divided on the nature of the manifestation described in 1 Corinthians 14, the entire chapter is perfectly intelligible when understood as relating to the use of unfamiliar languages requiring translation into the local dialect.[30]

Nor is there any indication that this phenomenon was a permanent feature of evangelism. It was indeed a sign, not to the disciples that they were filled with the Spirit, but "for unbelievers" (1 Cor. 14:22), i.e., to the world that the gospel is for all people of every language and "every nation under heaven" (Acts 2:5).

This impression is borne out by the fact that each of the three times over a period of more than 20 years when other languages are said to have been spoken was a time when the gospel broke out beyond the circle within which it had formerly been contained. Acts 2 reports the proclaiming of the Word to an audience predominantly Jewish—Jews of the Dispersion who had journeyed to Jerusalem for the Festival of Pentecost. Acts 10 reports the extension of the gospel to Gentiles who were proselytes to Judaism as typified by Cornelius and members of his household. Acts 19, the "Ephesian Pentecost," reports an encounter with those typical of converts from raw heathenism.

It is fair to say that in the historical or dispensational sense, Pentecost has not and cannot be repeated. Any historical era can have only one beginning. The signs that mark its inauguration— like the cloud, thunder, and earthquake that attended the giving of the law and covenant on Sinai—are not repeated although the era they memorialize continues.

---

30. Cf. Harvey J. S. Blaney, *Speaking in Unknown Tongues: The Pauline Position* (Kansas City: Beacon Hill Press of Kansas City, 1973); Charles D. Isbell, "Glossolalia and Propheteialalia: A Study of 1 Corinthians 14," WTJ, 10:15-22 (1975); and Richard S. Taylor, *Tongues: Their Purpose and Meaning* (Kansas City: Beacon Hill Press of Kansas City, 1973). That the languages of 1 Corinthians 14 were intelligible is argued also in W. T. Purkiser, *The Gifts of the Spirit* (Kansas City: Beacon Hill Press of Kansas City, 1975), pp. 62-68.

That Pentecost has an existential meaning as a pattern for Christians throughout the centuries seems to be suggested by Peter in vv. 37-39. In his response to the inquiry of the people, "Brothers, what shall we do?" (v. 37), Peter said, "Repent and be baptized, every one of you, in the name of Jesus Christ so that your sins may be forgiven. And you will receive the gift of the Holy Spirit" (v. 38).

That water baptism should be interposed in relation to the forgiveness of sins suggests a time interval, however brief, between repentance and forgiveness on the one hand, and "the gift of the Holy Spirit" in the sense of Pentecost on the other hand. Moffatt indicates this time interval by inserting the word "Then" in translating v. 38: "Then you will receive the gift of the Holy Spirit."

In its personal and subjective meaning, Pentecost has been, can be, and is repeated: in Samaria (8:14-17); in Damascus (9:17-19); in Caesarea (10:44-46); and in Ephesus (19:1-6). Of this enduring meaning, William Barclay writes:

> In the Old Testament and in Jewish thought there was much about the Spirit, but for the most part it is true to say that the power and action of the Spirit were connected with extraordinary and abnormal happenings. The great utterances and the great visions of the prophets, sudden manifestations of the splendour of God, were the work of the Spirit; but in the New Testament the Spirit has become even more precious, for the Spirit has become the moving, the controlling, and the upholding power for everyday life and everyday action.[31]

C. The Samaritan Revival, Acts 8:5-25

The events reported in Acts 8 are described by James D. G. Dunn as "The Riddle of Samaria."[32] They are a riddle only to one who operates with the assumption, as Dr. Dunn appears to, that the work of the Spirit is confined to the climactic moment of "outpouring" and that such outpouring represents in every case the first and only work of the Spirit in individual believers' hearts.

---

31. *The Mind of Saint Paul* (New York: Harper and Brothers, 1958), p. 181. See also Wood, *Pentecostal Grace*, pp. 22-23.

32. *Baptism in the Holy Spirit*, pp. 55-72. See, contra, Bruce, *Book of Acts*, p. 181, fn. 34, where he says concerning the reception of the Spirit by the Samaritans, "The prior operation of the Spirit in regeneration is not in view here." Cf. also Wood, *Pentecostal Grace*, pp. 70-71, 81: "If one accepts at face value the accounts in Acts 8:14-17, and Acts 19:1-7, the Samaritans and the Ephesians were believers prior to their reception of the Spirit" (p. 81).

Taken as reported, the revival in Samaria tends to refute the objection that the experience of the disciples in chapter 2 was not typical since their spiritual lives straddled two "dispensations": of the Son before Pentecost, and of the Spirit at and after Pentecost.

When the Church was scattered during the fierce persecution in Jerusalem, Philip the deacon went to a city in Samaria "and proclaimed Christ there" (v. 5). Evil spirits were cast out, many were healed, and "there was great joy in that city" (v. 8). A large company of people "believed Philip as he preached the good news of the kingdom of God and the name of Jesus Christ, [and] were baptized, both men and women" (v. 12).

"When the apostles in Jerusalem heard that Samaria had accepted the word of God, they sent Peter and John to them. When they arrived, they prayed for them that they might receive the Holy Spirit, because the Holy Spirit had not yet come upon any of them; they had simply been baptized into the name of the Lord Jesus. Then Peter and John placed their hands on them, and they received the Holy Spirit" (vv. 14-17).

In this instance there is every apparent intent to convey the fact of genuine faith certified by baptism, prior to the Holy Spirit "coming upon" these Christians. Nor was there any doubt of His coming when Peter and John later prayed for them and laid hands on them. Simon, who had practiced sorcery there and had gone along with the new Christian movement, offered money for power to induce the infilling of the Spirit—so obvious was it. For this he was sternly rebuked by Peter (vv. 9-11, 13, 18-24) and contributed an infamous name ("simony") to any attempt to buy ecclesiastical position or privilege. But to regard Simon as typical of the other Samaritan believers is as unfair as to judge the apostles by the character of Judas Iscariot.

D. The Conversion of Paul, Acts 9:1-19

Saul's Christian conversion took place on the road outside Damascus when he identified the One who encountered him there as Jesus of Nazareth and called Him "Lord." That "lord" *(kurios)* could be used by the Greek as we would use "sir" is indeed true. Yet for the Jew, *Kurios* was the title used in the Greek Old Testament for the one true God, and the earliest Christian confession was "Jesus is Lord" (Rom. 10:8-10). In his defense before the mob in Jerusalem, Paul indicates his submission to the control of Christ on the

Damascus road by his question, "What shall I do, Lord?" (Acts 22:10). When he testified to Herod Agrippa of his conversion (26:2-29), Paul indicated the Damascus road vision as the time— although in his earlier testimony (22:12-16) he had also related the subsequent visit of Ananias.[33]

Ananias, instructed to go to Saul, was reluctant until assured, "He is praying." When Ananias went, "placing his hands on Saul, he said, 'Brother Saul, the Lord—Jesus, who appeared to you on the road as you were coming here—has sent me so that you may see again and be filled with the Holy Spirit.' Immediately, something like scales fell from Saul's eyes, and he could see again. He got up and was baptized, and after taking some food, he regained his strength" (vv. 17-19).

E. The Case of Cornelius, Acts 10:1—11:18; 15:6-11

This is sometimes called the Caesarean or Gentile Pentecost. There are admitted ambiguities in the account. Luke's purpose in detailing the experience of Cornelius is his concern for the Gentile mission of the Church. This becomes clear in the timing of his repeated accounts of the event (11:1-18; 15:6-11). Peter's mission to Cornelius was to bring to him a message through which he and all his household would be saved (11:14). God gave them the same gift as He had given the Church in Jerusalem some two years before (v. 17). The Jerusalem church accepted this as evidence that God "has even granted the Gentiles repentance unto life" (v. 18).

At the Jerusalem Council some 13 years later, called to decide the status of Gentiles converted outside the ceremonial laws of Judaism, Peter again recounted his visit to Caesarea. The gift of the Holy Spirit was evidence that God "accepted" the Gentiles and "made no distinction" between Jewish and Gentile believers so that both groups are saved "through the grace of our Lord Jesus" (15:8-11). This again was accepted by the council as indicating the extension of the gospel to the Gentile world: "Simon has described

---

33. That Paul's conversion occurred on the road to Damascus at the time of the noon vision is cogently argued by Wood in his *Pentecostal Grace*, pp. 198-99, 268-71. In his fn. 100, Wood cites a wide range of scholarly opinion to support this view of which he says, "the preponderance . . . is clearly against" the view that Paul was not converted until his baptism by Ananias three days later (pp. 199, 234). John Wesley, on the other hand, remarks of the three days, "So long he seems to have been in the pangs of the new birth"—*Explanatory Notes, New Testament*, p. 428.

to us how God at first showed his concern by taking from the Gentiles a people for himself" (v. 14).

Donald S. Metz notes that "Cornelius is presented as an example by inference, rather than an example by direct assertion."[34] It would be too much to claim that prior to the coming of Peter, Cornelius had been in every way a full Christian disciple. On the other hand, he was certainly not a typical unconverted person.

Several hints are given as to the spiritual status of Cornelius. He was a "devout and God-fearing" man (10:2). His "prayers and gifts to the poor" had "come up as a remembrance before God" (v. 4). Peter was warned not to call impure what "God has made clean" (v. 15). His prayer was heard and answered (v. 31), and Peter says, "I now realize how true it is that God does not show favoritism but accepts men from every nation who fear him and do what is right" (vv. 33-34).

"You know the word," Peter continued, addressing Cornelius and the others with him, "which he sent to Israel, preaching good news of peace by Jesus Christ (he is Lord of all), the word which was proclaimed throughout all Judea, beginning from Galilee after the baptism which John preached" (10:36-37, RSV), a knowledge which could have been gained through the ministry of Philip in Caesarea (8:40; 21:8). The coming of the Holy Spirit upon Cornelius and his family was "as he had come on us at the beginning" (11:15). It was evidence that God, "who knows the heart, . . . accepted them by giving the Holy Spirit to them, just as he did to us. He made no distinction between us and them, for he purified their hearts by faith" (15:8-9).

The enduring importance of Peter's testimony lies in his clear identification of the effect of Pentecost as purifying or cleansing (RSV) the hearts of those "upon" whom the Holy Spirit comes. The phenomenon of speaking other languages which occurred in Caesarea (10:46) as it had in Jerusalem is completely ignored by Peter. This is a fact extremely hard to explain if such speaking is, as claimed, "the evidence of the baptism in the Spirit." For Peter, 20 years after Pentecost, the essential identification of the baptism or filling with the Holy Spirit is purity of heart. As Ralph Earle writes:

---

34. *Studies in Biblical Holiness* (Kansas City: Beacon Hill Press of Kansas City, 1971), p. 120. Cf. Wood, *Pentecostal Grace*, p. 91, where it is said of Cornelius, "As one who already sustained a trusting relationship to God, his heart was prepared to receive the Pentecostal Spirit."

Peter affirmed that two things happened both to the Jews at Pentecost and to the Gentiles at Caesarea: they were filled with the Holy Spirit, and their hearts were cleansed. Thus we affirm, with Peter, that when a person is filled with the Holy Spirit he not only receives power (1:8), but he also is cleansed from sin (15:8-9). . . . When the Spirit fills one's heart, He necessarily cleanses it; for He is the *Holy* Spirit, the sanctifying Spirit.[35]

The term *katharizō*, "purify," is in the aorist tense, suggesting an action completed and viewed as a unity. It is the same term used in Matt. 3:12, "purge" (KJV); Matt. 5:8, "pure in heart"; 2 Cor. 7:1, "purify"; Eph. 5:26, "cleansing"; 1 John 1:7, "purifies." It is used occasionally in a ceremonial sense in the New Testament, but its usual application has to do with cleansing from sin, corruption, or moral defilement—and always when the heart is the object of such purification.

F. The Disciples at Ephesus, Acts 18:24—19:6

This is sometimes called the Ephesian Pentecost. It represents the third stage in the breakthrough of the gospel into the Gentile world. Again, there is a dispensational problem with the mention of John's baptism. Yet the evidence of conversion prior to the filling with the Spirit is clear.

We are told that Paul had ministered in Ephesus and that he had left Priscilla and Aquila there when he went on to Jerusalem (18:19-21). Apollos preached there, and he is described as "a learned man, with a thorough knowledge of the Scriptures" (v. 24). Apollos "had been instructed in the way of the Lord, and he spoke with great fervor and taught about Jesus accurately, though he knew only the baptism of John. . . . When Priscilla and Aquila heard him, they invited him to their home and explained to him the way of God more adequately" (vv. 25-26).

When Paul returned to Ephesus, "he found some disciples and asked them, 'Did you receive the Holy Spirit when [or after, marg.] you believed?'" (19:2). The precise translation of the question has long been debated.[36] The alternate renderings are, "Have ye re-

---

35. BBC, 7:428.

36. Cf. Charles Ewing Brown, *The Meaning of Sanctification* (Anderson, Ind.: Warner Press, 1945), pp. 195-201. Wood argues that the context clearly favors "Have you received . . . ?" (*Pentecostal Grace*, pp. 82-83).

ceived the Holy Ghost since ye believed?" (KJV) and "Did you receive the Holy Spirit when you believed?" (RSV, NIV).

There are technical theological differences in the alternate translations. But in either case, the answer is "no," and there is no question raised as to the faith of the persons involved. They are called disciples (cf. 11:26), "the most distinctive name for the Christians in Acts."[37] Everett F. Harrison notes that the term "disciple" is used 30 times in Acts, "always in the sense of a member of the Christian community."[38] While the baptism of John fell short of the full meaning of Christian baptism, it was yet "a baptism of repentance for the forgiveness of sins" (Mark 1:4) and the baptism received by Jesus and the apostles. F. F. Bruce comments:

> But that these men were Christians is certainly to be inferred from the way in which Luke describes them as "disciples"; this is a term he commonly uses for Christians, and had he meant to indicate that they were disciples not of Christ but of John the Baptist (as has sometimes been deduced from v. 3), he would have said so explicitly. They may have received their knowledge of Christianity from a source similar to that from which Apollos received his; or they may have received it from Apollos and been baptized by him during his earlier days in Ephesus, when he knew only the baptism of John.
>
> At any rate, Paul's question, "Did ye receive the Holy Spirit when ye believed?" suggests strongly that he regarded them as true believers in Christ.[39]

The Ephesian disciples' confession of ignorance concerning the Holy Spirit might better be translated, "No, we have not even heard whether the Holy Spirit has been given" (19:2, NASB marg.). With it may be compared the statement of Dwight L. Moody to the effect that for seven years after his conversion he was as ignorant of the ministry of the Holy Spirit as the Ephesian disciples.[40]

With Paul's explanation, the Ephesians "were baptized into the name of the Lord Jesus" (19:5). Then "when Paul placed his

---

37. F. J. Foakes-Jackson and Kirsopp Lake, *The Beginnings of Christianity,* 5 vols., Part I, *The Acts of the Apostles* (London: Macmillan and Co., 1922), 4:237; cf. also *The Oxford Annotated Bible; Revised Standard Version* (New York: Oxford University Press, 1962), p. 1344, notes on Acts 19:1-2.

38. *Short Life of Christ,* p. 148.

39. *Book of Acts,* p. 385. Used by permission. Cf. also Wood, *Pentecostal Grace,* pp. 15-17 and 267-68, where receiving the Spirit is said to imply "receiving of the fulness of the Spirit" (p. 15).

40. *Secret Power* (Chicago: Fleming H. Revell Co., 1881), tract.

hands on them, the Holy Spirit came on them, and they spoke in tongues [marg., other languages] and prophesied" (v. 6). If, as is often claimed, the Ephesians did not become fully regenerate persons until "the Holy Spirit came on them," then Paul administered Christian baptism to those who were not fully Christian. That such has often been done since is indeed true. That Paul started the practice can hardly be accepted.

Paul's question had been, "Did you receive the Holy Spirit when you believed?" (v. 2). Jesus said, "The world cannot receive" Him (John 14:17, RSV). "Receive" *(lambanō)* is used 10 times in the New Testament in reference to the Holy Spirit, each time in such a way as to indicate some prior spiritual life. That there is an essential imparting of the Spirit at regeneration, which is being "born of the Spirit" (John 3:3-5), we have already seen. But in its full New Testament sense, "receiving" the Holy Spirit is apparently subsequent to regeneration.

G. Paul's Preaching and Testimony, Acts 20:32; 26:18

The term "sanctify" or "sanctified" as such occurs only twice in the Book of Acts, each time on the lips of the apostle Paul. G. Abbott-Smith defines the Greek word as meaning *"to make holy, consecrate, sanctify. . . . 1. to dedicate, separate, set apart for God. . . . 2. to purify,* make conformable in character to such dedication."[41]

In his farewell to the elders of the church at Ephesus, Paul says, "Now I commit you to God and to the word of his grace, which can build you up and give you an inheritance among all those who are sanctified" (20:32). A similar phrase is used in the apostle's explanation to King Agrippa concerning the scope of his message to the Gentiles as Christ had given it to him: "to open their eyes and turn them from darkness to light, and from the power of Satan to God, so that they may receive forgiveness of sins and a place [Gr., inheritance—so NASB] among those who are sanctified by faith in me" (26:18).

Here indeed is the broad scope of sanctification as indicating all God does by way of inner renewal in the redeemed heart. But there is also a more explicit meaning. The sanctification in question is said to be an inheritance—a possession by right of family

41. *A Manual Greek Lexicon of the New Testament,* 2d ed. (Edinburgh: T. & T. Clark, 1923), pp. 4-5.

membership—and it is said to be "by faith in" Christ Jesus. At this latter point, V. Raymond Edman writes:

> Life, however, is not achieved by longing for a better life and lingering at the Cross. There must be *appropriation* by faith of the Holy Spirit to fill life with the presence of the Lord Jesus. That obtainment is by faith, and not by works. Inquires the Scripture: "This only would I learn of you, Received ye the Spirit by the works of the law, or by the hearing of faith?" (Galatians 3:2). Just as salvation is by faith, so is the exchanged life. Just as we accept the Lord Jesus by faith as Saviour, so by simple faith we receive the fullness of the Holy Spirit. Just as we took the Lord as our sin-bearer, we take the Holy Spirit as our burden-bearer. Just as we take the Saviour as our penalty for sins that are past, we take the Holy Spirit for power over indwelling sins that are present. The Saviour is our atonement, the Holy Spirit is our advocate. In salvation we receive newness of life, by the Holy Spirit we find life more abundant. In each case the appropriation is by faith and by faith alone, wholly apart from any feeling on our part.[42]

---

42. *They Found the Secret,* p. 154.

5

Holiness in Romans

The Letter of Paul to the Romans, sometimes called "the fifth gospel," stands first among and is in all ways the greatest of the apostle's letters. It was a sound insight that placed Romans at the head of the Epistles, for it is an introductory summary of what follows. It was prepared and sent to Rome as an introduction to the apostle's teaching in preparation for a visit he hoped to make on the way to Spain (1:8-15; 15:23-29).

Romans was written at a watershed time in Paul's life. He felt that his work in Asia Minor, Macedonia, and Greece was completed. He had only to take an offering from the Gentile churches to the church in Jerusalem and then planned to move farther west. The westward direction set in the Macedonian call was to be continued.

Waiting at Corinth for the offering to be gathered gave Paul time and opportunity to write the main features of his doctrine of salvation. His purpose was to present the scope of his message and at the same time to clear away misconceptions from both Jewish and antinomian circles.

The influence of Romans in the Church is an eloquent testimony to its theological stature. It has emerged as a key factor in most of the great spiritual movements that have marked the course of the history of Christianity. It was a passage from Rom. 13:12-14 that sparked the conversion of Augustine. The key importance of Rom. 1:17, "The righteous will live by faith," for Luther and the Protestant Reformation is well known. While John Wesley was listening to a reading of Luther's Preface to the Book of Romans in a little Moravian gathering on Aldersgate Street in London, his heart was "strangely warmed" and he came to know personally that God for Christ's sake had forgiven his sins. And a key book in the shift of 20th-century theology from its humanistically liberal course toward neoorthodoxy was the 1914 commentary on the Book of Romans by Karl Barth.

I. THE STRUCTURE OF THE BOOK

The ground plan of Romans is both simple and sweeping. It divides into four main divisions:

(1) The doctrine of justification, 1:1—5:11—how forgiveness is possible in face of the fact that "all have sinned and fall short of the glory of God" (3:23).

(2) The doctrine of sanctification, 5:12—8:39—how it is possible for a sinful nature to be changed: "Now that you have been set free from sin and have become slaves to God, the benefit you reap leads to holiness, and the result is eternal life" (6:22).

(3) The doctrine of election, 9:1—11:36—salvation as the sheer gift of God's grace. It cannot be earned; it may be forfeited by unbelief.

(4) The doctrine of consecration, 12:1—16:27—the "behaving side" of the gospel that follows from the "believing side"; the practical applications of the gospel to life.

Norman P. Grubb makes an interesting observation concerning the structure of the first two sections of Romans and its relation to Christian experience:

> For most of us this deeper revelation of union has to come as a second experience. We can seldom see our outward sins and inner selves in one single exposure. The plainest proof of this is that the profound exposition of Romans 6—8 is given us separately and subsequently to chs. 1—5. It is not that there are two separate salvations, as it were. There is only one Saviour, one glorious process of restoration through His death, resurrection and ascension, one Holy Spirit. The two-foldedness is not on His side. But for most of us there has to be a two-fold appropriation of the two great deliverances that stream from the one Calvary, the deliverance from sin and wrath (1—5), the deliverance from sin and independent self (6—8). These could conceivably be experienced together, for both are there for the taking, but an appropriation which produces a real experience of both at the same time, and not merely a mental apprehen-

sion, is rare. In that sense there is a "second blessing," an entire sanctification subsequent to justification, an inner union according to Gal. 2:20.[1]

Approaching the relationship of justification and sanctification from a somewhat different point of view, Claude Thompson quotes the Scottish theologian John Baillie to the effect that "a justification which does not issue in sanctification is no true justification at all. That is, if it is only a good tree which produces good fruit, then our persistent failure to become more holy should raise a question even concerning our reconciliation with God."

Thompson adds, "Baillie becomes almost Wesleyan when he follows through on this vision: 'Of the few things I know, there is nothing that I know with a clearer and more immediate conviction than that I must not be *satisfied* with anything that is less than *perfect*' (*Invitation to Pilgrimage*, p. 71)."[2]

As noted above, 5:12—8:39 forms Paul's great classic passage on sanctification. It must be said that the apostle includes the whole process of inner transformation which begins in regeneration as initial sanctification and continues through entire sanctification into the final full redemption of body as well as soul (glorification).

Frederick Godet divides the section into three divisions: Holiness in Christ, 5:12—6:23; Holiness Without Law, c. 7; and Holiness by the Holy Spirit, c. 8.[3]

II. HOLINESS IN CHRIST

The first division, holiness in Christ, opens with a statement of the condition which requires the inner transformation that is sanctification. Rom. 1:1—5:11 had dealt with the catalog of human sins and the forgiveness and reconciliation that comes through justification by faith in Christ apart from the works of the law. Beginning with 5:12, Paul's terminology changes. From 5:12 to 8:10, the apostle uses the singular noun sin *(hamartia)* a total of 39

---

1. *The Liberating Spirit* (Fort Washington, Pa.: Christian Literature Crusade, 1955), p. 74.

2. *Theology of the Kerygma: A Study in Primitive Preaching* (Englewood Cliffs, N.J.: Prentice-Hall, 1962), p. 100.

3. *St. Paul's Epistle to the Romans*, trans. A. Cusin (Edinburgh: T. and T. Clark, 1884), p. 234.

times, of which 28 times the noun is used with the definite article, "*the* sin."[4]

A. M. Hills cites Whedon, Alford, Godet, Lange, and Sanday and Headlam in support of the thesis that "'the sin' . . . means a particular kind of sin, namely, 'indwelling sin,' 'inherited sin,' 'the sin principle,' 'depravity'."[5] It is not sins committed but sin inherited: "the principle of revolt whereby the human will rises against the divine will."[6] William M. Greathouse remarks: "Up to this point Paul has been dealing chiefly with the problem of sin as *guilt;* now he introduces the idea of sin as *revolt.*"[7]

A. The Problem, 5:12—6:1

Paul's contention here is that this human condition came about through one man, Adam (5:12-14). As already noted, the native sinfulness of human persons is a corrupt condition resulting from the loss of a personal fellowship with God. Theologians of many persuasions recognize what is generally known as "original sin." The concept is embedded deeply in the historic creeds, and their language persists in modern formulations. In another light, Daniel Day Williams writes:

> We must see that sin is a corruption at the root of our being, if we are to have any right understanding of it. What we call "sins," particular wrong actions, are for the most part to be understood as symptoms of the fundamental disorder which lies deep in the spirit.[8]

This corrupt condition is the cause of death, both spiritual—separation of the soul from God the Source of eternal life—and physical. "Nevertheless, death reigned from the time of Adam to the time of Moses, even over those who did not sin by breaking a command, as did Adam, who was a pattern of the one to come" (v. 14). The spiritual death and mortality that resulted from Adam's sin is not to be thought of as a penalty inflicted on those guilty, for

---

4. The exceptions are 5:13 (2); 6:14, 16; 7:7, 8*b*, 13*b*, 17; 8:3*b* (2), 10. While the definite article is omitted these 11 times, the sense is the same. Cf. William M. Greathouse, BBC, 8:114.

5. *Holiness in the Book of Romans,* published earlier as *The Establishing Grace* (Kansas City: Beacon Hill Press, 1950), p. 15.

6. Godet, *Romans,* p. 204.

7. Greathouse, BBC, 8:114.

8. *The Minister and the Care of Souls,* substance of the 1959 Sprunt Lectures (New York: Harper and Brothers, Publishers, 1961), pp. 73-74.

it is the lot of babies and children in their innocence as well as of adults. It is the consequence of our humanity deprived of its created relationship with the righteousness and holiness of God. The condition of corruption is the source of acts of rebellion: Each of us is "a sinner by choice, and an alien by birth."

But the conquest of sin and death is reversed by Christ. The "last Adam" (1 Cor. 15:45) stands in comparison, in contrast, and in contradiction to the first Adam. Like the first Adam, Christ is the Head of an entire race—the One affecting the many, the one act having universal consequences (vv. 12-14). While Paul's thought is broken in this paragraph, the intent is clear: "Adam . . . was a pattern of the one to come" (v. 14).

But the contrast is total. Because of Adam's one act of disobedience, sin and death reigned over all. Because of Christ's one act of obedience, God's grace and gift of life is offered to all (vv. 15-19): "For if, by the trespass of the one man, death reigned through that one man, how much more will those who receive God's abundant provision of grace and of the gift of righteousness reign in life through the one man, Jesus Christ" (v. 17).[9]

The contrast deepens into contradiction. Grace reverses what sin produces. "Consequently, just as the result of one trespass was condemnation for all men, so also the result of one act of righteousness was justification that brings life for all men. For just as through the disobedience of the one man the many were made sinners, so also through the obedience of the one man the many will be made righteous" (vv. 18-19). As Henry Alford indicates, the righteousness is as real and experiential as the sinfulness had been.[10]

"Where sin increased, grace abounded all the more, so that, as sin reigned in death, grace also might reign through righteousness to eternal life through Jesus Christ our Lord" (vv. 20-21, RSV). God's purpose is to cancel in Christ all the consequences of Adam's sin—replacing sin with righteousness, death with eternal life.

The consequence, then, is the total incompatibility of sin and grace. "What shall we say, then? Shall we go on sinning [lit., may

---

9. "The many" contrasted with "the one" has the force of "all." Cf. William Sanday and A. C. Headlam, "A Critical and Exegetical Commentary on the Epistle to the Romans," *International Critical Commentary* (New York: Charles Scribner's Sons, 1923), p. 140.

10. *The Greek New Testament*, 2:365.

we continue in sin] so that grace may increase? By no means! We died to sin; how can we live in it any longer?" (6:1-2). Grace and sin are mutually exclusive. Kenneth S. Wuest says, "The fundamental question [here] is not with regard to acts of sin but with respect to the believer's relationship to the sinful nature."[11] "Are we to be hospitable to the sin which has reigned since Adam's fall? Are we to give this sin a home? Shall we who have been justified continue in the same relationship with 'the sin' which we had before we came to Christ?"[12] The answer is a clear, ringing, "By no means!" "No, no!" (NEB).

B. The Provision, 6:2-23

The general principle set forth in the verses that follow 6:1-2 is to the effect that Christ died for us on the Cross not only for forgiveness of sins but to destroy (RSV) the "body of sin" (v. 6) and thus provide freedom from "the sin" (vv. 19, 22). As Vincent Taylor remarks, one of the curious blind spots in theology has been its strange failure to see sanctification as a result of the Atonement as well as justification.[13]

Paul here brings together and merges two great New Testament concepts: baptism, and the death of Christ. In this, he follows the example of Jesus himself who referred to His crucifixion as His baptism (Mark 10:38; Luke 12:50). Baptism has a twofold meaning in the New Testament: washing away the sins of the past (Acts 22:16), and a new state of union with Christ (Rom. 6:3). Therefore, baptism in the New Testament involves two elements: water, symbolizing the washing away of the sins of the past in order to unite with Christ (Acts 2:38); and the Holy Spirit as fire (Matt. 3:11; Luke 3:16; etc.), making actual what water baptism symbolizes in its forward look.[14] To be "baptized into Christ" means to be baptized with His Spirit into His death (Rom. 6:3).

1. *Crucifixion with Christ, vv. 4-10*

What baptism is in its full New Testament meaning must be

---

11. *Romans in the Greek New Testament* (Grand Rapids: William B. Eerdmans Publishing Co., 1955), pp. 91-93.

12. BBC, 8:127.

13. *Forgiveness and Reconciliation* (London: Macmillan and Co., 1956), pp. 144-230.

14. Cf. the treatment of these verses in Milton S. Agnew, *More than Conquerors* (Chicago: The Salvation Army, 1959), p. 59.

realized in our experience—the passion of our Lord repeated in us. To follow Christ fully means to deny self and take one's cross (Matt. 16:24). The path of the cross involves three stages: (1) Gethsemane, the consecration expressed in the words, "Yet not as I will, but as you will" (Matt. 26:39); (2) Golgotha, the cleansing of "cocrucifixion," dying to sin (Rom. 6:3-6); and (3) the Garden of the Empty Tomb, commitment to the risen life (vv. 4-5, 7-8).

What is "our old man" (KJV and literal) or "our old self" (RSV, NIV) that was crucified with Christ? Is it the old unregenerate state, or is it the remains of "the sin," original or inherited corruption? Opinions differ, and the biblical evidence (comparing Eph. 4:22 and Col. 3:9) is insufficient for a dogmatic answer. Rom. 6:6 may be interpreted either way. Eph. 4:22 seems to differentiate between the "old self" and the "former way of life," and as it is usually translated its "putting off" stands as an imperative for believers. Col. 3:9 would appear to identify the "old self" with the sinful life.

It is at least possible that we need not choose: that the "old self" is the whole former course of life *and* the sinful condition that lies behind it. Paul is not here concerned to develop a "one-two" pattern of Christian experience, but to sketch the totality of redemption encompassing both regeneration and entire sanctification. As Paul here considers the whole potential of sanctification under the analogy of crucifixion and resurrection, he deals with the whole problem of sin under the symbol of the "old man" or the "old self."

Certainly what was crucified with Christ is not the "self" in a psychological sense. It is the fictitious self-sovereignty of the person standing apart from God. Everett Lewis Cattell expresses a proper caution at this point:

> Those who are striving for the deeper life in the Spirit often call for the death of self. One realizes what is meant, but nevertheless the language is inaccurate. The self can never die. It is eternal. It is the center of the soul and must live forever. God created it and has no desire that it should be eradicated. It is inaccurate to speak of the death *of* self, but it is entirely proper to speak of death *to* self. There is a world of difference. Selfishness is that pattern of life which inevitably results when the self stands apart from God in any degree.[15]

---

15. *The Spirit of Holiness* (Grand Rapids: William B. Eerdmans Publishing Co., 1963), p. 26.

The Christian's "fourfold death" in this passage has been sketched as follows:

(1) We died in provision when Jesus died on the Cross (v. 6).

(2) We died in purpose when we embraced Christ as Savior. Implied in Christian conversion is consent not only to abandon sin but to accept all for which Christ died.

(3) We died in profession in Christian baptism.

(4) We die to sin in personal experience as an actual fact when "sanctifying grace destroys 'the body of sin.'"[16]

It is well to recall that the essential meaning of death in Scripture is a clean-cut separation. Physical death is the separation of the spirit/soul from the physical body. Spiritual death is the separation of the human self from God, the Source of life. The "second death" (Rev. 20:14) or eternal death is everlasting separation of the finally impenitent from God. "Death to sin" is a clean-cut separation from sin; as conversely to be "alive to God" means united to God in Christ Jesus (Rom. 6:11).[17]

The end result of our crucifixion with Christ is that the body of sin might be "destroyed, and we might no longer be enslaved to [the] sin" (6:6, RSV). The body of sin is not to be thought of in physical terms. As C. H. Dodd comments:

> It is important to bear in mind the characteristic sense in which Paul uses the term body, which is most clearly brought out in 1 Cor. 15. It is not the structure of flesh and blood as such. The flesh-and-blood structure may pass away, leaving not a vestige, and yet the body remain self-identical. As it now partakes of the perishable substance of "flesh," it may in future partake of the imperishable substance of "glory" or splendour, and yet remain the same "body." Such is Paul's metaphysic. The body is the individual self as an organism (neither flesh nor spirit being individual, and "soul" being merely the animating principle of the flesh, or physical structure). Thus the sinful body is the self as the organization of the sinful impulses inherent in the flesh.[18]

The term "destroyed" must not be weakened. Here the NIV translation, "rendered powerless," is more interpretation than

---

16. William M. Greathouse, "Romans," *Search the Scriptures,* vol. 6 (Kansas City: Nazarene Publishing House, n.d.), p. 28 (hereafter cited SS; cf. BBC, 8:140-41.

17. Cf. Grubb, *Liberating Spirit,* p. 78.

18. "The Epistle of Paul to the Romans," *The Moffatt New Testament Commentary* (New York: Harper and Brothers, 1932), p. 90. Used by permission.

translation. *Katargein* is used variously in the New Testament. Its use in 1 Cor. 6:13; 15:26; 2 Cor. 3:13; Eph. 2:15; 2 Thess. 2:8; and Heb. 2:14[19] shows the depth and intensity of the term. Herman Cremer says of Paul's use of *katargein,* "With him it always denotes a complete, not a temporary or partial ceasing. Elsewhere it signifies a putting out of activity, out of power or effect; but with St. Paul it equals *to annihilate,* to put an end to, to bring to naught."[20] When Paul "speaks of the destruction of the sinful body he wishes to stress the end of the inner sinful condition."[21]

2. Faith and Consecration, vv. 11-13

What Christ provided for us on the Cross and in His resurrection life is to be realized in us by our active response: "In the same way, count yourselves dead to sin but alive to God in Christ Jesus. Therefore do not let sin reign in your mortal body so that you obey its evil desires. Do not offer the parts of your body to sin, as instruments of wickedness, but rather offer yourselves to God, as those who have been brought from death to life; and offer the parts of your body to him as instruments of righteousness" (6:11-13).

"Count yourselves—" (v. 11) is *logizesthe heautous.* It has been pointed out that *logizomai* is a bookkeeping term. It does not mean to suppose what is not true. It means to take account of what is.[22] It represents the "reckoning of faith" described in Rom. 4:1-12 in relation to Abraham's justification and here used with regard to the

---

19. Where the NIV itself uses "fading away," "abolishing," "destruction," "destroy," "destroyed."

20. *Biblico-Theological Lexicon of New Testament Greek,* p. 261; quoted by Ralph Earle in Kenneth Geiger, comp., *Insights into Holiness* (Kansas City: Beacon Hill Press, 1962), p. 86.

21. Franz J. Leenhardt, *The Epistle to the Romans: A Commentary* (Cleveland: World Publishing Co., 1961), p. 162. By confusing Paul's use of the term "old man" or "old self" with the empirical, psychological human self, J. Sidlow Baxter concludes that the crucifixion and death here are legal and not experiential. Such an exegesis loses touch completely with the context, particularly in the latter part of the chapter. The whole matter is clarified when it is seen that the apostle has in view here not the self which is the center of consciousness, the core of personal being, but the fictitious self-sovereignty that is the essense of original sin. Cf. Baxter's treatment in *A New Call to Holiness,* republished in *Christian Holiness Restudied and Restated* (Grand Rapids: Zondervan Publishing House, 1977).

22. Cf. Ralph Earle, *Word Meanings in the New Testament,* vol. 3, "Romans" (Kansas City: Beacon Hill Press of Kansas City, 1974), p. 89; and in Geiger, *Insights into Holiness,* p. 87.

appropriation by faith of the freedom from sin and union with God provided in the atonement and resurrection of Christ. It does not stand for a whitewash that "imputes" a righteousness which does not in fact exist. It stands for crediting to one's account (by God in response to faith) a cleansing that has in actual fact taken place.[23]

Faith therefore is a "reckoning" as real and actual what God has declared without waiting for supporting evidence. Faith is the condition on which the heart is made pure, the soul is sanctified, the promise of the Spirit is received (Acts 15:8-9; 26:18; Gal. 3:14). It is not a matter of overcoming God's reluctance but of accepting His willingness. In this context it relates both to a death *of* sin within and a death *to* sin without. In the lines of Hartley Coleridge, faith

> . . . *is an affirmation and an act*
> *That bids eternal truth be present fact.*[24]

But faith such as this is possible only in conjunction with obedience to a call to consecration: "Do not yield your members to sin as instruments of wickedness, but yield yourself to God as [those] who have been brought from death to life, and your members to God as instruments of righteousness" (v. 13, RSV).

"Yield" here is *paristimi.* In its first use, it is in the present tense: "Do not be presenting your members [a constant yielding] as instruments of unrighteousness unto sin." The second use is in the aorist tense: "But yield yourselves [in contrast, a decisive act] unto God" (cf. KJV). The same term is used in 12:1, also in the aorist, "Therefore, I urge you, brothers, in view of God's mercy, to offer your bodies as living sacrifices, holy and pleasing to God—which is your spiritual worship."

Paristimi is used in *koinē* Greek (the common, everyday language in which the New Testament was written) in two frames of reference. It is used in the sense of a military enlistment; and it is used in the sense of offering a sacrifice at an altar. In both instances, it involves a decisive act, a finality of commitment, and a

---

23. Cf. Gleason L. Archer, Jr., *The Epistle to the Romans: A Study Manual* (Grand Rapids: Baker Book House, 1959), p. 35.

24. Quoted by William R. Inge, *Faith and Its Psychology* (New York: Charles Scribner's Sons, n.d.), p. 229.

transfer of control or ownership of all of life. Dougan Clark writes in reference to v. 13:

> The essence of consecration is in the sentence, "Yield your-selves unto God." When you yield yourselves you yield every-thing else. All the details are included in the one surrender of yourself: "Yield yourself unto God." Consecration is not to God's *service,* not to His *work,* not to a life of *obedience* and *sacrifice,* not to the *Church,* not to the *Christian Endeavor,* not to the *missionary cause,* not even to the *cause of God:* it is to God HIMSELF. Consecration is the willingness, and the resolution, and the purpose to be, to do, and to suffer all God's will.[25]

3. A New Master, vv. 14-23

To be "not under law, but under grace" (v. 14) means own-ership by a new Master. Just as we were freed from sin by death (v. 7), in a change of metaphor we are freed from sin by becoming slaves in obedience to righteousness (vv. 15-18). This is a human analogy, but as we were once in an ongoing and ever-increasing bondage to sin, we are now to offer our bodies "in slavery to righteousness leading to holiness" (v. 19; *hagiasmos,* "sanctification, holiness"; Paul's first use of the term in Romans since the phrase "Spirit of holiness" in 1:4).

The service of (literally, slavery to) sin and the service of righteousness are mutually exclusive (v. 20). Each has its own distinctive end (*telos,* the essential and inherent outcome of; KJV and RSV). The *telos* of sin is death (v. 21). The *telos* of service to God is holiness and eternal life (v. 22). Both death and eternal life are present and contrasting realities. Death is the "wages"—a word meaning the daily subsistence allowance of a Roman soldier. Eter-nal life is the gift of God "in Christ Jesus our Lord" (v. 23).

III. HOLINESS APART FROM THE LAW

Romans 7, most of which falls in Godet's second division, "Holiness Without Law," is notorious for its difficulty. Commen-tators are sharply divided in their interpretations. The chapter divides into three rather clearly marked sections. Each deals with law in one sense or another, and the varying connotations of *nomos* (law) serve to increase the perplexities. Verses 1-6 are an analogy

---

25. Quoted by Hills, *Holiness in Romans,* p. 40; italics and capitals in the original.

from the law of marriage; vv. 7-13 describe the unexpected consequences of the law of God; and vv. 14-25 deal with the inadequacy of law and self-discipline in conquering sin. These are captioned by Greathouse, "Freedom from the law," "The function of the law," and "The futility of the law."[26]

A. Freedom from the Law, 7:1-6

Verses 1-6 in effect complete the thought of c. 6. We are freed from sin by death (6:1-14); we are freed from sin by a change of masters (6:15-23); and we are freed from sin by marriage to Another (7:1-6).

As is also true of the following two sections, vv. 1-6 are subject to various interpretations. One of the most helpful is offered by Sanday and Headlam.[27] Verses 1-3 sketch the main features of the analogy. "The law is binding on a person only during his life" (v. 1, RSV)—law regulates only those living in the conditions or relationships it covers. A wife is bound by the law of marriage to her husband as long as he lives. But when the husband dies, the woman "dies" as a wife. She becomes a widow, and as such is free to wed another. The law of the married state no longer applies to her.

The application is made in vv. 4-6. The wife is the believer. The husband who dies is the old self, the Adamic principle, crucified with Christ. The second husband is Christ. The purpose of the union is that "we might bear fruit to God" (v. 4) and "serve in the new way of the Spirit, and not in the old way of the written code" (v. 6).

B. The Function of the Law, 7:7-13

The second section deals not with the law of marriage but with the law of God that is "holy, righteous and good" (v. 12). It introduces the thought that controls the balance of the chapter—the law can no more sanctify than it could justify (c. 4).

The purpose of the law is to make known what sin is (v. 7). But the law has unexpected results. It not only reveals sin, it aggravates and inflames the perverse, sinful condition of the unsanctified

---

26. BBC, 8:146-61.

27. *Romans,* p. 173. As C. H. Dodd points out, we die *to* the law; the law cannot die (*Romans,* ad loc.).

heart: "But [the] sin, seizing the opportunity afforded by the commandment, produced in me every kind of covetous desire. For apart from law, sin is dead. Once I was alive apart from law; but when the commandment came, sin sprang to life and I died" (vv. 8-9). Charles R. Erdman writes:

> Paul reverts in memory to a time, when, as a proud young Pharisee, he was at ease, confident that he was keeping the law of God because he was so carefully observing its outward forms. However, there came a day when there dawned on his mind the full spiritual meaning of the law, specifically of the commandment, "Thou shalt not covet." The result was twofold. First, it revealed to Paul how much of evil desire really lay lurking in his heart. This he never before had realized. There was, however, an even more terrible result. The very command, "Thou shalt not," made him the more eager to do the thing forbidden. Before the commandment came, sin was "dead"; it was comparatively dormant, inert, and inoperative; but when the commandment came, it gave an impulse to sin. "Sin revived, and I died," that is, I died to my complacent self-satisfaction. I died to true holiness and happiness and hope; I fell deeper and deeper into guilt; I faced only misery and doom and eternal death.[28]

C. The Futility of the Law, 7:14-25

Around the third division the tide of controversy has swept with greatest force. Paul continues the use of the first person, "I," "me," "myself," "my." But where in vv. 7-13 he had used the first person with the past tense, now he uses the first person with the present tense: "I am unspiritual," "I do not understand what I do," "Nothing good lives in me," "Evil is right there with me," etc.

It is this consistent use of the present tense that gives occasion for the most debate. Was Paul speaking of his present spiritual experience at the time he wrote? Is this a valid picture of the regenerate life? A distinguished line of scholars from Luther to Nygren would say it is. An even longer line from James Arminius on would disagree. Paul, the latter group would say, is looking back on his struggles as an awakened but as yet unregenerate man, his unavailing efforts to achieve the righteousness of the law by his own efforts. As C. H. Dodd describes it:

---

28. *The Epistle of Paul to the Romans* (Philadelphia: Westminster Press, 1925), pp. 79-80. Used by permission.

He is continuing an argument to show that under grace a man is free from the power of sin. He has already said that the Christian has died to sin, and moves in a new sphere of life. He has compared him to a slave bought by a new master, and to a widow set free to marry again. It would stultify his whole argument if he now confessed that, at the moment of writing, he was a miserable wretch, a prisoner to sin's law (verses 24, 23). He would have thought it quite abnormal that any Christian should feel so, and there is nothing in his own confessions elsewhere to lead us to suppose that, with all his sense of struggle and insecurity, he ever had such an experience as this after his conversion. We conclude that Paul is clinching his argument by the undeniable evidence of his own experience that he was once dead in trespasses and sins, but has now found life and liberty.[29]

This then is not the normal regenerate state. In broadest terms, it is the struggle of an awakened person with the sinful impulses of his own unredeemed heart, a struggle carried on by his own strength of will. Paul takes back nothing he had already said in 6:18, 22 about being "set free from sin," nor does he undercut what he will say in 8:1-11. William M. Greathouse writes:

Clearly, the **wretched man** is the awakened sinner, struggling in vain for deliverance from indwelling sin. To apply these verses to the Christian believer would be to admit practically that the grace of Christ is as powerless against sin as is the law. The thrust of the whole argument is to demonstrate that the grace of God in Christ can do "what the law could not do" (8:3), to show that under grace a man has been freed from sin.[30]

However, we may interpret this passage on two levels. There is an echo of this struggle in the experience of any who strive for a consistently victorious life by means of their own self-discipline or their own strength of will. All who depend on self-effort for dealing with inner sin are represented here. These words do away completely with any scheme of sanctification that relies on "suppression" or "counteraction" as a matter of self-effort. Such is only a path to futility. Again Greathouse writes:

A concession, however, must be granted. Paul's thesis throughout chapter 7 is clear: *the law cannot sanctify.* To the extent a Christian believer is depending upon his own self-effort for sanctification, to *that extent* he is under the law. Having begun in the Spirit he is seeking to be made perfect by the

---

29. *Romans,* pp. 107-8.
30. BBC, 8:159.

flesh (Gal. 3:3). Not until he ceases "from his own works" does he enter the rest of heart holiness (Heb. 4:9-10). Something of this struggle therefore continues until by the baptism with the Holy Spirit his obedience is made perfect in love.[31]

The term "law" *(nomos)* here and elsewhere in the balance of this chapter and in c. 8 picks up a new connotation for Paul, as indeed it may for us in present usage. It no longer stands for the law of God set forth in the Scriptures, or even God's law in general terms. It is "this law at work: When I want to do good, evil is right there with me" (7:21). It is "another law" (v. 23), "the law of sin." Barrett describes it as "a law-like rule, which as an evil double of the Mosaic law can bear the same name."[32] It is "a controlling power imposing itself on the will," a "uniform tendency" or "principle."[33]

Verses 7-25, which seem so much like a digression or interruption in Paul's thought, are not really so. Before his case has been made complete, he must consider the possibility that there is some other alternative to Christ and His Spirit as the source of Christian sanctification.

Could the Mosaic law accomplish the desired end? No, the law can no more free the person from inner sin than it could justify him in the first place—the alternative considered and dismissed in 4:9-25. The law reveals the sinful condition of the heart but cannot cure it.

Could conscience ("the law of my mind," v. 23), desire to do good (v. 21), self-discipline, or strength of character bring deliverance? No, such a course leads only to frustration. Its outcome is the despairing cry of v. 24: "What a wretched man I am! Who will rescue me from this body of death?" No "what" nor "it" can suffice; a Deliverer is necessary. The answer is the first part of v. 25: Rescue comes only from "God—through Jesus Christ our Lord!" This looks ahead to c. 8. The latter half of v. 25 summarizes the case in vv. 14-24, "I of myself" (RSV) or "I, left to myself" (Moffatt), in desire "am a slave to God's law, but in the sinful nature [Greek, *sarx;* flesh] a slave to the law [principle or power] of sin." The slavery to the sinful nature can be shattered only in the deliverance so clearly sounded in c. 8.

31. "Romans," SS, pp. 30-31; cf. BBC, 8:160.

32. C. K. Barrett, "The Epistle to the Romans," *Black's New Testament Commentaries* (London: Adam and Charles Black, 1957), p. 149.

33. Godet, *Romans,* p. 296; and Greathouse, "Romans," SS, p. 32.

William Barclay calls 7:14-25 "a demonstration of inadequacies":

(i) It demonstrates *the inadequacy of human knowledge*. If to know the right thing was to do the right thing, then life would be easy. But knowledge by itself does not make a man a good man. . . .

(ii) It demonstrates the inadequacy of *human resolution*. To resolve to do a thing is very far from doing it. There is in human nature an essential weakness of the will. . . . The human will unstrengthened by Christ is bound to crack.

(iii) It demonstrates *the limitations of diagnosis*. Paul knew quite clearly what was wrong; but he was quite unable to put it right. He was like a doctor who could accurately diagnose a disease but who was quite powerless to prescribe a cure. Jesus is the one person who not only knows what is wrong, but who can also put the wrong to rights. It is not criticism He offers but help.[34]

IV. Holiness by the Holy Spirit

The almost despairing cry of 7:24 is abundantly answered in c. 8. The words of anticipation in 7:25 are followed up and filled out in the exultant lines of 8:1-11. Here is revealed the power from on high that is necessary to realize in experience all that was implied in c. 6 by way of death to sin and new life and service in Christ. That power is the power of the Holy Spirit, "by whom Christ crucified and risen reproduces Himself in the believer."[35]

A. The Spirit of Life in Christ, 8:1-2

Romans 8 is the great "Holy Spirit chapter" of the book. In the seven chapters preceding, Paul mentioned the Spirit four times (1:4; 2:29; 5:5; 7:6). Here he speaks of the Spirit 19 times in 39 verses. The person and work of the Holy Spirit is central to Paul's doctrine of salvation. Stephen Neill goes so far as to say that "Paul's doctrine of the Spirit is far more central and characteristic than his doctrine of justification by faith."[36]

---

34. "The Letter to the Romans," *The Daily Study Bible* (Edinburgh: Saint Andrew Press, 1962), pp. 102-3.

35. Godet, *Romans*, p. 295.

36. *The Interpretation of the New Testament*, 1861-1961, The Firth Lectures, 1962 (London: Oxford University Press, 1964), p. 189.

Rom. 7:14-25 deals with the frustration of man "in himself" in relation to the purpose of God. Rom. 8:1-2 opens the door of faith and hope to those who, by contrast, are "in Christ": "Therefore, there is now no condemnation for those who are in Christ Jesus, because through Christ Jesus the law of the Spirit of life set me free from the law of sin and death." The Spirit of life as a controlling Power ("law") delivers totally from "the body of sin" whose death warrant had been signed at Calvary (6:6), that which makes one "carnal, sold under sin" (7:14, RSV), "the law of sin" (7:23), "this body of death" (7:24), or "the sinful nature" (7:25).

Concerning Paul's use of the term *nomos* (law) in relation to "the Spirit of life," Godet points out that it is in the general sense in which he had used it in 7:21, 23—as a controlling power or principle. Paul had affirmed the power of indwelling sin. Now he affirms that the power of that indwelling sin has been met and mastered by a greater power: the power "of the Spirit of life in Christ Jesus" (8:2, RSV). "The apostle deliberately contrasts *law* with *law,* that is to say here: power with power."[37] As Greathouse says, "Paul now gives testimony to the experience of entire sanctification. In Christ he has found the sanctifying power of the Holy Spirit, liberating him from the principle of sin and death."[38]

This emerging emphasis on the work of the Holy Spirit is what makes this chapter, as Skevington Wood has said, "the Pentecost of Romans."[39] Henry Van Dusen writes:

> Indeed, the Spirit is, above all, the agency of moral transformation ("sanctification"), and that transformation is into the likeness of Christ, because the Holy Spirit which is the Spirit of God *is* the Spirit of Christ. The radical and all-embracing character of this insight is revealed in the alternative use as though interchangeable, of the variant terms "Spirit," "Spirit of God," "Spirit of Christ," "Holy Spirit"; so that, at the heart of that greatest of all the discourses of Paul which itself stands as the very pivot of all his thought, the eighth chapter of Romans, he declares confusingly but rightly, "Ye are not in the flesh, but in the Spirit, if so be that the Spirit of God dwell in you. Now if

---

37. Godet, *Romans,* p. 297.

38. "Romans," SS, p. 32.

39. *Life by the Spirit,* formerly *Paul's Pentecost* (Grand Rapids: Zondervan Publishing House, 1963), p. 12.

any man have not the Spirit of Christ, he is none of his" (Rom. 8:9).[40]

Greathouse writes, "As the Nicene Creed invites us to confess, He [the Holy Spirit as the Spirit of life] is 'the Lord and Giver of life.' He was the Life Giver in creation (Gen. 1:2). He is the Life-Giver in the new birth (John 3:5). Here He is the Life-Giver in sanctification, bringing to an end the tyranny of the flesh and delivering us into that perfect love which is the fulfillment of God's law (4)."[41]

B. What the Law Could Not Do, 8:3-4

Paul goes on to explain that Christ does by His Spirit what the Mosaic law could not do: "For what the law was powerless to do in that it was weakened by the sinful nature, God did by sending his own Son in the likeness of sinful man to be a sin offering. And so he condemned sin in sinful man, in order that the righteous requirements of the law might be fully met in us, who do not live according to the sinful nature but according to the Spirit" (8:3-4).

That "the sin" [lit.] "in sinful man" was condemned does not mean it was merely disapproved. It was doomed. The law disapproved sin but could not destroy it. Godet says, "Grace does not save by patronizing sin, but by destroying it."[42] Sin is not condoned but condemned to death. God, "that is, passed sentence upon it."[43] Greathouse writes:

> Paul returns to the idea of the powerlessness of the law to sanctify (8:3a). But God has broken the impasse! Through the Incarnation and Cross, God has himself, in the person of His Son, *pronounced the doom of sin!* He has utterly routed the foe on the very battlefield where he had entrenched himself—in human personality (8:3b). In Christ God has completely sanctified human nature![44]

C. The Contrast of Flesh and Spirit, 8:5-8

Verses 5-8 develop the total contrast in Paul's thought be-

---

40. *Spirit, Son, and Father* (New York: Charles Scribner's Sons, 1938), pp. 66-67. Used by permission.

41. BBC, 8:164.

42. *Romans,* p. 296.

43. Vincent Taylor, *The Epistle to the Romans* (London: Epworth Press, n.d.), p. 50.

44. "Romans," SS, pp. 32-33; cf. BBC, 8:166.

tween "flesh" and "Spirit." "Flesh" [*sarx*, translated "the sinful nature" in the NIV] and the Spirit stand in stark opposition to each other, a point repeated and elaborated in Gal. 5:16-25.

Paul's use of *sarx* has been the despair of Bible students. He uses it at times in a purely physical sense, as equivalent to humanity (e.g., Rom. 1:3; 9:3). But in the 16 times Paul contrasts flesh and Spirit, he uses *sarx* to denote that corruption in human nature which is itself sinful.[45]

If "the sinful nature" is understood as an element in fallen humanity that is not an inherent or intrinsic part of *human* nature, then "the sinful nature" as used by the NIV may be accepted as a reasonable defining paraphrase for *sarx* or flesh. It must be kept clearly in mind, however, that this "sinful nature" is dealt with decisively and eliminated from present Christian experience by the sanctifying Lordship of the Holy Spirit: "But you are not in the flesh, you are in the Spirit, if in fact the Spirit of God dwells in you" (8:9, RSV); and "Those who belong to Christ Jesus have crucified the sinful nature with its passions and desires" (Gal. 5:24).

In any case, "flesh" *(sarx)* must never be confused with "body" *(sōma)*. It is not material and tangible. As Barclay says, "The flesh to Paul was not a physical thing; it was a spiritual thing. The flesh was human nature in all its sin and weakness, and impotence and frustration; the flesh is all that man is without God and without Christ."[46] John Knox writes:

> When [Paul] speaks of "the flesh" he is referring to that in ourselves from which come our "immorality, impurity, licentiousness . . . strife, jealousy, anger, selfishness . . . envy, drunkenness . . . and the like." And what is this but our alienation from God and our true selves, that is to say, our existential "brokenness" and "fallenness" and, in consequence, our moral impotence and our sinfulness? . . . "Flesh" is a way of referring, again from within our experience, to the "old man," man in Adam, to whom as natural men we belong. "The flesh" is the "old" "fallen" world as it makes its presence and power felt within our souls.[47]

---

45. Cf. C. Ryder Smith, *The Bible Doctrine of Man* (London: Epworth Press, 1951), pp. 153 ff. Cf. also Richard Howard, *Newness of Life* (Kansas City: Beacon Hill Press of Kansas City, 1975), for an in-depth study of *sarx* (flesh) and its varied meanings.

46. *Romans*, DSB, p. 105.

47. *Life in Christ Jesus* (Greenwich, Conn.: Seabury Press, 1961), p. 83.

The condition reflected by the phrase "the sinful nature" operates through the mind-set that results in a life marred by sin: "Those who live according to the sinful nature have their minds set on what that nature desires" (8:5a). On the contrary, "Those who live in accordance with the Spirit have their minds set on what the Spirit desires" (v. 5b). Gleason Archer says, "This verb 'to mind' is *phroneō*: to have something as the prevailing mood of mind, habit of thought, or direction of moral interest. What are you really interested in? This is your 'mind'—*phronēma*—the word used in verses 6 and 7."[48]

"The mind of sinful man is death" (8:6a). In another context, Knox writes:

> Sin has about it the "smell" of death. It partakes of the nature of death. Indeed, it *is* death already present in us, and not only threatening our life, but already poisoning and destroying it. Who needs to be told of the destructiveness of lustfulness or drunkenness, of jealousy or selfish pride? But these are only the manifestations, the outbreakings, of an inner distortion and corruption which is Death itself at work within our souls. When Paul says, "To set the mind on the flesh is death," we know what he means.[49]

Because to Paul sin equals spiritual death, the apostle goes on: "The mind of sinful man is death, but the mind controlled by the Spirit is life and peace" (v. 6). Just as death on the one hand and life and peace on the other are mutually exclusive realities, so are "the mind of sinful man" and "the mind controlled by the Spirit."

The essence of the sinful nature is that it is "hostile to God. It does not submit to God's law, nor can it do so" (v. 7). The hallmark of the sinful nature is both its unwillingness and its inability to submit to the law of God. In this there is a contrast with the human nature. The impulses and tendencies arising from the sinful nature always lead to acts of sin. There is no possibility of expressing them in harmony with God's will. On the other hand, the impulses and tendencies that arise from human nature are such that they may be expressed in harmony with God's law. In fact, the law of the Lord is given precisely to give guidance and direction to human impulses and tendencies so that they are expressed in constructive rather than destructive ways.

---

48. *Epistle to the Romans*, p. 45.
49. *Life in Christ Jesus*, p. 85.

So total is the antagonism of *sarx* (flesh) and Spirit that "those who are in the flesh cannot please God" (v. 8, RSV). A. M. Hills writes:

> This word "flesh" cannot mean "body" here. Enoch dwelt in the body: "And before his translation he had this witness borne to him that he had been well-pleasing to God." Jesus dwelt in a body; and the Father said: "This is my beloved Son, in whom I am well pleased." No; *"in the flesh,"* like the phrase "after the flesh," means to be in subjection to *this sin principle,* which perverts and deranges all our sensibilities, prompting obedience to them rather than obedience to right reason, illuminated by the Holy Spirit. *"Cannot please God."* That settles it. This principle of sin that infests our being must be condemned and executed, so that we may be wholly loyal and well-pleasing to God.[50]

D. The Indwelling Spirit, 8:9-14

The question is, of course, how that "execution" is to take place. The "condemnation" has already taken place in the Incarnation (8:3). Paul's answer is given in v. 9*a*, "But you are not in the flesh, you are in the Spirit, if in fact the Spirit of God dwells in you" (RSV). This is a reminiscence of 7:5-6: "While we were living in the flesh, our sinful passions, aroused by the law, were at work in our members to bear fruit for death. But now we are discharged from the law, dead to that which held us captive, so that we serve not under the old written code but in the new life of the Spirit" (RSV).

The change in condition from "in the flesh" to "in the Spirit" comes about "if in fact the Spirit of God dwells in you." Sanday and Headlam comment on the phrase "dwells in": *"Oikein en* denotes a settled permanent penetrative influence. Such an influence, from the Spirit of God, St. Paul assumes to be inseparable from the higher life of the Christian."[51]

Nor is the Spirit remote and inaccessible. Paul immediately comments: "And if anyone does not have the Spirit of Christ, he does not belong to Christ" (8:9*b*). The question is not one of the presence or absence of the Spirit but of the measure of His control. All we have in the spiritual life we have through the agency of the Holy Spirit, the Spirit of Christ. In promising the "Helper, the Holy

---

50. *Holiness in Romans,* p. 72. Cf. Wood, *Pentecostal Grace,* p. 85: "The idea of 'having' is not the same as 'dwelling.'"

51. *Romans,* p. 196.

Spirit" (John 14:26, NASB), Jesus had said, "He lives with you and will be in you" (John 14:17). What is in view in the expressions "dwell in" and "be in" is a new order of relationship in which the promise implied in regeneration (initial sanctification) is brought to fruition in entire sanctification.

The indwelling Spirit does not cancel the mortality of the body; He brings life to the human spirit (8:10). Yet the indwelling Spirit is, to use Paul's term in Eph. 1:14, the "deposit guaranteeing" the resurrection of the body itself (8:11).

As the indwelling Spirit does not free us from liability to physical death, neither does He set aside the need for a constant and consistent disciplining of the body. "We have an obligation" (v. 12)—not to the sinful nature, for to live according to the flesh is to die spiritually (v. 13, RSV). Our obligation is "by the Spirit [to] put to death the misdeeds of the body." The same apostle who testifies in v. 2 to having been set free from "the law [power] of sin and death," says in 1 Cor. 9:27, "I beat my body and make it my slave so that after I have preached to others, I myself will not be disqualified for the prize." As Greathouse writes:

> Such an experience as Paul has been describing has its own imperatives. Our obligation is to live on the plane of the Spirit (8:12). This means we must "go on putting to death" our bodily impulses by dwelling in the Spirit (8:13). Observe Paul's terminology: "The flesh" has ceased to be (8:9a), "the body" must be kept under the discipline of the Spirit (8:13). (Cf. 1 Cor. 9:27.)
>
> We therefore conclude: original sin must be *eradicated* (annihilated, destroyed): our human impulses must be *subjugated* (subdued, subjected). *Both are by the Spirit.*[52]

Though no longer "in the flesh," "controlled . . . by the sinful nature," the sanctified Christian is still "in the body" and under the necessity of keeping it subject to the law of God. This means "put[ting] to death"—a clear-cut separation from—the "misdeeds of the body," i.e., acts contrary to God's law arising out of the human nature with all its instincts, urges, propensities, drives, and needs. In this we are to be "led by the Spirit of God" as befits the children of God (8:14).

E. The Spirit and Our Infirmities, 8:26

The sinful nature is hostile to God, and as such the believer

---

52. "Romans," SS, pp. 33-34.

cannot longer be "in the flesh." The human nature is subject to God's law, and in its weakness depends upon the help of the Spirit (v. 26). The Spirit frees us from sin (v. 2), but He "helpeth our infirmities" (v. 26, KJV).

The distinction between sin and "infirmity" is not easy to make, but it is essential. Those who follow Augustine and Calvin tend to lump together all human weakness and imperfection with sin and sinfulness. But the New Testament not only here but elsewhere makes a distinction. Christ came to "save his people from their sins" (Matt. 1:21), but as our High Priest He is able to "sympathize with our weaknesses," including our liability to temptation (Heb. 4:15).

The term "help" in 8:26 is an enlightening one. It literally means "to take hold of the other side with" one. The Holy Spirit does not cancel out our infirmities; He enables us to cope with them.

V. CONSECRATION

Romans 12 marks the transition from doctrine to ethics, from the "believing side" of the gospel to the "behaving side." Paul closes his discussion of doctrine with a song (11:33-36); he opens his discussion of ethics with a summons (12:1-2). It would be a serious mistake to separate the two parts of the Epistle. Paul's doctrine is misunderstood if it is not seen to demand ethical action, and his ethical guidelines rest at every point on his theology.[53]

Rom. 12:1-2 echoes the call to consecration sounded in 6:13, 19. Indeed, the same term is used, a fact often obscured in translation. The term is *paristimi,* used in 6:13, 19 in the connotation of yielding oneself for service and in 12:1 in the context of an offering for sacrifice. In both contexts, the common element is a transfer of ownership and control.

A. The Call to Consecration, 12:1-2

Just as in 6:13, the appeal to consecration is made on the basis of a new life in Christ—"brought from death to life"—directed toward those who had apprehended God's mercy, who are "broth-

---

53. Cf. Barrett, *Romans,* p. 230.

ers" by a common faith, and whose offering is "holy and pleasing to God" and an act of "spiritual worship."

Gerald Cragg emphasizes the parallel between the "living sacrifice" of Christian consecration and the sacrifices of the Old Testament:

> We can claim, then, that the highest privilege of the new life of discipleship is to use all our powers in God's service; yet there are demands which we cannot evade. Under the old dispensation it was decreed that "no maimed and worthless sacrifice" could be offered to God; we must accept a standard equally exacting. Under the Jewish law all ritual requirements had to be fulfilled; under the Christian gospel it is sacrilege complacently to bring to God lives whose stains have not been cleansed by repentance and renewal. How can we come before him who is "of purer eyes than to behold evil" (Hab. 1:13) if "our sins are still fresh upon us"? From what Paul has said it follows that we are the Lord's; on this account we should be holy: to be careless in God's service is more grievous sacrilege than it ever was to offer unclean beasts upon the altar. Moreover, that holiness which is to be the mark of the life devoted to God is not expressed in esoteric ritual observances, but in the disciplines of ordinary experience. Not apart from daily life, but in its midst, we serve God "without fear, in holiness and righteousness before him, all the days of our life" (Luke 1:74-75). This is the true worship of God; it is the "service" appropriate to beings in whom intellectual and moral qualities unite.[54]

To offer one's body means to offer "the whole human person, including its means of expressing itself in common life."[55]

While there is analogy with the Jewish ceremony, there is also distinction. The Christian's consecration is to be a living sacrifice. Ernest Best explains:

> He asks for a *sacrifice* of a different nature—their *very* selves: it is not enough for a Christian to offer things, his possessions, his time, his talents, to God; he must *offer* himself. Such a *sacrifice* is *living* because the Christian possesses new life (5:12-21; 6:1-14); it is also *living* in the sense that once an animal is sacrificed it is dead, but the Christian's sacrifice of himself is a continuously living action.[56]

Such a living sacrifice has both a negative and a positive

---

54. IB, 9:581.

55. Barrett, *Romans*, p. 231.

56. "The Letter of Paul to the Romans," *The Cambridge Bible Commentary on the New English Bible* (Cambridge: University Press, 1967), p. 138.

outcome. The call to consecration is a sharp, decisive imperative— the aorist form of the verb "to offer, yield, or present." The grammatical form implies an act brought to completion. The results that follow are in the present tense and imply a continuing condition. The completed sacrifice "continuously" lives on.

The negative outcome is a discontinuity in spirit and practice from "the world." In J. B. Phillips' unforgettable paraphrase, Paul says, "Don't let the world around you squeeze you into its own mould." Barclay paraphrases, "Don't try to match your life to all the fashions of this world; don't be like a chameleon which takes its colour from its surroundings; don't go with the world; don't let the world decide what you are going to be like."[57] Erdman says, "The phrase 'this world,' or 'age,' pictures the sphere or form of life from which God is excluded, the spirit of which is selfishness, the prince of which is Satan. One who belongs to God must not be controlled by worldly precepts, by selfish motives, by sinful impulses."[58]

The positive outcome of consecration is a deep inner renewal —"be transformed by the renewing of your mind" (12:2). Best comments that the Christian's transformation "must begin at the very centre of being—the *mind*."[59] Franz Leenhardt writes:

> The mind here implies much more than the intellectual faculty of apprehension; *nous* includes the personality viewed in its deepest aspects and suggests, as it were, man's awareness of his total situation in the universe. Metaphysical and moral self-consciousness will be renewed because a new reality will now confront it. This transcendent reality is Jesus Christ.[60]

This is the renewal of the fallen human self begun in regeneration. It is a renewal into the image of Christ. It now rises to a new level and continues toward "the whole measure of the fullness of Christ" (Eph. 4:13). "Now the Lord is the Spirit, and where the Spirit of the Lord is, there is freedom. And we, who with unveiled faces all reflect the Lord's glory, are being transformed into his likeness with ever-increasing glory, which comes from the Lord, who is the Spirit" (2 Cor. 3:17-18). Erdman says:

> One who belongs to God . . . must be "transformed" by accepting the will of Christ as the controlling principle of his

---

57. *Romans,* DSB, p. 170.
58. *Romans,* p. 132.
59. *Romans,* p. 139.
60. *Romans,* p. 305.

life and by allowing the continual indwelling of the Spirit of Christ as the dominating power of his life. His character and conduct will not be determined by a mere imitation of Christ, but by the transforming energy of a divine, indwelling presence, irradiating his whole being.[61]

By this renewal, write Sanday and Headlam, "the intellectual or rational principle will not longer be a *nous sarkos* (Col. ii.18—carnal mind), but will be filled with the Spirit" and thus "renewed and purified."[62]

B. A Sanctified Offering, 15:16, 29

In Rom. 15:16, Paul affirms again his mission as a "minister of Christ Jesus to the Gentiles with the priestly duty of proclaiming the gospel of God, so that the Gentiles might become an offering acceptable to God, sanctified by the Holy Spirit." It is "the sanctifying work of the Spirit" (2 Thess. 2:13; 1 Pet. 1:2) that renders the sacrifice of consecration acceptable to God. As Wilbur T. Dayton notes, Paul "does not consider his task done whenever a given number of people have heard the gospel proclaimed. The apostle must stay with the people until the gospel bore fruit not only in a forgiveness of sins but in a genuine purification and dedication of life through the Holy Spirit that would make the people a suitable present to God."[63]

Paul unveils his plan to visit Rome and the reason for the delay in 15:23-32. Conscious of the uncertainties of life, he yet says, "I know that when I come to you I shall come in the fulness of the blessing of Christ" (v. 29, RSV)—a beautiful description of the experience unfolded so completely in the letter. Gerald Cragg comments:

> The fulness of the blessing of Christ is a singularly happy phrase. It suggests, for one thing, the many-sided completeness of the gift that Christ brings to men. What area of life does he not touch into richer vitality? Is there any region where he disappoints our hopes? Only when men bring us a thin and attenuated gospel is there any inconsistency between Paul's words and our actual experience. Again, the phrase points to the distinctive quality as well as the comprehensive sufficiency

---

61. *Romans,* p. 132.

62. *Romans,* p. 354.

63. "The Epistle of Paul to the Romans," *Wesleyan Bible Commentary* (Grand Rapids: William B. Eerdmans Publishing Co., 1965), 5:90; hereafter cited as WesBC.

of what Christ does for us. To enrich, but with satisfaction that passes into triumphant joy, is the characteristic work of the gospel. Moreover, this kind of experience has its sole source in Christ. To the N. T. writers Christ was not one among a number of alternative sources of such a blessing; there was "none other name under heaven given among men, whereby we must be saved" (Acts 4:12).[64]

---

64. IB, 9:652.

6

Holiness in Corinthians, Galatians, and Ephesians

That Romans is Paul's definitive treatment of the doctrines of salvation would generally be conceded. However, his keen pastoral concern for the spiritual development of the churches under his care shows clearly in all his writings. Paul's other letters tend to be "occasional" pieces: that is, they were written to meet the need of some particular occasion or problem in the various churches to which they were addressed. Yet the issues that arise usually root back in the area of Christian commitment and life. For this reason, the other writings of the apostle (with the possible exception of Philemon) all add data to aid our understanding of the doctrine, experience, and ethics of holiness.

I. THE CORINTHIAN LETTERS

The Corinthian correspondence of the apostle Paul shows as clearly as any and more clearly than most the tension that may exist between the potential of Christian experience and its actuality. As Bethune-Baker says, "Though St. Paul addressed the first generation of Christians as 'saints' or 'holy', it is clear from his letters to them that they were so potentially only, and that he applied the term to them as set apart (called out from the rest of men) for a holy purpose, rather than possessed of personal holiness."[1]

---

1. *The Early History of Christian Doctrine*, p. 357; quoted by Jones, *Concept of Holiness*, p. 118.

Thus as in Rom. 1:7, so in 1 Cor. 1:2; 2 Cor. 1:1; Eph. 1:1; Phil. 1:1; and Col. 1:2, all believers are addressed as "saints" and "holy." "To the church of God in Corinth, to those sanctified in Christ Jesus and called to be holy . . ." (1 Cor. 1:2) is Paul's address to a church in which existed some glaring ethical faults as well as some damaging doctrinal aberrations. The term translated "saints" is *hagioi* and literally means "holy ones."

Paul S. Rees has pointed out that today the term "saint" is apt to suggest either one *canonized* as by the Roman church or one *cleansed* and exemplifying outstanding piety. In the New Testament, however, "saint" describes one *claimed*, called out from the world in the fellowship of the Spirit, a member of the Body of Christ.[2]

A. A Christological Emphasis, 1 Cor. 1:30

The Christological emphasis in holiness is preserved in Paul's comment in 1 Cor. 1:30: "It is because of him [God] that you are in Christ Jesus, who has become for us wisdom from God—that is, our righteousness, holiness and redemption." It is important to establish clearly the truth that as Christ is our wisdom, our righteousness, and our redemption, so He is our sanctification, our holiness.

H. J. Stolee, a Lutheran scholar who would not agree with the usual Wesleyan interpretation of holiness, sounds an essential note when he says, "True holiness is active, but . . . it does not spring from activity. Christ enthroned is the source. The Spirit-filled disciple is the most humble, yet the most bold. In his own eyes he is 'less than the least.' His life is Spirit-filled because it is Christ-filled."[3]

We must never lose our sense of the centrality of Christ in the concept of Christian holiness. There is no tension between Christ and the Holy Spirit. Father, Son, and Spirit are all involved in every level of Christian experience. As Samuel Chadwick writes:

> The fullness of God is in Christ, and Christ lives in men through His Spirit. He is Himself the gift. He brings all the

---

2. *The Adequate Man: Paul in Philippians* (Westwood, N.J.: Fleming H. Revell Co., 1959), p. 18.

3. *Speaking in Tongues* (Minneapolis: Augsburg Publishing House, 1963), p. 141.

blessings of grace, and Wisdom, and Power, but He is the Blesser and the Blessing. There is in the soul a very true sense of a divinely real Presence. The Spirit makes the Presence real. This is the crowning mystery and glory of Grace. The Christian religion is not a set of doctrines about Christ, neither is it a rule of life based on the teaching and example of Christ. It is not even an earnest and sincere endeavour to live according to the mind and spirit of Christ. It is Life, and that Life is the Life of Christ. It is a continuation of the Life of the Risen Lord in His Body which is the Church, and in the sanctified believer. "Christ liveth in me" is the essence of the Christian religion as set forth in the New Testament. It is not a system, but a Presence; the Spirit of Christ indwelling the spirit of man.[4]

B. Assurance, 1 Cor. 2:12

It is noteworthy that John Wesley most often cited 1 Cor. 2:12 as evidence for assurance of Christian perfection: "We have not received the spirit of the world but the Spirit who is from God, that we may understand what God has freely given us." That there is a "witness of the Spirit" to entire sanctification is nowhere stated in the New Testament as clearly as Paul states the witness of the Spirit to a filial relationship to God in Rom. 8:16. Yet the words cited here, as later in 1 John 3:23; 4:13, would lend biblical support to the idea of such assurance.

C. A Classification, 1 Cor. 2:14—3:3

An implied classification of spiritual strata has been seen in 1 Cor. 2:14—3:3, where Paul speaks of three classes of persons: (1) natural (KJV), unspiritual (RSV), "without the Spirit" (2:14); (2) carnal (KJV), of the flesh (RSV), "worldly" (3:1-3); and (3) "spiritual" (2:15-16).

The "natural" person, "unspiritual" and "without the Spirit," is the person apart from the saving grace of God. The "carnal," "of the flesh," or "worldly" are "infants in Christ" (3:1) whose spiritual deficiency is revealed in the jealousy and quarrelling among them and in their conduct as "mere men" (v. 3). The "spiritual" person is the ideal, able to accept and discern "the things that come from the Spirit of God," possessing "the mind of Christ" (2:14, 16).

---

4. Quoted by Robert E. Coleman, *The Spirit and the Word* (Wilmore, Ky.: Asbury Theological Seminary, 1965), p. 8.

D. Temples of God, 1 Cor. 3:16-17; 6:19-20

The concept of a human "temple of God" appears twice in the early chapters of 1 Corinthians. In 3:16-17 the plural is used and the entire church is intended: "Don't you know that you yourselves are God's temple and that God's Spirit lives in you? If anyone destroys God's temple, God will destroy him; for God's temple is sacred, and you are that temple."

In 6:19-20 the physical body of the individual believer is identified as "a temple of the Holy Spirit," a powerful incentive to sexual purity (cf. vv. 12-18): "Do you not know that your body is a temple of the Holy Spirit, who is in you, whom you have received from God? You are not your own; you were bought at a price. Therefore honor God with your body." As Donald S. Metz comments, "When the Holy Spirit resides in a temple, it belongs to God. . . . This indwelling Spirit is a Gift from a holy God and cannot dwell in a polluted sanctuary."[5]

E. One Body, 1 Cor. 12:13

First Corinthians 12 deals with the gifts of the Spirit within the framework of the unity of the Church. One verse has been pivotal in debate about the baptism with the Spirit. First Cor. 12:13 has been taken to indicate that the baptism with the Spirit occurs at regeneration and the initiation of the believer into the Body of Christ: "For we were all baptized by one Spirit into one body— whether Jews or Greeks, slave or free—and we were all given the one Spirit to drink."

Admittedly, "by one Spirit" may be translated "in one Spirit" or "with one Spirit." However, the NEB is truer to the context by inserting a comma: "For indeed we were all brought into one body by baptism, in the one Spirit, whether we are Jews or Greeks, whether slaves or free men, and that one Holy Spirit was poured out for all of us to drink." The Spirit is the Agent, not the medium of baptism, and by "the washing of regeneration" (Titus 3:5) symbolized in water baptism places all believers in the one Body. If "Spirit" is the medium of baptism ("baptized in" or "with"), then a hopeless confusion of figures arises when it is suggested that all "drink" of the Spirit. The idea that we "drink" of the Spirit has affinities with John 7:37-39.

---

5. BBC, 8:370.

F. The Hymn to Love, 1 Corinthians 13

First Corinthians 13 is Paul's classic "Hymn to Love," the basis of Henry Drummond's *Greatest Thing in the World.* [6] It is the "more excellent way" (KJV) or "the most excellent way" (12:31). It was esteemed by John Wesley as a true picture of Christian perfection.[7] In a sense true to the best in New Testament theology, "Christ" or "holiness" are interchangeable with *agapē* (love), and either "Christ" or "holiness" may be read in place of "love" throughout the chapter.

Commissioner Samuel Logan Brengle of the Salvation Army wrote:

> Do you want to know what Holiness is? It is *pure* love. Do you want to know what the Baptism of the Holy Ghost is? It is not a mere sentiment. It is not a happy sensation that passes away in a night. It is a baptism of love that brings every thought into captivity to the Lord Jesus; that casts out all fear; that burns up doubt and unbelief as fire burns tow; that makes one "meek and lowly in heart;" that makes one hate uncleanness, lying and deceit, a flattering tongue, and every evil way with a perfect hatred; that makes Heaven and Hell eternal realities; that makes one patient and gentle with the froward and sinful; that makes one "pure, peaceable, easy to be entreated, full of mercy and good fruits, without partiality and without hypocrisy;" that brings one into perfect and unbroken sympathy with the Lord Jesus Christ in His toil and travail to bring a lost and rebel world back to God.[8]

Henry Drummond, in a penetrating insight drawn from a chemical analogy, says, "Souls are made sweet not by taking the acid fluids out, but by putting something in—a great Love, a new Spirit, the Spirit of Christ. Christ, the Spirit of Christ, interpenetrating ours, sweetens, purifies, transforms all. This only can eradicate what is wrong."[9]

Bishop J. Paul Taylor quotes a memorable paragraph from Henry Howard's *Something Ere the End* (p. 34):

---

6. And other addresses (London: Collins' Cleartype Press, n.d.).

7. Cf. sermon on "The More Excellent Way," *Sermons on Several Occasions,* 2 vols. (New York: Lane and Scott, 1852), 2:266-73.

8. *Helps to Holiness* (London: Salvationist Publishing, 1896), p. 8; cf. William S. Deal, *Problems of the Spirit-filled Life* (Kansas City: Beacon Hill Press of Kansas City, 1961), p. 26.

9. *Greatest Thing in the World,* p. 38.

There is no despot like love. It will brook no rival, take no denial, effect no compromise. Love cannot be brow-beaten, or bullied, or bribed to abandon its quest. It will wait with a patience that no opposition can wear down, no insolence discourage, no indifference turn sour. Its ingenuity is infinite, its resources inexhaustible, its endurance unending. It will spare itself no pain or tears or blood to gain its beneficent ends. It will keep on pursuing the object of its desire with unfaltering foot, with unquenchable ardor, with undying hope.[10]

Archibald Hunter recognizes the difficulty of adequately defining *agapē*, the most typical New Testament term translated "love," or at least of finding a single English word that conveys its meaning. He writes:

In a world where "charity" has almost become "a dirty word" and "love" can cover almost everything from Hollywood to heaven, "caring" perhaps is least inadequate. But the meaning of *agape* is not in doubt. As *eros* in Greek is the love which passionately desires and, at its lowest, lusts, and *philia* means friendship, mutual affection with kindred spirits, so *agape* is the love which seeks not to possess but to give. It is self-spending love.[11]

G. Purity and Perfection, 2 Cor. 7:1

Second Cor. 7:1 presents what Daniel Steele called "the Wesleyan paradox"—that sanctification is both progressive and critical: "Since we have these promises, dear friends, let us purify ourselves from everything that contaminates body and spirit, perfecting holiness out of reverence for God."

Here, "purify" is in the aorist tense and indicates an act viewed as complete and entire. "Perfecting," on the other hand, is a present participle and suggests a continuing process. Grammatically, it is possible to argue that the aorist of "purify" controls the time element of "perfecting," and both are to be regarded as instantaneous and complete. Many interpret it in this sense.[12]

Other Wesleyan scholars interpret the passage in the sense of both crisis and process. "Holiness" is *hagiōsunē*, a grammatical form that normally suggests the manifestation of sanctification

---

10. *Holiness the Finished Foundation*, p. 168.

11. *The Gospel According to St. Paul*, rev. ed. of *Interpreting Paul's Gospel* (Philadelphia: Westminster Press, 1966), p. 46.

12. Cf. the statement to this effect in Purkiser, Taylor, and Taylor, *God, Man, and Salvation*, p. 468 and fn. 13.

(*hagiasmos*) in personal conduct. Steele writes, "The duty . . . of perfecting holiness is a progressive work."[13] J. Harold Greenlee translates the verse, "Let us cleanse ourselves from every defilement of flesh and spirit, bringing holiness to completion . . ."[14] Frank G. Carver writes:

> In this Corinthian passage the present participle **perfecting** emphasizes the practical ethical progress toward the full likeness of Christ (cf. 3:18; 1 John 3:2). This is to be a continuing part of the daily lives of those who live **in the fear of God** (cf. 5:10-11). There is a paradox here. Those who have been brought into a sanctified relationship to God in Jesus Christ (cf. 1 Cor. 1:2, 30; Heb. 2:11; 10:10, 14, 29; 13:12) must ever reach for the ethical ideal of that relationship; holiness is both a gift and a task. It means, Become what you are![15]

Defined as cleansing from inner sin, holiness is perfected in the instant of entire sanctification. Defined as conformity to the nature of Christ, cleansing is the essential qualification for the process of attaining that "fulness of Christ" (Eph. 4:13).

H. Consecration, 2 Cor. 8:5

An interesting sidelight on the nature of Christian consecration appears in Paul's discussion of the offering being raised among the Gentile churches for the Jerusalem Christian community. Paul writes of the Macedonians that "they did not do as we expected [e.g., they went beyond our expectation], but they gave themselves first to the Lord and then to us in keeping with God's will" (2 Cor. 8:5). Consecration involves a self-dedication *in toto* to the Lord—a decisive act at a given moment. It then leads to ongoing results—"then to us [in relation to the work of the Kingdom] in keeping with God's [specific] will."

I. Perfection, 2 Cor. 13:9

A different "perfection passage" occurs in 13:9: "We are glad whenever we are weak but you are strong; and our prayer is for your perfection." Here "perfection" is not *teleios* as in Matt. 5:48. It

---

13. Daniel Steele, *Milestone Papers* (New York: Phillips and Hunt, 1878), p. 107.

14. In *Further Insights into Holiness*, pp. 77-78.

15. BBC, 8:567.

is *katartizō* and means "to render fit, complete *(artios)* . . . right ordering and arrangement . . . to supply what is necessary."[16]

The implication of words such as these is stated by H. L. Goudge in his *Commentary on I Corinthians:*

> It is often said that we "cannot be perfect here." Now, it is true that we cannot in this world reach our full spiritual stature. . . . It is also true that, as a matter of fact, "in many things we stumble all" (James 3:2). But it is not at all true that a certain amount of sin is unavoidable. Every sin looked at separately might and ought to have been avoided by the Christian. What is unavoidable cannot be, in the true sense, sin. Much popular language really denies that God's salvation is complete. But this is contrary to the universal teaching of the Scripture (Isaiah 60:21; Jeremiah 31:33-34; Romans 8:1-5) which assures us that our failures are due not to any incompleteness of the work of salvation on the Divine side, but to our own failure to respond to it (II Cor. 6:1). . . . God's salvation ever brings the power to obey Him. If we are really unable, we cannot be in a state of salvation at all.[17]

Similar expressions are found in Vincent Taylor, *Forgiveness and Reconciliation:* "Beyond doubt the New Testament teaches the absolute necessity of ethical and spiritual perfection, or if we prefer the word, attainment. It knows nothing of a reconciliation with God that does not make this goal an object of passionate desire."[18] Speaking of John Wesley's teaching, W. E. Sangster says, "His more general claim that the whole tenor of the New Testament points to the necessity of ethical and spiritual perfection, seemed to us to be beyond dispute."[19]

II. Galatians

Galatians is Paul's passionate defense of Christian liberty against those who would continue to argue the claims of the ceremonial or cultic provisions of the Old Testament. The letter has traditionally been grouped with Romans and 1 and 2 Corinthians

---

16. Vine, EDNTW, 3:175.

17. Quoted by Roy S. Nicholson, *The Arminian Emphasis* (Owosso, Mich.: Owosso College, n.d.), p. 134.

18. Quoted by Atkinson, *Beauty of Holiness*, p. 73.

19. *The Path to Perfection* (New York: Abingdon-Cokesbury, 1943), p. 185; cf. also Atkinson, ibid.

and dated about the middle 50s of the first Christian century. An alternate view would place the letter earlier and in fact make it Paul's first—written on the eve of the Council of Jerusalem in c. 50 A.D. "Galatia" (1:2) would then be the political province rather than the geographical area of that name, and the churches would include Perga, Pisidian Antioch, Iconium, Lystra, Derbe, etc. (cf. Acts 14:21-25). As A. M. Hunter writes:

> But the really strong argument for putting Galatians before the Council is the letter's complete silence about the Apostolic Decree of Acts 15. This Decree settled the point at issue in Galatia, viz. that Gentile believers need not be circumcised. If Paul had been writing after the Council, all he had to do was to quote it and silence all controversy.[20]

A. Crucified with Christ, Gal. 2:20

The concept of crucifixion with Christ found in Rom. 6:6 occurs again in Gal. 2:20—"I have been crucified with Christ and I no longer live, but Christ lives in me. The life I live in the body, I live by faith in the Son of God, who loved me and gave himself for me." Macgregor comments, "When men come to die with Christ on the cross, He comes to live in them by the Spirit."[21] Raymond T. Stamm writes:

> Crucifixion with Christ means three things: (a) Participation in the benefits of Christ's death, including freedom from law, forgiveness for past sins, and a passionate urge never to sin again (Rom. 4:24-25; II Cor. 5:14-15; Col. 2:12-15, 20; 3:1-4). (b) A moral, spiritual fellowship with Christ in his death and resurrection, which takes the Christian's "I will" captive to "the mind of Christ," replacing the law as a design for living (II Cor. 10:3-6; Phil. 3:10; Rom. 6:11-11). (c) A partnership with Christ in his creative suffering, which requires the Christian to "complete what remains of Christ's afflictions" for the sake of his body the church (Col. 1:24-25; 3:5; Rom. 8:17).[22]

In this case, the KJV "I am crucified with Christ" better represents the idea of the continuing result of this crucifixion implied in the perfect tense of the verb than does the translation "I have been crucified" (RSV, NIV).[23]

---

20. *Introducing the New Testament*, p. 114.
21. Quoted, NBC, p. 1006.
22. IB, 10:489.
23. Cf., ibid.

Many commentators would apply these words to an initial conversion experience. But the context, as in Romans 6, is the impossibility of sin in a justified life: "If, while we seek to be justified in Christ, it becomes evident that we ourselves are sinners, does that mean that Christ promotes sin? Absolutely not!" (v. 17). Rebuilding what had been destroyed and thereby being a law-breaker is obviated by dying to the law in crucifixion with the Savior (vv. 18-20).

Again, as in Romans 6, what is crucified is not the self which is the core of personal identity. As E. Stanley Jones writes:

> The false, unnatural world of sin and evil, the false self, organized around egoism, has to die. When Paul said, "I have been crucified with Christ," he meant that false world and that false self were crucified. He didn't mean his self, his real self was annihilated, cancelled, for in the next breath he says: "It is no longer I who live." He was cleansed by the crucifixion of the false self, this body of death that had clung to him.[24]

What is to die, Richard E. Howard comments, is not "one's essential selfhood or what is often termed self-crucifixion. It is rather the old, inner self, helplessly and hopelessly depraved by sin, that dies. Paul's terminology is strange to modern ways of thinking, yet it depicts a truth that is well known in human experience."[25]

In an eloquent testimony, Jones writes: "I laid at His feet a self of which I was ashamed, couldn't control, and couldn't live with; and to my glad astonishment He took that self, remade it, consecrated it to Kingdom purposes, and gave it back to me, a self I can now live with gladly and joyously and comfortably."[26]

Paul S. Rees cites the experiential value of Gal. 2:20 in the life of Prebendary Webb-Peploe of the Anglican church:

> Listen to that distinguished minister of the Anglican Church, Prebendary Webb-Peploe, who for many years thrilled with his scholarly expositions of Scripture the thousands who attended the Keswick Convention in England's "Lake District": "For many years I was a minister and faithful preacher of the doctrine of justification, but I had no joy for every moment, no rest in the midst of trouble, no calm amid the burdens of this life; I was strained and overstrained until I felt that I was breaking down." Then came new light from God and the response to

---

24. *Victory Through Surrender* (New York: Abingdon Press, 1966), pp. 36-37.
25. BBC, 9:51.
26. *Mastery: The Art of Mastering Life* (New York: Abingdon Press, 1955), p. 97.

it in faith. There was the testimony given to him privately by Sir Arthur Blackwood. There was the illuminated text on the wall: "My grace is sufficient for thee." There was the instant, half-irritated reaction of his frustrated soul, "It is *not* sufficient, it is *not* sufficient!" There was the quiet, desperate cry, "Lord, let Thy grace be sufficient!" There was the rebuking Inner Voice that said, "You fool, how dare you ask God to *make* what *is?*" There was the chastened response, "O God, whatever Thou does say in Thy Word I believe, and please God, I will step out upon it." There was the further revealing, reassuring word of Galatians 2:20, "not I, but Christ liveth in me."

And then—the release! The release from a divided mind and a distressed heart! Said Webb-Peploe: "When the truth came—'not I, but Christ liveth in me'—the rest of faith was practically known in my life."[27]

B. Faith and the Promise of the Spirit, Gal. 3:2-3, 14

The function of faith in experiencing all that is meant by "the promise of the Spirit" is indicated in Galatians 3. In rhetorical questions that imply their own answers, Paul asks, "I would like to learn just one thing from you: Did you receive the Spirit by observing the law, or by believing what you heard? Are you so foolish? After beginning with the Spirit, are you now trying to attain your goal by human effort?" (vv. 2-3). Rather, God "redeemed us in order that the blessing given to Abraham might come to the Gentiles through Christ Jesus, so that by faith we might receive the promise of the Spirit" (v. 14).

C. Flesh and Spirit, Gal. 5:17-24; 6:14

Galatians 5 includes a classic statement of the inner strife between "flesh and Spirit" which with Romans 7 has often been taken as normative for the highest Christian life: "For the sinful nature [Gr., *sarx;* flesh, KJV, RSV] desires what is contrary to the Spirit, and the Spirit what is contrary to the sinful nature. They are in conflict with each other, so that you do not do what you want" (v. 17). That *sarx* ("the sinful nature") here is not bodily or physical as indicated in the apostle's detailed listing of the "acts of the sinful nature": "sexual immorality, impurity and debauchery; idolatry and witchcraft; hatred, discord, jealousy, fits of rage, selfish ambition, dissensions, factions and envy; drunkenness, orgies, and the

---

27. *Adequate Man,* p. 81.

like. I warn you, as I did before, that those who live like this will not inherit the kingdom of God" (vv. 19-21).

In total contrast with "the acts of the sinful nature" is "the fruit of the Spirit . . . love, joy, peace, patience, kindness, goodness, faithfulness, gentleness and self-control" (vv. 22-23).

The crucifixion of 2:20 emerges again in 5:24 where the subject of the crucifixion is "the sinful nature with its passions and desires." Such a crucifixion pertains to "those who belong to Christ Jesus." Belonging to Christ Jesus in its full scope involves three stages: (1) We are Christ's by creation—He made us; (2) we are Christ's by the Cross, by redemption—He purchased us; and (3) we are Christ's by consecration—the self-yielding of those already "alive from the dead" (Rom. 6:13).

Just as Rom. 7:14-25 must be interpreted in harmony with its context in Romans 6 and 8, so Gal. 5:17 must be interpreted in harmony with v. 24. The inner strife—so far as "the sinful nature" is concerned—is ended when that sinful nature is crucified. To think of "crucifixion" as nothing but a continual "dying" that never results in "death" is to miss the biblical as well as the natural meaning of the term.

Paul comes back to the concept of crucifixion a third time in Galatians 6:14—"May I never boast except in the cross of our Lord Jesus Christ, through which the world has been crucified to me, and I to the world." Through the Cross the world has become as a dead thing, and the crucified Christian "dies to" the world.

III. EPHESIANS

Ephesians and Colossians have been called the "twin Epistles." Approximately half the verses in Ephesians can be traced to parallels in Colossians. It is possible that Ephesians is a circular letter, written shortly after Colossians and developing some of its ideas more completely. As it stands in our English Bibles, it is the first of four "Prison Epistles"—including Philippians, Colossians, and Philemon—and written from Rome in the early 60s.

The primary emphasis in Ephesians is on the Church, developed under three metaphors each related to the Spirit:

(1) The Church is the building or temple of God, to be His habitation through the Spirit (2:20-21).

(2) The Church is the Body of Christ—to grow in the unity of

the animating Spirit into the fullness of Christ (1:23; 2:14-16; 4:4, 12, 16; 5:23, 30).

(3) The Church is the Bride of Christ, "loved by Him to the point of sacrificial surrender, cleansed by Him through a baptism resulting in unblemished consecration (a baptism of water which represents the inner baptism of one Spirit)" (5:25-27; cf. 1:13-14; 3:16; 5:23, 30; 6:18).[28]

A. The Holy Spirit in Ephesians

Ephesians lays special stress on the work of the Holy Spirit in the Church. Twelve times in six short chapters and at least once in each chapter, Paul speaks of the Holy Spirit. As believers, we are "marked in him with a seal, the promised Holy Spirit, who is a deposit guaranteeing our inheritance until the redemption of those who are God's possession" (1:13-14). Paul says, "I keep asking that the God of our Lord Jesus Christ, the glorious Father, may give you the Spirit of wisdom and revelation, so that you may know him better" (v. 17).

All of us "have access to the Father by one Spirit" (2:18), and we "are being built together to become a dwelling in which God lives by his Spirit" (v. 22). The "mystery of Christ . . . has now been revealed by the Spirit" (3:4-5). Paul prays that God "may strengthen you with power through his Spirit in your inner being, so that Christ may dwell in your hearts through faith" (vv. 16-17).

We are to "keep the unity of the Spirit through the bond of peace" because "there is one body and one Spirit" (4:3-4). We must not "grieve the Holy Spirit of God, with whom you were sealed for the day of redemption" (4:30), but rather must "be filled with the Spirit" (5:18). In our Christian armory we have "the sword of the Spirit, which is the word of God" and we are to "pray in the Spirit on all occasions with all kinds of prayers and requests" (6:17-18).

B. Chosen to Be Holy, Eph. 1:4

Ephesians 1:3-14 has been titled "A Hymn of Salvation."[29] It stresses the source of salvation blessing, v. 3; salvation enacted

---

28. Outline adapted and quotation from H. Wheeler Robinson, *The Christian Experience of the Holy Spirit* (New York: Harper and Brothers Publishers, 1928), p. 140.

29. By John Wick Bowman; cited by Taylor, BBC, 9:142.

before time began, vv. 4-6; and salvation realized in time, vv. 7-14.[30]

God's eternal purpose for His people is strongly stated: "For he chose us in him before the creation of the world to be holy and blameless in his sight" (1:4). The choice (election) is not unconditional and arbitrary, for "the elect are constituted, not by absolute decree, but by acceptance of the conditions of God's call."[31]

As E. F. Scott writes, "Those who are 'holy' are also to be morally blameless. Their calling by God lays on them the obligation to lead a life which God Himself will be able to approve."[32] Willard H. Taylor comments:

> **Holy** *(hagios)* expresses the positive experiential purpose of God's choice. More than ceremonial holiness is meant here; that is, more than a mere difference stemming from a divine separation. **Holy** expresses the inner, moral difference which prevails when God's grace is operative in the heart. This fact is abundantly indicated in the second word describing the result of the choice, namely **blameless** *(amomos)*. . . . **Holy** refers to the inner spiritual quality, whereas **without blame** refers to the outer conduct of the life.[33]

C. Prayer for the Church, Eph. 3:14-21

Paul's great prayer for the Church in 3:14-21 includes four petitions directly related to the fulfillment of God's purpose that believers be "holy and blameless." The first is that the Father "may strengthen you with power through his Spirit in your inner being" (v. 16). Taylor observes:

> The phrase **to be strengthened** is an aorist infinitive *(krataiothenai)*, suggesting crisis or punctiliar action. Paul seems to be speaking of that second experience of the Christian in which "the Holy Spirit of Promise, the Lord of Pentecost, the Spirit of Counsel and Might" cleanses and empowers the heart. This is no surface work. It happens **in the inner man,** in "the true and enduring self."[34]

---

30. BBC, 9:143.

31. Ibid., p. 146.

32. "The Epistles of Paul to the Colossians, to Philemon, and to the Ephesians," *The Moffatt New Testament Commentary* (New York: Harper and Brothers Publishers, 1930), p. 141.

33. BBC, 9:147-48.

34. Ibid., p. 195; the quotation is from F. F. Bruce, *The Epistle to the Ephesians* (New York: Fleming H. Revell Co., 1961), p. 67.

This strengthening is "so that Christ may dwell in your hearts through faith" (v. 17). William Barclay says, "The word that Paul uses for Christ *dwelling* in our hearts is the Greek word *katoikein* which is the word used for permanent, as opposed to temporary, residence."[35] Moule comments that Christ's coming in this sense is "so deep and great, as to constitute practically a new arrival, and remaining where He so arrives not as a Guest, precariously detained, but as a Master resident in His proper home."[36]

The believer so indwelt by Christ through the Spirit will be "rooted and established in love [and] . . . have power, together with all the saints, to grasp how wide and long and high and deep is the love of Christ, and to know this love that surpasses knowledge" (vv. 17-19). Charles Hodge, a staunch Calvinist, writes, "This love of Christ, though it surpasses the power of our understanding to comprehend, is still a subject of experimental knowledge. We may know how excellent, how wonderful, how free, how disinterested, how long-suffering, it is, and that it is infinite. . . . Those who thus know the love of Christ towards them purify themselves even as he is pure."[37]

The final petition is that "you may be filled to the measure of all the fullness of God" (v. 19). Francis W. Beare says, "This is the culminating petition of the prayer, the final issue of all the gifts which the writer has desired for his readers. Its substance is that their life should advance in all respects from the partial to the complete, that they should attain to the completeness which belongs to God and which God imparts through Christ."[38] Being "filled with the Spirit" (5:18) and "filled to the measure of all the fullness of God" represents the "fulness of the blessing of Christ" about which Paul wrote in Rom. 15:29, RSV.

D. A General Appeal, Eph. 4:17-24

Paul's "General Appeal"[39] in 4:17-24 has been variously interpreted. The most significant differences in interpretation have to

---

35. "The Letter to the Ephesians," DSB, p. 154.

36. Handley C. G. Moule, *Ephesians Studies*, 2d ed. (London: Pickering and Inglis, n.d.), p. 129.

37. *Commentary on the Epistle to the Ephesians* (Grand Rapids: William B. Eerdmans Publishing Co., 1950), pp. 189-90.

38. IB, 10:680.

39. The title proposed by Beare, IB, 9:696.

do with the understanding of the meaning of the terms "old man" and "new man" (KJV, RSV) or "old self" and "new self, created to be like God in true righteousness and holiness"; and with the interpretation of the infinitives "to put on" and "to put off."[40] The problem arises because the Greek infinitive may be understood as a simple declarative or as carrying the force of an imperative.

The RSV translates the infinitives as imperatives: "Put off your old nature which belongs to your former manner of life and is corrupt through deceitful lusts, and be renewed in the spirit of your minds, and put on the new nature, created after the likeness of God in true righteousness and holiness" (vv. 22-24). The NIV, on the other hand, translates the passage in such a way as to maintain the ambiguity of the original: "You were taught, with regard to your former way of life, to put off your old self, which is being corrupted by its deceitful desires; to be made new in the attitude of your minds; and to put on the new self, created to be like God in true righteousness and holiness"—"the holiness which is no illusion" (Phillips).

The issue is whether Paul is describing the change from an unregenerate to a Christian life as a fact already accomplished, or whether he is addressing an injunction to Christians to deal decisively with a corrupted nature in an experience of entire sanctification. The infinitives "to put off" and "to put on" are aorists, suggesting a definite, dateable action. Archibald Hunter says, "The metaphors come from putting clothing on and off, and the tenses of the verbs in the Greek refer to a change which is to be made once for all."[41] Putting on "the new self, created to be like God in true righteousness and holiness" seems very much like one of Paul's varied descriptions of what he described in 1 Thess. 5:23 as being sanctified "wholly."

The "putting off" and "putting on" are therefore definite actions resulting in a continuing process suggested by the words "be renewed in the spirit of your minds" (23, RSV). Beare says concerning "put off" (v. 22) and "put on" (v. 24). "Both these infinitives are aorists, referring to a change that is made once for all; **be renewed,** on the other hand, renders a present infinitive denoting a continuing process (cf. II Cor. 4:16, 'Our inner nature is being renewed

40. Cf. the complete discussion by Taylor in BBC, 9:217-22.
41. LBC, 22:68.

day by day')."[42] Taylor says, "A parallel Pauline verse is Rom. 12:2: 'And continue to be transformed by the renewing of your mind' (lit.). This renewal is not the result of human effort; it is the work of the Holy Spirit upon the human spirit. The transformation comes as the individual surrenders himself to the leadership of the Spirit."[43]

E. Filled with the Spirit, Eph. 5:18

The exhortation to be "filled with the Spirit" (5:18) is in the present tense and could well be translated "Go on being filled with the Spirit." It is also passive—the filling is to be received, not accomplished; and it is plural—all believers are to be filled. "Let the Holy Spirit take full possession."[44]

Nor is this injunction found in a distinctively theological passage. It is rather right at the heart of a paragraph dealing with some of the most practical, down-to-earth matters of Christian living: being careful how one lives; not unwise, but wise; making the most of every opportunity; understanding what the Lord's will is; renunciation of drunkenness; speaking to each other with psalms, hymns, and spiritual songs; and constant thankfulness to the Father. Taylor observes:

> The day-by-day experience of the Christian man must be that of being **filled with the Spirit.** The verb **filled** is a present imperative and can be translated "be continually filled with the Spirit." But it stands to reason that a Christian cannot *go on being filled* until he has first been filled at some given time, as was true on the Day of Pentecost. Ralph Earle comments, "This is not to be a transitory experience, but an abiding one." ("Gleanings from the Greek New Testament," *Nazarene Preacher,* XXXIX [October, 1964], 38). The verbs in the present tense which appear in 19-21 suggest that Paul is not here calling his readers to the crisis of being sanctified wholly, but rather to the subsequent life in which the Holy Spirit fills us moment by moment, having already been "sealed with the Holy Spirit of promise" (1:13, NASB; cf. 4:20).[45]

---

42. IB, 10:699.
43. BBC, 9:221-22.
44. Hunter, LBC, 22:71.
45. BBC, 9:235.

F. Christ's Sanctifying Love, Eph. 5:25-27

In Paul's exhortation to mutual submission in the Christian home (5:21—6:9) there is a profound statement of the purpose and effect of Christ's love for His Church: "Husbands, love your wives, just as Christ loved the church and gave himself up for her to make her holy, cleansing her by the washing with water through the word, and to present her to himself as a radiant church, without stain or wrinkle or any other blemish, but holy and blameless" (5:25-27).

Grammarians differ as to the interpretation of the aorist participle "cleanse" in relation to the main verb "sanctify." The RSV, NASB, and Taylor would translate "having cleansed."[46] Beare would agree with the KJV and NIV translations, making the cleansing coordinate with sanctifying or "making holy." He says that "having cleansed" in the RSV is "better rendered 'by cleansing'; the aorist expresses coincidental action."[47] Henry Alford says, "*Hagiase* [sanctify] and *katharisas* [cleanse] might be contemporaneous, and indeed this is the more common usage of past participles with past finite verbs in the N.T." He goes on to say, however, that since the sanctifying (in his opinion) is a gradual process, the cleansing must precede it.[48]

Scholars of Wesleyan persuasion who prefer the antecedent action of the cleansing would relate this to initial sanctification in cleansing from "acquired depravity." This is indeed a necessary interpretation if the "washing with water through the word" be identified with water baptism or with what water baptism signifies. It is at least possible, however, that the water here is used symbolically of the Holy Spirit in relation to the sanctifying power of the Word stated by Jesus in John 17:17.

Taylor's preference for "having cleansed" has been noted. He also writes:

> The phrase **by the word** cannot be construed to mean either the baptismal formula or the confession of the recipient of baptism; it refers to the gospel or the word of God. It is also to be attached to the word **sanctify** rather than to **cleanse**. In keeping with this analysis, the translation would be: "Christ sanctified His Church by the word, having cleansed it with the

---

46. Ibid., pp. 242-43; cf. NIV fn.
47. IB, 10:723.
48. *Greek New Testament,* 3:137.

washing of water." In John 17:17, it is recorded that Christ prayed, "Sanctify them through thy truth: thy word is truth." The word of God is the means or instrument by which the deeper purification beyond conversion is accomplished. This second blessing is administered by the Holy Spirit upon acceptance by faith of the meritorious death of Christ by the converted Christian.[49]

In any event, two important truths stand out: (1) sanctifying the Church is one of the reasons for the self-giving of Christ on the Cross (cf. Heb. 13:11). We are sanctified by His blood as well as justified by His blood as in Rom. 5:8. (2) The effect of sanctification is to render its subjects "radiant," "holy and blameless." This is not "faultless," a condition no finite being can enjoy in this life. It is to be without the blame of sin in heart or life.

---

49. BBC, 9:243.

7

Holiness in Philippians, Colossians, Thessalonians, and the Pastoral Epistles

I. PHILIPPIANS

Paul's letter to the church at Philippi is one of the warmest and most personal in the New Testament. It was written as an expression of thanksgiving for the generosity of the Philippians in ministering to the apostle's needs during his Roman imprisonment. Bengel stated that it could be summarized in two phrases: "I rejoice . . . Rejoice ye."[1]

Although written from prison, Philippians breathes an atmosphere of serenity and praise. Archibald Hunter says it reminds him of a letter written by Martin Niemoller from a concentration camp in Germany to a friend in Britain: "In the old days I used to be a bearer of the Gospel; now that Gospel is bearing me."[2]

While neither primarily doctrinal nor ethical, Philippians contains both elements. Certainly one of the most notable Christological passages from Paul's pen is the "kenosis" passage in 2:3-10.

---

1. Cf. William Barclay, DSB, p. 9.
2. *Introducing the New Testament*, p. 128.

A. To the Saints, Phil. 1:1

As is true in six of Paul's nine letters addressed to churches (as compared with those addressed to individuals), the apostle speaks of the recipients as saints (1:1; cf. 2 Cor. 1:1; Eph. 1:1; Col. 1:2; or called [to be] saints, Rom. 1:7; 1 Cor. 1:2). John Allen Knight points out that the term

> literally "holy" ones (hagiois), refers to those who have been set apart to the service of Christ, separated and different from the world. They belong to, and are to be like, God. They are His purchased possession and His peculiar property. The term is the equivalent of believers or regenerated ones, and indicates those who have been "washed" from sin and set on the road in love to moral and spiritual maturity (1 Cor. 6:9-11; 1 Pet. 1:2). . . . In this sense every believer experiences initial sanctification (1 Cor. 1:2; 6:11). "It is the Spirit who sanctifies; but He does so inasmuch as He roots us in Christ and builds us up in Christ. Therefore saints are sanctified by, or of, the Spirit; but they are sanctified (or holy) in Christ Jesus." Entire sanctification takes place when the heart is cleansed from all sin and filled with the Holy Spirit (Acts 15:8-9).[3]

"'Saints' in its New Testament sense means not people wearing halos but committed Christians."[4]

B. The Mind of Christ, Phil. 2:5-11

Ernest F. Scott calls these verses "the great passage which is the chief glory of the Epistle to the Philippians."[5] His primary reference is, of course, to the unsurpassed Christology of the great "kenosis" passage, vv. 6-11. NIV sets these lines in poetic form, suggesting that Paul may be quoting here from an ancient Christian hymn.

The apostle introduces the high theology of this passage with words that have a very practical import: "Your attitude should be the same as that of Christ Jesus" (v. 5), or "Let this mind be in you, which was also in Christ Jesus" (KJV). This was one of John Wesley's frequent descriptions of Christian perfection. The term translated "mind" is phronein and "signifies the general mental attitude

---

3. BBC, 9:288.
4. Archibald Hunter, LBC, 22:85.
5. IB, 11:46.

or disposition."[6] "The word denotes rather a general disposition of the mind than a specific act of thought directed at a given point."[7]

There is a parallel here with Rom. 8:6-7 where the same term *(phronēma)* is used in the phrase "the mind of the Spirit." The mind-set of the Spirit is the mind-set of Christ and is to characterize the Christian. Scott says of the believers to whom Paul writes, "What they require as Christians is an inward disposition which will direct them in all they do."[8]

C. Perfection: Goal and Experience, Phil. 3:12-15

In Phil. 3:12-15, Paul contrasts a perfection which is a goal to be fully realized only at the resurrection with a maturity or perfection that is possible now: "Not that I have already obtained all this [i.e., the resurrection from the dead], or have already been made perfect, but I press on to take hold of that for which Christ Jesus took hold of me. Brothers, I do not consider myself yet to have taken hold of it. But one thing I do: Forgetting what is behind and straining toward what is ahead, I press on toward the goal to win the prize for which God has called me heavenward in Christ Jesus. All of us who are mature [*teleios,* the same term translated 'perfect' in v. 12] should take such a view of things."

John Wesley's translation of v. 12 and his comment on it are valuable: *"Not that I . . . am already perfected*—There is a difference between one that is perfect and one that is *perfected.* The one is fitted for the race (verse 15); the other, ready to receive the prize."[9] E. F. Scott says, "The word also signifies a state of fulfillment, when something has become in fact what it was ideally meant to be."[10]

Paul S. Rees writes concerning the term "perfect" *(teleios)* in v. 15:

> Not *absolute* perfection: that were fantastic. Not *legal* perfection: that were to return to the law and to retreat from grace. Not *service* perfection: that were to overlook obvious awkward-

---

6. Marvin R. Vincent, "Epistles to the Philippians and to Philemon," *International Critical Commentaries* (Edinburgh: T. and T. Clark, 1897), p. 57.

7. Ibid., p. 8.

8. IB, 11:48.

9. *Explanatory Notes upon the New Testament,* p. 735. See also Wesley's sermon on Phil. 3:12 in which he contrasts "what perfection is not" with what it is (*Sermons on Several Occasions,* 1:355-68).

10. IB, 11:88.

ness and clumsiness. Not *behavioral* perfection: that were to fly in the face of a hundred flaws in our manners. Not *sinless* perfection: that were to imply a status identical with our "unfallen" Lord.

What then? Let's call it *affectional* and *dispositional* perfection. It is God's own gift to totally committed children of His, who, renouncing self-pleasing and men-pleasing, are imbued with a passionate eagerness to please Him in all things.[11]

In the verses immediately preceding v. 12 there is a hint of one of the many things Christian perfection may mean: singleness of purpose. "To will one thing" is Sören Kierkegaard's well-known equivalent of "pure in heart." When that one thing is the will of God, the definition is not far wrong. Total commitment to the full will of God and fitness for doing that will are close to the heart of biblical holiness. As Oswald Chambers remarked, "Perfection does not mean the full maturity and consummation of a man's powers, but perfect fitness for doing the will of God."[12] E. Stanley Jones comments on the same point:

> The man who cannot say: "This one thing I do," has to say, "these many things I dabble in." For his soul forces are not fused into one—he is a dabbler instead of a doer. The Holy Spirit cleanses from conflict as well as from contamination. The scattered rays of the sun, not concentrated, set nothing afire; but when they are brought through a burning glass and concentrated at one point, they set that point ablaze.[13]

II. COLOSSIANS

Colossians is a letter to a church threatened by a heresy that downgraded the uniqueness of Christ's work and that imposed a false asceticism upon believers. Paul therefore lays a twofold stress on the person and work of Christ (cc. 1—2) and the implications of the new life in Christ (cc. 3—4).

---

11. *Prayer and Life's Highest* (Grand Rapids: William B. Eerdmans Publishing Co., 1956), p. 61. It should be noted that Dr. Rees uses the term "sinless" in the above quotation in the sense in which Wesley said, *"Sinless perfection* is a phrase I never use, lest I should seem to contradict myself" (*Plain Account,* p. 54). The contradiction would arise from Wesley's recognition that "sin, improperly so called" includes involuntary transgressions of divine laws, known and unknown (ibid.)

12. *If Thou Wilt Be Perfect,* p. 117.

13. *Mastery,* p. 232.

A. The Purpose of Reconciliation, Col. 1:22-23

In Col. 1:22-23, Paul states as the purpose of reconciliation to God "to present you holy in his sight, without blemish and free from accusation—if you continue in your faith, established and firm, not moved from the hope held out in the gospel." John B. Nielson writes:

> These words establish scriptural holiness. Biblical righteousness and holiness are found in the motive or intention. Paul (Rom. 13:10; Gal. 5:14) agrees with Jesus (Mark 12:28-31). The three words [holy, unblameable, and unreproveable in the KJV] indicate a spiritually perfect condition as well as position; they are practically synonymous. When the motive is pure, when love is the sole guiding principle of conduct, the believer is **unreprovable,** blameless, **holy.** Entire sanctification is "Love Enthroned."[14]

Francis Beare comments on these verses: "To the new relationship with God there corresponds the inward transformation in those whom Christ now brings before him. The words belong to the vocabulary of sacrifice. Christ presents us before God, and we freely offer ourselves, as 'a living sacrifice, holy and acceptable to God, which is (our) spiritual worship' (Rom. 12:1)."[15]

B. Presenting Everyone Perfect, Col. 1:28

The purpose of Paul's preaching and teaching is "so that we may present everyone perfect in Christ" (v. 28). The thrice-repeated "everyone" (Gr., warning every man, teaching every man . . . in order to present every man) is probably an oblique reference to a Gnostic notion that only a few were capable of the highest spiritual attainment or perfection. In contrast, Paul stresses the potential of all to be "perfect in Christ"—not, let it be said, perfect "in themselves" but in their relation to Christ.

C. Spiritual Circumcision, Col. 2:9-15

Along with the idea of perfection is that of fullness. Fullness for the believer is tied to the fullness of God in Christ: "For in Christ all the fullness of the Deity lives in bodily form, and you have been given fullness in Christ, who is the head over every

---

14. BBC, 9:385.
15. IB, 11:175.

power and authority. In him you were also circumcised, in the putting off of the sinful nature [*tou sōmatos tēs sarkos*, lit., the body of the flesh, e.g., the carnal nature], not with a circumcision done by the hands of men but with the circumcision done by Christ, having been buried with him in baptism and raised with him through your faith in the power of God, who raised him from the dead" (2:9-12).

The concept of spiritual circumcision or the circumcision of the heart is one that we have already met in Deut. 10:16 and 30:6 where it is associated with deliverance from a rebellious spirit ("do not be stiff-necked any longer") and living and loving God with all the heart and soul ("The Lord your God will circumcise your hearts and the hearts of your descendants, so that you may love him with all your heart and with all your soul, and live").

In the reference to baptism here as in Romans 6, there would seem to be more in view than water baptism alone. The full meaning of death with Christ and the resurrection life that follows implies a personal experience of the baptism with the Spirit which Christ alone ministers to His people.

In any event, there is a clear statement of the "putting off" (the same word used in 2:15 of "powers and authorities" and in 3:9 of "the old man" [KJV], "your old self"), of the "sinful nature." Here that "putting off" is the effect of "the circumcision done by Christ," not "a circumcision done by the hands of men." Circumcision becomes a symbol of cleansing, and cleansing is the condition of the completeness or fullness of Christ in the life of the believer.

Writes E. F. Scott, "The material rite [of circumcision] was only the symbol of a condition that must be effected in man's inward being; this higher circumcision consists in 'the putting off of the body of the flesh,' i.e., of the whole carnal nature."[16] F. F. Bruce says, "This is an inward purification, which to Paul was the true circumcision."[17] Nielson writes, "**Circumcision** is a figure of the grace of our sanctification."[18] Vincent comments, "In spiritual circumcision,

---

16. *Epistles of Paul to Colossians, Philemon, and Ephesians,* p. 44. See the chapter on "Circumcision of the Heart" in Wood, *Pentecostal Grace,* pp. 137-68. Wood's study is a classic.

17. "Colossians," NICNT (Grand Rapids: William B. Eerdmans Publishing Co., 1957), pp. 234-35.

18. BBC, 9:402.

through Christ, the whole, corrupt carnal nature is put away like a garment which is taken off and laid aside."[19]

The whole of our deliverance is related to the triumph of Christ on the Cross: "When you were dead in your sins and in the uncircumcision of your sinful nature, God made you alive with Christ. He forgave us all our sins, having canceled the written code, with its regulations, that was against us and that stood opposed to us; he took it away, nailing it to the cross. And having disarmed the powers and authorities, he made a public spectacle of them, triumphing over them by the cross" (2:13-15); or in Phillips' vivid paraphrase, "And then, having drawn the sting of all the powers and authorities ranged against us, he exposed them, shattered, empty and defeated, in his own triumphant victory!"

D. The Risen Life, Col. 3:1-14

The ethical implications of the risen life are spelled out in part in 3:1-14. They involve "putting to death" sins with a physical basis—"whatever belongs to your earthly nature": "sexual immorality, impurity, lust, evil desires and greed, which is idolatry"—and "putting away" what have been called dispositional sins: "such things as these: anger, rage, malice, slander, and filthy language from your lips" (vv. 5, 8). It is worth noting that the verbs for "putting to death" and "putting away" ("rid yourselves of") are in the aorist tense with its inevitable suggestion of a crucial, decisive act.

Paul's expression in vv. 9-10 parallels Eph. 4:22-24: "Do not lie to each other, since you have taken off your old self [lit., your old man] with its practices and have put on the new self [lit., the new—'man' or 'self' is omitted], which is being renewed in knowledge in the image of its Creator."

Here, for the third and last time, Paul uses the debated expression "old man." As we have seen, it may be taken to represent either the totality of the old unregenerate life, or the sinful "nature" or condition of an unsanctified heart. It may indeed represent both: "the whole of the former sinful life as well as the cause or root from which that life springs."[20] Paul's use of the expression

---

19. Marvin R. Vincent, *Word Studies in the New Testament* (Grand Rapids: William B. Eerdmans Publishing Co., 1965 reprint), 3:488.

20. W. T. Purkiser, *Sanctification and its Synonyms* (Kansas City: Beacon Hill Press, 1961), p. 89.

"put off" in 2:11 in regard to "the body of the flesh" or "the sinful nature" would seem to indicate that the carnal nature is included, as well as a career of sinning. In any event, "putting to death" and "putting away" both physical and dispositional sin is coordinate with putting off the old man and putting on the new.

The resulting renewal, described in Eph. 4:24 as a nature or condition "created to be like God in true righteousness and holiness," is said in Col. 3:10 to be "in the image of its Creator." The allusion would seem to be to renewal or restoration of what is commonly called "the moral image of God" that had been lost or at least defaced in the Fall.

The negative aspects of the ethic of the risen life are balanced with the positive: "Therefore, as God's chosen people, holy and dearly loved, clothe yourselves with compassion, kindness, humility, gentleness and patience. Bear with each other and forgive whatever grievances you may have against one another. Forgive as the Lord forgave you. And over all these virtues put on love, which binds them all together in perfect unity" (vv. 12-14).

The use of the same verb in the Greek (*endusamenoi, endusasthe*) translated "have put on" in v. 10 and "clothe yourselves with" in v. 12 suggests that "compassion, kindness, humility, gentleness and patience" form a description of dispositional and ethical aspects of the new nature "which is being renewed in knowledge in the image of its Creator." The parallel with the fruit of the Spirit in Gal. 5:22-23 is apparent: kindness, gentleness, patience, and above all, love.

III. THE THESSALONIAN LETTERS

The Thessalonian letters, while grouped with the shorter letters of Paul in the traditional arrangement of the New Testament, are among the earliest written—possibly antedated only by Galatians. They reveal Paul's early concern that his converts experience the full scope of the redemption possible in Christ.

The two letters were probably written close together toward the end of A.D. 50, during the early part of Paul's extended stay in Corinth. Acts 17:1-9 tells of Paul's brief but highly successful mission in Thessalonica. The bond required of Jason and other friends of Paul was probably a peace bond that prevented the apostle from returning in person. In his stead, he sent Timothy, and it was

Timothy's return with good news from Thessalonica that was the occasion for the writing of 1 Thessalonians (cf. 3:1-6).

Timothy's report included a description of the strong personal spiritual life of the Thessalonian converts. It also conveyed their concern for more teaching about the coming of Christ particularly in relation to those Christians who would die before the Parousia (the New Testament term commonly used for the Second Advent). Paul's letter thus revolves around two themes: the second coming of Christ (each chapter in 1 Thessalonians ends with a reference to this event); and the apostle's concern for the full sanctification of his converts.

A. Holiness as Subsequent to Conversion, 1 Thess. 1:1—3:9

First Thessalonians provides some of the strongest evidence in the New Testament for a second epochal work of grace in the Christian experience. This grows out of Paul's unqualified testimony to the clear experience of conversion in evidence in the Thessalonian church—together with his evident concern for a further work of God in their lives.

The spiritual life of the Thessalonian disciples was vigorous and normal. These believers were exemplary in character and conduct. Through the first two and a half chapters, in a mood of exultant gratitude, Paul describes the current spiritual condition of the church:

> We always thank God for all of you, mentioning you in our prayers. We continually remember before our God and Father your work produced by faith, your labor prompted by love, and your endurance inspired by hope in our Lord Jesus Christ.
> Brothers loved by God, we know that he has chosen you, because our gospel came to you not simply with words, but also with power, with the Holy Spirit and with deep conviction. You know how we lived among you for your sake. You became imitators of us and of the Lord; in spite of severe suffering, you welcomed the message with the joy given by the Holy Spirit. And so you became a model to all the believers in Macedonia and Achaia. The Lord's message rang out from you not only in Macedonia and Achaia—your faith in God has become known everywhere. Therefore we do not need to say anything about it, for they themselves report what kind of reception you gave us. They tell how you turned to God from idols to serve the living and true God, and to wait for his Son from heaven, whom he raised from the dead—Jesus, who rescues us from the coming wrath.

You know, brothers, that our visit to you was not a failure *(1:2—2:1)*.

You are witnesses, and so is God, of how holy, righteous and blameless we were among you who believed *(2:10)*.

And we also thank God continually because, when you received the word of God, which you heard from us, you accepted it not as the word of men, but as it actually is, the word of God, which is at work in you who believe. For you, brothers, became imitators of God's churches in Judea, which are in Christ Jesus: You suffered from your own countrymen the same things those churches suffered from the Jews *(2:13-14)*.

For what is our hope, our joy, or the crown in which we will glory in the presence of our Lord Jesus when he comes? Is it not you? Indeed, you are our glory and joy *(2:19-20)*.

First Thessalonians 3:6-9 conveys the substance of Timothy's report:

But Timothy has just now come to us from you and has brought good news about your faith and love. He has told us that you always have pleasant memories of us and that you long to see us, just as we also long to see you. Therefore, brothers, in all our distress and persecution we were encouraged about you because of your faith. For now we really live, since you are standing firm in the Lord. How can we thank God enough for you in return for all the joy we have in the presence of our God because of you?

B. A Prayer for Holiness, 1 Thess. 3:10-13

At this point of climax in his rejoicing, Paul reveals his concern for the further advancement of his Thessalonian friends: "Night and day we pray most earnestly that we may see you again and supply what is lacking in your faith. . . . May the Lord make your love increase and overflow for each other and for everyone else, just as ours does for you. May he strengthen your hearts so that you will be blameless and holy in the presence of our God and Father when our Lord Jesus comes with all his holy ones" (3:10, 12-13).

Paul could testify himself to conduct that was holy (*hosiōs*, 2:10) and blameless; his concern is that his followers may likewise be blameless in holiness *(en hagiōsunē)* in the presence of God when the Lord Jesus comes again. Writes John W. Bailey:

The ultimate goal toward which the prayer is directed is that the Lord may establish **your hearts unblamable in holiness before our God and Father.** A similar and even more comprehensive prayer is voiced in 5:23. But again nothing is being sought for these new disciples that is not also a part of the very life of the apostle. The Thessalonians knew how holy and righteous and blameless the missionaries had been in their lives among them (2:10). Also, as God himself knew the lives of his messengers (2:10), so it is the prayer of Paul and his fellow writers that these new converts may be known and recognized of God as blameless in their holiness, when they are before him **at the coming of our Lord Jesus with all his saints.**[21]

Arnold E. Airhart adds an important qualification:

> The whole emphasis of this prayer is upon the inwardness of personal character. It is implied that the character required to make the Thessalonians ready to stand before Christ at His coming is more than a certain blamelessness of outward behavior or service. God's requirement is rather a blamelessness in inward devotion to God, and inward moral purity. Their hearts, their whole personalities, inwardly as well as outwardly, must be pure before God.[22]

Increasing and overflowing love and God's inward strengthening are the means indicated here to effect the blamelessness in holiness essential to the apostle's concern. It is divine love *(agapē)* poured out into our hearts by the Holy Spirit (Rom. 5:5). As Airhart says:

> This love is the Spirit's instrument for the expulsion of that which is impure and incompatible from the heart; its necessary outcome is full obedience to the will of God. A "holiness" which comes some other way than by a baptism of divine love will be spurious—sanctimonious, censorious, legal. True holiness will be manifested in love for **one . . . another,** and for **all men.** Divine love is "the bond of perfectness" (Col. 3:14); it is the energy of all true holiness. It is the means to spiritual stability, since all else is transient.[23]

C. God's Will and God's Call, 1 Thess. 4:3-8

In 4:3-8, Paul relates the idea of sanctification in the will of God to the problem of sexual morality—a connection which could not be made were sanctification, as has been claimed, merely a matter of imputation or position. The ethical content is unmistakably clear: "It is God's will that you should be holy; that you

---

21. IB, 11:289-90. Used by permission.
22. BBC, 9:471.
23. Ibid., 9:472.

should avoid sexual immorality; that each of you should learn to control his own body in a way that is holy and honorable . . . For God did not call us to be impure, but to live a holy life. Therefore, he who rejects this instruction does not reject man but God, who gives you his Holy Spirit" (vv. 3-4, 7-8).

Some ambiguity shadows the interpretation of *heautou skeuos,* "his own vessel" (NASB) in v. 4. A number, including Wesley, Weymouth, NBV, and the RSV, interpret "vessel" to be "wife." Others, including Phillips, Barclay, the NEB and NIV, favor "body." The latter interpretation brings these verses into parallel with Rom. 12:1-2, where the body is to be presented "holy and pleasing to God."

Where the NIV has "be holy," "a way that is holy," and "live a holy life," the Greek uses one or another form of *hagiasmos,* "sanctification" or "holiness." "To be impure" in v. 7 is a rendering of *akatharsia,* literally, "uncleansed." Both God's will and God's call are to holiness or sanctification.

The propriety of this warning about sexual morality as given to those of such clear Christian commitment is explained by William Neil:

> The fact is that one of the most difficult hurdles that any pagan convert had to clear was the Christian attitude to sex. He had been brought up in a world where polygamy, concubinage, homosexuality, and promiscuity were accepted as a matter of course. . . . Many of the religious cults were frankly sexual in character, with phallic rites and sacramental fornication as part of their worship.[24]

Airhart adds:

> The illegitimate or intemperate satisfaction of sensual appetite remains an area of temptation in all healthy and normal Christians, but the unsanctified Christian is perilously vulnerable to such appeals. There is a resurgent paganism in our own time with its smutty entertainment, pornographic literature, laxity in marriage vows, promiscuity, overall obsession with sex, and general permissiveness in sex relationships. In times like these the New Testament teaching on sexual purity is desperately needed, and the New Testament experience of sanctification, with its full devotion to the will of God, is the real answer. The immoral code of our time is fostered and condoned by such entrenched philosophies as naturalism and evo-

---

24. "St. Paul's Epistles to the Thessalonians," *Torch Bible Commentaries* (New York: The Macmillan Co., 1957), p. 74.

lutionism. Gospel dynamite is required to break up these respectable havens of vice.[25]

And William Barclay comments:

Paul believed that God was calling men to holiness. He tells the Thessalonians that God calls them to a holy life (1 Thessalonians 4:7). The root meaning of the word holy *(hagios)* is *different.* To be holy is to be different; it is to have a different standard, a different peace and beauty from the stained, frustrated, defeated life of the world. God calls men to a life in which there has opened out the possibility of a new victory over sin and a new loveliness and beauty. . . . Now in Christ God calls to men to realize that they cannot earn, but can only accept in wonder, His rescuing and redeeming love. The moment a man realizes that, the tension of life is gone.[26]

Phillip Hughes sees in the call of God a reference to the theological concept of election. He reminds us that election in the New Testament is election to be like Christ and cites 1 Thess. 4:7, together with 1 Pet. 1:2, where we are said to have been "chosen according to the foreknowledge of God the Father, by the sanctifying work of the Spirit, for obedience to Jesus Christ and sprinkling by his blood." "The purpose of God's election in Christ is that we should be 'conformed to the image of His Son' (Rom. 8:29)," he says.[27]

The Source of the sanctification or holiness so important to purity of heart and life is the Holy Spirit—literally, "the Spirit of him, the Holy"—or as Phillips, "It is not for nothing that the Spirit God gives us is called the *Holy* Spirit." The verb for "give" is in the present tense. "Thus, the emphasis is on the dynamic, continuing relationship with the Holy Spirit, rather than on the past act of giving."[28] Airhart points out that "in this is seen the utter incompatibility of a life of impurity and sin with the life in Christ." It is the Holy Spirit himself who is "the Fountain of true holiness" whose peculiar work is to sanctify. "If the Spirit's ministry is not rebuffed (cf. 5:19) but rather lovingly received, He will lead unerringly to the entire sanctification of the whole person."[29]

---

25. BBC, 9:475.

26. *Mind of Saint Paul*, pp. 50-51.

27. *But for the Grace of God: Divine Initiative and Human Need* (Philadelphia: Westminster Press, 1964), pp. 87-88.

28. BBC, 9:478, n. 8.

29. Ibid., p. 479.

D. Sanctified Through and Through, 1 Thess. 5:19-24

Paul closes his first letter to the Thessalonians with a series of short, clear instructions and another incisive prayer for their full sanctification:

"Do not put out the Spirit's fire; do not treat prophecies with contempt. Test everything. Hold on to the good. Avoid every kind of evil.

"May God himself, the God of peace, sanctify you through and through. May your whole spirit, soul and body be kept blameless at the coming of our Lord Jesus Christ. The one who calls you is faithful and he will do it" (5:19-24).

Verse 23 is the passage in the New Testament that gives the chief basis for the phrase "entire sanctification": "sanctify you through and through." It is the climax of the ethical and experiential concerns of the entire latter half of the Epistle. It is the God of peace who sanctifies: peace here taking on its deeper biblical meaning of health, soundness, wholeness, and well-being.

It should be noted that the entire context of the prayer in v. 23 testifies to the ethical meaning attached to the term "sanctify" (derived from *hagiazō*). Joseph Thayer states that to sanctify means both to separate from things profane and dedicate to God, and also to purify both externally and internally by a reformation of the soul.[30] We have already noted the New Testament emphasis on sanctification as purification. It is preeminent here.

The main verb (*hagiasai*, sanctify) is an aorist. While too much must not be claimed for this grammatical form, it does suggest "not continuing action or process, but an action which takes place and is conceived of as completed."[31] Airhart indicates that this is not to say there is no process preceding sanctification nor a continuing growth *in* holiness after the crisis. "Paul *is*, however, praying for the purifying action of God in the lives of these believers so that they will say, 'The work has been done; we have been, and are now, entirely sanctified.'"[32]

Bishop J. Paul Taylor quotes John Fletcher in respect to the temporal aspect of sanctification:

---

30. *Greek-English Lexicon of the New Testament* (New York: American Book Co., 1889), p. 6.

31. Airhart, BBC, 9:500.

32. Ibid.

Where is the absurdity of this doctrine of the instantaneous destruction of indwelling sin? If the light of a candle
brought into a dark room can *instantly* expel the darkness; and
if, upon opening your shutters at noon, your gloomy apartment
can instantaneously be filled with meridian light; why might
not the instantaneous rending of the veil of unbelief, or the
sudden and full opening of the eye of your faith, instantly fill
your soul with the light of truth, and the fire of love; supposing
the Sun of righteousness arise upon you with healing in his
wings.[33]

The scope of the purification envisioned in the apostle's
prayer is indicated by two Greek terms, *holoteleis* and *holoklēron.*
Holoteleis is translated "through and through," "wholly" (KJV,
RSV), "in every part" (NEB), or "entirely" (NASB). Bailey notes that
"this word is not found elsewhere in our Greek Bible, but its usage
in the few instances known in literature leaves no doubt of its
meaning. It is formed from *holos* (all) and *telos* (end), and suggests
finality as well as completeness."[34]

Holoklēron is a predicate adjective modifying "spirit, soul and
body." It is translated "whole" and "means complete in all its parts
(*holos*, whole, *kleros*, lot or part). There is to be no deficiency in any
part."[35] Thayer defines it as "ethically free from sin";[36] and Arndt
and Gingrich say it means "undamaged, intact, whole, complete,—blameless, sound."[37] Again the emphasis is on totality,
completeness; and again the body is included with spirit and soul
as an object of sanctification (cf. Rom. 12:1; 1 Thess. 4:4). As
Airhart writes, "The cleansing is to reach into every part of man's
nature: his affections, his will, his imagination, the springs of his
motive-life. His body is included as the temple of the Holy Spirit (1
Cor. 6:19) and as the vehicle and instrument of personal life (cf.
Rom. 6:12-13, 19)."[38]

The purpose of entire sanctification is that the people of God
may "be kept blameless at [or until] the coming of our Lord Jesus
Christ." The use of the term "be kept" *(tērētheiē),* along with the

---

33. *Holiness the Finished Foundation,* p. 101.

34. IB, 11:314.

35. A. T. Robertson, *Word Pictures in the New Testament* (New York: Harper and
Brothers, 1931), 4:39.

36. *Lexicon,* in loc.

37. *Greek-English Lexicon,* in loc.

38. BBC, 9:501.

aorist of "sanctify," indicates that entire sanctification is not to wait for the Parousia, but to be accomplished in preparation for it. The New Testament consistently relates holiness or sanctification to preparation for Christ's coming again (Heb. 12:14; 1 John 3:1-3).

The prayer concludes with a note of encouragement and assurance: God who calls us to holiness (4:7) is faithful and will do that for which the apostle prays (v. 24).

E. Full Salvation, 2 Thess. 2:13

Paul's second letter to the Thessalonian church followed close on the heels of the first. Its occasion was apparently a report that had come to the apostle following delivery of the first letter. Further misconceptions of the Second Coming had arisen, and Paul deals forthrightly with these.

One important sanctification passage occurs in 2:13, "But we ought always to thank God for you, brothers loved by the Lord, because from the beginning God chose you to be saved through the sanctifying work of the Spirit and through belief in the truth."

Here salvation in its full scope is seen to depend upon both divine and human elements. The divine element is "the sanctifying work of the Spirit" (the Greek is literally "in sanctification of Spirit"). The human element is "belief in the truth." God's elective choice is not arbitrary. It is the gracious provision of salvation for those who believe (John 3:16; Rom. 1:16). It is accomplished not through our striving or effort, however sustained or earnest, but "through the sanctifying work of the Spirit."

IV. THE PASTORAL EPISTLES

The grouping of Paul's Epistles in the New Testament ends with four personal letters: two written to Timothy, and one each to Titus and Philemon.

Philemon was a wealthy slaveholder to whom Paul returned a runaway slave, Onesimus, converted through Paul's influence in Rome. The short letter is not a theological document. It does illustrate the compassion of the apostle and the way in which Christian love was eventually to undermine the universally unquestioned institution of human slavery in the Roman Empire.

The letters to Timothy and Titus offer valuable insights into the continuing concerns of the apostle for the churches under the influence of these younger men. Here are found helpful clues concerning the thinking and teaching of the Early Church.

A. The Goal of Sound Teaching, 1 Tim. 1:5

One of Paul's concerns in his first letter to Timothy was to offset the influence of false teachers—probably representing a variety of Gnosticism. It contrasts the "myths and endless genealogies" (v. 4) promoted by the false teachers with what Paul deems the fundamentals: "The goal of this command [to forbid teaching false doctrines] is love, which comes from a pure heart and a good conscience and a sincere faith" (1:5).

"Goal" here is *telos* and means also purpose or intended end. In place of the sophistries of the false teachers, Paul stresses the primacy of love. This is no new note; we have found it not only in Paul but throughout the Gospels. The essence of piety is *agapē*—unconditional love like the love of God for us. It is this kind of love that is "poured out . . . into our hearts by the Holy Spirit" (Rom. 5:5).

Love "comes from a pure heart." Here, again, is no novel idea. We have found it in Matt. 5:8, in Acts 15:8-9, and will encounter it again in 2 Tim. 2:22 and 1 Pet. 1:22. *Kardia* (heart) is the whole of the inner life, purpose, will, and motivation as well as affection. It must be pure (*katharas*, derived from the characteristic New Testament word for cleansing, purifying, purging). A clean heart, in any meaningful definition, is a heart made free from the stain of inherited sin.

Love is conditioned also by "a good conscience" (*syneidēseōs agathēs*). Conscience is an important New Testament concept. It is consistently related to the moral life both as offering guidance and providing an impulse toward right conduct. Yet conscience can be weak (1 Cor. 8:10, 12), seared (1 Tim. 4:2), or defiled (Titus 1:15). It convicts of sin (John 8:9; Rom. 2:15). A good, clear conscience void of offence is essential in normative Christian living (Acts 23:1; 24:16; 2 Cor. 1:12; 1 Tim. 1:18-20; 3:9; 2 Tim. 1:3; 1 Pet. 2:19, KJV).

Love also depends upon "a sincere faith." There is a close connection between love and faith in the New Testament, and between faith and a good conscience. Faith carries a double meaning of trustful believing and dependability or faithfulness. Each has implications for the expression of a pure heart.

B. Called to a Holy Life, 2 Tim. 1:8-10

Second Timothy was the last letter to come from Paul's pen. It is a warm, personal message with mingled concern for its recipient and keen desire for the support of his presence. Paul's faith is facing the ultimate test, but facing it with serenity and triumph.

In a very personal context, the apostle writes: "So do not be ashamed to testify about our Lord, or ashamed of me his prisoner. But join with me in suffering for the gospel, by the power of God, who has saved us and called us to a holy life—not because of anything we have done but because of his own purpose and grace. This grace was given us in Christ Jesus before the beginning of time, but it has now been revealed through the appearing of our Savior, Christ Jesus, who has destroyed death and has brought life and immortality to light through the gospel" (1:8-10).

Many of Paul's characteristic themes appear in these verses. God has saved us and has called us to a holy life. Salvation and our holy calling are none of our effort or striving. They are of God's own grace and His purpose in Christ conceived before the world began but now manifested in the appearing of Christ Jesus, who by His death and resurrection destroyed death and brought to light life and immortality through the gospel. J. Glenn Gould writes of our "holy calling" (KJV, RSV):

> This means more than a holiness that exists in name only or is merely imputed to the believer by the supreme holiness of God; it means that the believer is loosed from his sins and delivered from their guilt and power. God's call is to an experience and life that involve a complete consecration on the believer's part and a complete inner cleansing on God's part.[39]

C. Prepared for Every Good Work, 2 Tim. 2:19-22

Still concerned with the encroachment of false teachers, some of whom were claiming that the resurrection was already past and were destroying the faith of some members of the church, Paul writes:

> Nevertheless, God's solid foundation stands firm, sealed with this inscription: "The Lord knows those who are his," and, "Everyone who confesses the name of the Lord must turn away from wickedness."
>
> In a large house there are articles not only of gold and

---

39. Ibid., pp. 629-30.

silver, but also of wood and clay; some are for noble purposes
and some for ignoble. If a man cleanses himself from the latter,
he will be an instrument for noble purposes, made holy, useful
to the Master and prepared to do any good work.

Flee the evil desires of youth, and pursue righteousness,
faith, love and peace, along with those who call on the Lord out
of a pure heart *(2:19-22).*

Paul's illustration of the house and its vessels has been crit-
icized for ineptness, and there is some ambiguity as to what a man
is to cleanse himself from, but the main thrust of the passage is
clear. "Grammatically," says E. F. Scott, "this [the phrase *purge
himself from*] should mean separation from the 'base vessels'—i.e.
unworthy men, and some would find here a warning against association with heretics, or doubtful members of the Church. But the
phrase, 'purge,' or 'cleanse' oneself, points to inward purification."[40] The one who thus cleanses or purges himself will become "a vessel unto honour, sanctified, and meet [fitted] for the
master's use, and prepared unto every good work" (v. 21, KJV).

Righteousness, faith, love, and peace are the goals of those
who call on the Lord out of a pure heart (v. 22). Far from questioning the possibility of a heart made pure, Paul identifies Timothy
and his companions as those whose prayers spring from such
hearts.

D. Truth That Leads to Godliness, Titus 1:1-3, 15

Titus, along with Timothy, was one of Paul's associates or
assistants. He is not mentioned by name in Acts but frequently in
the letters. He had served various missions for the apostle, and at
the time of writing this letter was on the island of Crete to care
for the organization of the churches there. Shortly after, he was
sent to Dalmatia, possibly as the emissary of the apostle from his
last imprisonment in Rome (2 Tim. 4:10).

Paul characterizes the purpose of his apostleship as "for the
faith of God's elect and the knowledge of the truth that leads to
godliness—a faith and knowledge resting on the hope of eternal
life, which God, who does not lie, promised before the beginning
of time, and at his appointed season he brought his word to light
through the preaching entrusted to me by the command of God
our Savior" (1:1-3).

---

40. "The Pastoral Epistles," *The Moffatt New Testament Commentary* (New York:
Harper and Brothers, n.d.), p. 114.

The parallel in 2 Tim. 1:9-11 is striking. There is the same emphasis on the eternal purpose and promise of God, its temporal manifestation in Christ and the preaching of the gospel. The faith of God's elect constitutes them as saved persons, and godliness *(eusebeia)* is paralleled by the calling "to a holy life." *Eusebeia* is one of the distinctive terms in the Pastoral Epistles (1 Tim. 2:2; 3:16; 4:7, 8; 6:3, 5, 6, 11; 2 Tim. 3:5). It is found elsewhere only in Acts 3:12 and 2 Peter (1:3, 6, 7; 3:11). It means "that piety which, characterized by a Godward attitude, does that which is well-pleasing to Him."[41]

In the context of rejecting "Jewish myths" (1:14), Paul says, "To the pure, all things are pure, but to those who are corrupted and do not believe, nothing is pure" (v. 15). E. F. Scott comments, "His meaning is that ritual purity is at best artificial. Nothing really counts except the clean heart, and to those who have it all the distinctions of clean and unclean (in ritual) are meaningless. . . . There is something in inward purity which cleanses everything, so that ceremonial rules cease to have any value."[42]

E. The Grace of God, Titus 2:11-14

Paul returns to one of his best-loved themes in 2:11-14—"For the grace of God that brings salvation has appeared to all men. It teaches us to say 'No' to ungodliness and worldly passions, and to live self-controlled, upright and godly lives in this present age, while we wait for the blessed hope—the glorious appearing of our great God and Savior, Jesus Christ, who gave himself for us to redeem us from all wickedness and to purify for himself a people that are his very own, eager to do what is good."

Fred D. Gealy writes:

> **The grace of God** which **has appeared** is nothing less than the Christian gospel or event in its entirety, an event which centers in and revolves around the two "appearings" of the Savior, the first and the final. When God as grace first appeared, it was to give **himself for us to redeem us from all iniquity;** when he appears again, in accord with our blessed hope in glory, it will be to receive us as a purified **people of his own.**[43]

---

41. Vine, EDNTW, 2:162.
42. "Pastoral Epistles," p. 161.
43. IB, 11:538.

Noteworthy in these verses is the emphasis on renouncing ungodliness and worldly passions and living self-controlled, upright, and godly lives in this present age (v. 12). This parallels the emphasis of the father of John the Baptist that the messianic salvation will "enable us to serve him without fear in holiness and righteousness before him all our days" (Luke 1:74-75). There is a fullness of salvation to be experienced in this present life. It is possible only through "our great God and Savior, Jesus Christ, who gave himself" both to "redeem us from all wickedness" and to "purify for himself a people" who are "his very own, eager to do what is good" (vv. 13-14).

The ultimate purpose of the Savior's incarnation and sacrifice is that He may "set us free from all our evil ways and make for himself a people of his own, clean and pure, with our hearts set upon living a life that is good" (v. 14, Phillips). The effect of such purification is explained in v. 12, "to live a life of self-mastery, of integrity, and of godliness in this present world" (Moffatt). The people thus made "clean and pure" are to be the Master's special possession—not "peculiar" in the modern sense of the word as the KJV unfortunately suggests, but belonging specially to God. Their goodness is not merely in what they do not do. They are "eager to do what is good."

8

Holiness in the General Epistles and Revelation

The letters of Paul are followed by a grouping of eight letters known as "General Epistles." They include the anonymous Book of Hebrews, a letter from James, two by Peter, three by John, and a short note by Jude. In terminology strikingly similar to that of Paul but with varying emphases, they add their witness to the nature of and need for sanctification in the Christian life. Revelation, the great New Testament apocalypse, climaxes the entire Bible with its vision of the dissolving horizons of time and the endless expanse of eternity.

I. HEBREWS

The Book of Hebrews was written to Christians facing the onset of severe persecution and tempted to seek shelter under the protection of their former Jewish faith. The theme of the book is the superiority of Christ in comparison to the Old Testament way of salvation. Its purpose is to encourage these believers to go forward rather than backward. It stresses particularly the fullness of Christ's provision for sin's pollution and power in contrast with the limitations of animal sacrifices in the Jewish Temple.

One of the chief contributions to our theme found in Hebrews is the linking of perfection and sanctification. As Oscar Cullmann has argued, the author makes the two virtually synonymous.[1] There is a strong feeling of the holiness imperative, a sense of urgency in the alternative "on to perfection" (6:1, KJV) or "back unto perdition" (10:39, KJV). E. C. Blackman summarizes the teaching of Hebrews at this point:

> The main theme of the Letter to the Hebrews is the work of Christ as priest and sacrifice. It can be stated as the provision of "purification for sins" (1:3), implying the imagery of sacrifice, as in 2:17b; 5:1 and in the whole central argument of chs. 5-10. But the metaphor changes to that of sanctification when Christ is referred to as the sanctifier (2:11; 7:26-27; 13:12). These metaphors are used interchangeably, as we see from 9:11-14— a peak point in the argument—and 9:22-23. The point of contrast here between Christian and Jewish mediatory rites is that whereas the latter effected outward sanctification, Christ offers an inward one ("conscience"; v. 14b) which fits men for God's service, or, more precisely, for the sharing of God's own holiness (*hagiotes;* 12:10), which is the greatest need of man. The vision of God is not possible for the unholy (12:14). "Sanctification" is a synonym for "perfection," a key word in this letter (2:10; 10:14; 11:39—12:2). This sanctification or perfection is due to Christ, who identified himself with man, made man fit for God's presence, and pioneered a way thither as "forerunner" (6:20; 10:19 ff; cf. 3:1a).[2]

A. Christ and His Brothers, Heb. 2:10-11

In the great incarnation passage of c. 2, the author establishes the identity of Christ and His people with the statement: "In bringing many sons to glory, it was fitting that God, for whom and through whom everything exists, should make the author of their salvation perfect through suffering. Both the one who makes men holy *[hagiazō]* and those who are made holy are of the same family. So Jesus is not ashamed to call them brothers" (2:10-11).

This passage is noteworthy because it affirms a qualitative identity between Sanctifier and sanctified. H. Orton Wiley says, "It is very evident therefore that He who leads many sons to glory does so by sanctifying them, and that the only way to glory for the sons of God is through sanctification."[3] F. F. Bruce comments,

---

1. *The Christology of the New Testament,* rev. ed., trans. Shirley C. Guthrie and Charles A. M. Hall (Philadelphia: Westminster Press, 1963), p. 100.

2. IDB, 4:211. Used by permission.

3. *The Epistle to the Hebrews* (Kansas City: Beacon Hill Press, 1959), p. 90.

"Sanctification is glory begun, and glory is sanctification completed."[4]

Wiley has an important statement on the full meaning of the infinitive *hagiazein:*

> The word *hagiazein* "to sanctify," is used in both an objective and a subjective sense. In its objective sense it has reference to the work which Christ has done *for* us in expiating sin or in making atonement. This objective and provisional aspect is sometimes referred to as "the finished work of Christ." But this is not the full sense of the word sanctification, for it also has its subjective aspect, by which is meant that which Christ works *in* us by His Holy Spirit. It is not enough to say that Christ has provided an atonement *for* us; we need Christ *in* us as much as we need His atoning work *for* us. It is not alone what Christ did on the Cross that saves us; it is what He does *in* us by virtue of what He did *for* us on the Cross. Christ not only expiates our sins; He dwells within us through the Holy Spirit; and it is His personal presence within that sanctifies us in the deeper sense of the word *hagiazein.* Here the word *hagios* or "holy" signifies not only the act of purifying or cleansing, but the indwelling presence of Christ in His cleansed temple; and it is this presence within that sanctifies and makes us His possession.[5]

Richard S. Taylor writes, "Jesus, the God-man, by the Incarnation, now shares with man the fatherhood of God as Creator; by sanctifying His own disciples He shares with them the holiness of the Father. A family likeness is thereby established. This likeness to God through sanctification is the deeper meaning of sonship in the NT."[6]

B. The Rest of Faith, Hebrews 3—4

Heb. 3:7 introduces an extended comparison between what had been given Israel under the law and what is open to believers under grace in what the author calls God's "rest" or "the rest of faith." Believers have embarked on a "new exodus." William Neil writes, "It was no mere play on words that made Jesus call his own death an Exodus, a Deliverance (Luke 9.31), or speak at the Last Supper of a New Covenant (Mark 14.24). Nor was it fanciful

---

4. "The Epistle to the Hebrews," NICNT (Grand Rapids: William B. Eerdmans Publishing Co., 1964), p. 45.

5. *Hebrews,* p. 92.

6. BBC, 10:37.

allegorism that suggested to St. Paul that Christ was our Passover (1 Cor. 5.7), and that Christian Baptism could be compared with the Crossing of the Red Sea (1 Cor. 10.2)."[7]

But the full meaning of the Exodus was not accomplished in deliverance from the bondage of Egypt. Its full meaning was completed in possession of the Promised Land. The failure in faith at Kadesh-barnea is viewed as a warning to believers not to commit a similar sin by failing to enter the "rest" of which Canaan was a type (3:7-19).

"Therefore, since the promise of entering his rest still stands, let us be careful that none of you be found to have fallen short of it. . . . Now we who have believed enter that rest . . . For if Joshua had given them rest, God would not have spoken later [in Ps. 95:7-11] about another day. There remains, then, a Sabbath-rest for the people of God; for anyone who enters God's rest also rests from his own work, just as God did from his. Let us, therefore, make every effort to enter that rest, so that no one will fall by following their example of disobedience" (4:1, 3, 8-11).

Alexander Purdy notes that the writer understands and applies Ps. 95:7-11 in two stages. "His readers must not harden their hearts as did the wilderness generation, for it was unbelief which caused their failure to enter God's rest (vss. 12-19); the promise of the divine 'rest' remains open to the people of God and the danger of unbelief is quite as serious now as then (4:1-13)."[8]

There have been three major interpretations of "the rest of faith" in Hebrews 4. One has been that it is heaven, the Christian's ultimate goal. Another is that it is the way of salvation by faith rather than by the works of the law. The third is that it is the Christian's higher life, a synonym for entire sanctification. Taylor notes that the "Sabbath-rest for the people of God" has "often been understood as a second work of Grace. Among the Quakers the terminology of Hebrews has been maintained and forms the basis of Philip Doddridge's stanza:

---

7. "The Epistle to the Hebrews," introduction and commentary, in *Torch Bible Commentaries* (London: SCM Press, 1955), p. 48. Cf. W. T. Purkiser, *Hebrews, James, Peter,* "Beacon Bible Expositions" (Kansas City: Beacon Hill Press of Kansas City, 1974), 11:40-43. Hereafter cited as BBE.

8. IB, 11:624.

> "Now rest, my long divided heart;
> Fixed on this blissful center, rest;
> Nor ever from thy Lord depart,
> With Him of every good possessed."[9]

That the rest is not heaven would seem to be indicated by the fact that "we who have believed enter that rest" (v. 3). Nor is it likely that the rest is the Christian way of faith rather than the Jewish way of works and law, unless one concludes that the readers were not at that time genuine Christians. Rather, the contrast between Hebrews 3 and 4 is quite similar to the contrast between Romans 7 and 8. Thomas Hewitt says that the rest of Canaan "is a type of consecration rest, that is, of the rest which comes from a surrender of the mind, will and heart to God's power and influence which enables the believer to conquer sin."[10]

The rest envisioned is obviously not the rest of inactivity, "the heavy slumber which follows over-taxing toil, nor . . . inaction or indolence." It is rather, says F. B. Meyer, "the rest which is possible amid swift activity and strenuous work; . . . perfect equilibrium between the outgoings and incomings of the life; . . . a contented heart; . . . peace that passeth all understanding; . . . repose of the will in the will of God; and . . . the calm of the depths of the nature which are undisturbed by the hurricanes which sweep the surface, and urge forward the mighty waves."[11]

Major Allister Smith recalls the key significance of this concept in the life of J. Hudson Taylor:

> Hudson Taylor, the founder of the China Inland Mission, and one of the greatest missionaries the world has known, remained a defeated Christian until he learned the secret of looking to Jesus for his sanctification. He had his eyes opened by a letter from a friend who wrote that victory came by "abiding, not striving or struggling; looking off unto Him; trusting Him for present power; trusting Him to subdue all inward corruption; resting in the love of an almighty Saviour, in the conscious joy of a complete salvation, a salvation from all sin (this is His Word); . . . willing that His will should truly be supreme."

---

9. BBC, 10:51. Cf. the chapter on "The Promised Land Motif" and "Pentecostal Language as Canaan Land Language" in Wood, *Pentecostal Grace*, pp. 33-95.

10. "The Epistle to the Hebrews," introduction and commentary, TNTC (Grand Rapids: William B. Eerdmans Publishing Co., 1960), p. 92.

11. *The Way into the Holiest* (New York: Fleming H. Revell Co., 1893), p. 56.

Taylor suddenly realized that faith was not strengthened by striving, but by resting in the faithful One. "If we believe not, he abideth faithful." He confessed: "I have striven in vain to rest in Him. I'll strive no more. For has He not promised to abide with me, never to leave me, never to fail me?"[12]

C. On to Perfection, 6:1-3

Heb. 6:1 is one of the outstanding "perfection" texts of the New Testament. Taking their cue from 5:14, most modern translations parallel the NIV: "Therefore let us leave the elementary teachings about Christ and go on to maturity [teleiotēta], not laying again the foundation of repentance from acts that lead to death, and of faith in God, instruction about baptisms, the laying on of hands, the resurrection of the dead, and eternal judgment. And God permitting, we will do so" (vv. 1-3).

The propriety of "maturity" here need not be debated. It is only fair, however, to point out that teleios, from which teleiotēta here comes, properly means "complete," "conveying the idea of goodness without necessary reference to maturity."[13] Teleiotēta itself is translated "perfect unity" by the NIV in Col. 3:14, the only other place it appears in the New Testament. Teleios is not only used with the meaning of mature in the New Testament, but it is used in contexts where "mature" is inappropriate as, for example, of God himself (Matt. 5:48), Christ (Heb. 5:9), Christ's atoning work (Luke 13:32, KJV), the "law that gives freedom" (Jas. 1:25, NIV), the heavenly tabernacle (Heb. 9:11), and the will of God (Rom. 12:2).

D. Saved to the Uttermost, Heb. 7:25

Chapter 7 deals with the priesthood of Christ in comparison and contrast with that of Melchizedek. One aspect of Christ's priesthood, unique in kind as that of Melchizedek, is that Christ lives forever. "Therefore he is able to save completely those who come to God through him, because he always lives to intercede for them" (v. 25).

"Completely" (KJV, "to the uttermost") translates eis to pan-

---

12. The Ideal of Perfection (London: Oliphants, Ltd., 1963), p. 67. See Wood, Pentecostal Grace, pp. 47-50, for evidence that John Wesley identified the "rest of faith" with Christian perfection.

13. EDNTW, 3:174.

teles, a term that means completeness more than duration (Luke 13:11). Phillips translates it, "This means that he can save fully and completely those who approach God through him." The *Amplified Bible* combines ideas of completeness and duration: "completely, perfectly, finally and for all time and eternity."[14]

E. Cleansing by the Blood, Heb. 9:13-14; 10:10, 14

Heb. 9:13-14 identifies "sanctify" with cleansing and stresses the infinitely better purification provided by the sacrifice of Christ in comparison with the sacrifices of the Old Testament: "The blood of goats and bulls and the ashes of a heifer sprinkled on those who are ceremonially unclean sanctify them so that they are outwardly clean. How much more, then, will the blood of Christ, who through the eternal Spirit offered himself unblemished to God, cleanse our consciences from acts that lead to death, so that we may serve the living God!" As William Barclay notes, "The ancient sacrifices cleansed a man's body from ceremonial uncleanness; the sacrifice of Jesus cleansed men's souls."[15]

Heb. 10:10, 14 states again that Jesus himself in His full submission to the will of the Father is the offering whereby we are sanctified: "And by that will, we have been made holy through the sacrifice of the body of Jesus Christ once for all. . . . because by one sacrifice he has made perfect forever those who are being made holy."

"Made holy" in each of these verses is from *hagiazō.* In v. 10, it is in the perfect tense, describing a state of affairs completed and enduring to the time. In v. 14, it is in the present tense which the NIV interprets as reflecting a continuing action, but which Hewitt says may be "iterative and means 'those who from age to age receive sanctification.'"[16]

Oscar Cullmann is impressed by the conjunction of perfection and sanctification in v. 14. He writes:

> Just as the High Priest concept applied to Jesus is so fulfilled that the purely cultic in general must be raised to a higher level, so must the purely cultic concept *teleioun* [to make perfect] applied to him necessarily include also the sense of mak-

14. (Grand Rapids: Zondervan Publishing House, 1958), in loc.
15. "The Epistle to the Hebrews," DSB, p. 114.
16. *Hebrews,* p. 159.

ing morally perfect. This happens in a really human life—in Jesus, the High Priest, who is made perfect; and in the brothers, the sanctified, who are made perfect by him (Heb. 2:11).[17]

He adds, "'For by a single offering he has perfected for all time those who are sanctified' (10.14). *Teleioun* (to make perfect) is almost a synonym for *hagiazein* (to sanctify). Thus 2.11 reads, 'For he who sanctifies and those who are sanctified have all one origin.'"[18]

F. Holiness, the Indispensable Grace, Heb. 12:10, 14-17

In 12:10, 14-17 two aspects of holiness are given:

> Our fathers disciplined us for a little while as they thought best; but God disciplines us for our good, that we may share in his holiness. . . . Make every effort to live in peace with all men and to be holy; without holiness no one will see the Lord. See to it that no one misses the grace of God and that no bitter root grows up to cause trouble and defile many. See that no one is sexually immoral, or is godless like Esau, who for a single meal sold his inheritance rights as the oldest son. Afterward, as you know, when he wanted to inherit this blessing, he was rejected. He could bring about no change of mind, though he sought the blessing with tears.

"Holiness" in v. 10 is *hagiotēs*, defined by W. E. Vine as "the abstract quality of holiness,"[19] and is used only here in the New Testament.[20] It is, as F. F. Bruce says, "positive holiness of life that is meant" in contrast with the sanctifying work of cleansing earlier in the book.[21] Although different terms for "partaking" are used here and in 2 Pet. 1:4 ("participate in the divine nature"), the thought is parallel. As Taylor says, "This is God's supreme aim and wish for man, and is the objective of all His redemptive deeds. We may not share God's natural attributes which belong solely to Deity—as omniscience, omnipotence, etc. But we may be like Him in holiness, since this is a moral quality possible (through grace) to all personal moral agents."[22]

---

17. *Christology of the NT*, p. 93.

18. Ibid., p. 100.

19. EDNTW, 2:226. Cf. Purkiser, BBE, 11:107-10.

20. *Hagiotēs* occurs in some mss. in 2 Cor. 1:12, but *haplotēs*, "simplicity, singleness," is used there in the preferred texts.

21. *Hebrews*, p. 359.

22. BBC, 10:159.

There is an interesting parallel in the sequence of ideas in 12:12-14 with Isa. 35:3-8. In both passages there is a call to "strengthen the feeble hands, [and] steady the knees that give way" (Isa. 35:3) followed by reference to pursuing "the Way of Holiness" which the "unclean" will not travel (v. 8).

"Peace with all men" has unsuspected meaning. William Barclay writes:

> In Hebrew thought and language peace was no negative thing; it was intensely positive. It was not simply freedom from trouble. It was two things. First, it was everything which makes for a man's highest good; it meant the highest welfare that a man could enjoy; it meant that in which manhood finds its highest peace. . . . Second, *peace* means right relationship between man and man. It means a state when hatred is banished, and when each man seeks nothing but his neighbour's good; it means the bond of love, forgiveness and service which ought to bind men together.[23]

Alexander Purdy adds another dimension to the concept of peace. It is more, he says, than "the absence of dissension and quarreling in the brotherhood." It rather "means the quiet security of the dedicated and cleansed life, which will, to be sure, have its social consequences in peaceful human relationships."[24]

The conjunction of peace and sanctity is significant. Charles R. Erdman says, "For peace almost anything may be sacrificed, but not purity."[25] Wiley adds, "The word *diokete*, 'follow,' carries with it not only a desire for peace but the willingness to go far to obtain it; and the word *hagiasmon*, 'sanctification,' is an implied warning that we are not to seek peace to the extent of compromising 'the sanctification' without which no man shall see the Lord. Thus Westcott says, 'The Christian seeks peace with all alike, but he seeks holiness also, and this cannot be sacrificed for that.'"[26]

Both E. C. Wickham[27] and Thomas Hewitt[28] notice the similar conjunction of peace and purity in the Beatitudes of Jesus in Matt. 5:8-9:

---

23. *Hebrews*, DSB, pp. 205-6.

24. IB, 11:743-44.

25. *The Epistle to the Hebrews: An Exposition* (Philadelphia: Westminster Press, 1934), p. 126.

26. *Hebrews*, p. 395.

27. "The Epistle to the Hebrews," *Westminster Commentaries* (London: Methuen and Co., 1910).

28. *Hebrews*, pp. 196-97.

> *Blessed are the pure in heart,*
> *for they will see God.*
> *Blessed are the peacemakers,*
> *for they will be called sons of God.*

"Without holiness [lit., the sanctification] no one will see the Lord" and such holiness is, as F. F. Bruce writes, and "as the words themselves make plain, no optional extra in the Christian life but something which belongs to its essence. It is the pure in heart, and none but they, who shall see God (Matt. 5:8.)"[29]

Sanctification, or holiness, it should be remembered, is the great biblical term for the entire working of the Holy Spirit in us whereby we are inwardly renewed and made free from sin. It begins in regeneration or the birth of the Spirit and is brought to a new and higher plane in the fullness of the Spirit or entire sanctification (1 Thess. 5:23-24). "Although he lives in the world," says William Barclay of one who is sanctified, he "must always in one sense be different from the world and separate from the world. His standards are not the world's standards, nor is his conduct the world's conduct. His ideal is different; his reward is different; his aim is different. His aim is, not to stand well with men, but to stand well with God."[30] His "supreme aim," adds Hewitt, "must be devotedness to God, which alone produces purity of heart and life and *without which no man shall see the Lord.*"[31]

To "see the Lord" has been interpreted in three ways: (1) to see God now in a beatific vision (Matt. 5:8); (2) to worship God acceptably—the typical Old Testament sense where to "behold the face of the Lord" is the idiom for true worship and "to see a person's face" is to be favorably received by him (to "cause one's face to shine upon" another is to bestow blessing or favor upon him); or (3) eschatologically, to stand uncondemned in the presence of the Son of Man at His coming again. This latter is the emphasis of 1 John 3:2-3: ". . . Everyone who has this hope in him purifies himself, just as he is pure." It will be seen that these are not mutually exclusive. All three may be implied.

Three reasons are given in vv. 15-17 for making every effort to

---

29. *Hebrews*, p. 364.
30. *Hebrews*, DSB, p. 207
31. *Hebrews*, p. 196.

live in peace with all men and to be holy. Each is introduced with a negative particle *mē* translated "that" or "lest" and meaning "in order that it may not be:"

(1) In order that "no one misses the grace of God" (v. 15). This may mean either failing to obtain a grace offered, or falling back from a grace possessed.[32]

(2) In order that "no bitter root grows up to cause trouble and defile many" (v. 15). These words are interpreted both sociologically—a person who causes bitterness and dissension in the fellowship; and psychologically—the inner sin that troubles the believer and poses an obstacle to many in his orbit of influence.

(3) In order that "no one is sexually immoral, or is godless like Esau" (v. 16). There is difference of opinion as to the application here of *pornos*, which NIV translates "sexually immoral." If it be taken literally, it would tie this passage in with Paul's discussion of sanctification and sexual morality in 1 Thess. 4:3-6. William Manson, on the other hand, prefers to think of it as relating to religious infidelity, or "spiritual lapse from the truth of God" and "not mere sensuality."[33]

"Godless" (KJV, "profane") in this sense means to be common, unconsecrated, literally, "open to common tread" as a public thoroughfare would be. It is used as the opposite of "holy." Wickham writes: "It would mean here 'without the religious sense.' Esau in the story showed this lack in treating so lightly his birthright with its religious import, the priesthood of the family and the mysterious promises."[34] As such, he "was rejected"—"The technical Greek term for the rejection of a candidate for office on scrutiny as disqualified."[35]

That Heb. 12:14 must not be interpreted in a narrowly sectarian sense should be obvious. Heaven is not closed to all who do not understand or accept a Wesleyan definition of entire sanctification. Heb. 12:14 must always be interpreted in the light of Rom. 5:9, "Since we have now been justified by his blood, how much more shall we be saved from God's wrath through him!" and 1 John 1:7,

---

32. Cf. Wiley, *Hebrews*, p. 396.

33. *The Epistle to the Hebrews*, The Baird Lecture, 1949 (London: Hodder and Stoughton, Ltd., 1951), p. 85.

34. *Hebrews*, p. 114.

35. Ibid.

"But if we walk in the light, as he is in the light, we have fellowship with one another, and the blood of Jesus, his Son, purifies us from every [marg., all] sin." Each child of God is provisionally sanctified wholly as long as he walks "in the light."

At the same time, the imperative is clear. No Christian is spiritually secure who acquiesces in anything less than the best God has provided for him. To "make every effort" implies pursuit of an attainable and vitally important goal.

G. Sanctified by His Blood, Heb. 13:11-13

In 13:11-13, Wickham sees the author's final conclusion that not only is Christianity superior to Judaism, but the two are incompatible.[36] The author writes: "The high priest carries the blood of animals into the Most Holy Place as a sin offering, but the bodies are burned outside the camp. And so Jesus also suffered outside the city gate to make the people holy [sanctify the people, RSV] through his own blood. Let us, then, go to him outside the camp, bearing the disgrace he bore."

The point made by Paul in Eph. 5:25-27 and by the author of the Book of Hebrews in 10:10, 14 is repeated here: Sanctification is possible only through the sacrifice of Christ on the Cross. Sanctification as well as justification is the purchase of Calvary. "The people" is always used in Scripture with the sense of "God's people." It is by or through His blood that they are made holy.

The call to "go to him outside the camp" would in contemporary terms be a call to consecration in self-identification with Christ in a way reminiscent of our Lord's own words: "If anyone would come after me, he must deny himself and take up his cross and follow me" (Matt. 16:24). We go out not to "it" but to "Him."

H. A Benedictory Prayer, Heb. 13:20-21

Close to the end of Hebrews is a benedictory prayer with deep meaning—"one of the most beautiful and inclusive benedictions that the Scriptures contain:"[37] "May the God of peace, who through the blood of the eternal covenant brought back from the dead our Lord Jesus, that great Shepherd of the sheep, equip you

---

36. Ibid., p. 127. Cf. Purkiser, BBE, 11:117-19.

37. Erdman, *Hebrews*, p. 136.

with everything for doing his will, and may he work in us what is pleasing to him, through Jesus Christ, to whom be glory for ever and ever. Amen" (13:20-21).

"Equip you" (*katartisai,* "make you perfect," KJV) is explained by Thomas Hewitt as a term that

> could be used for the reconciliation of factions, or the repairing of broken bones. Its fundamental meaning is "repairing what is broken" or "restoring what is lost". According to Westcott, it "includes the thoughts of the harmonious combination of different powers (Eph. iv.12), of the supply of what is defective (1 Thes. iii.10), and of the amendment of that which is faulty". If this threefold definition could legitimately be applied to the word in this verse, then in a single word the author provides the solution to all the problems within the Church.[38]

Richard S. Taylor writes, "Clearly this is spiritual equipment for the full, unhindered performance of the will of God. 'With everything good'!—a pure heart by the infilling of the Holy Spirit; and the aorist tense suggests a full and completed divine action. What an apt description of entire sanctification as a second definite work of grace!"[39]

II. James

The letter of James is the "wisdom book" of the New Testament. Its emphasis is on the practical applications of Christian faith and experience to the issues of life. James deals with such subjects as temptation, the rich and the poor, faith and works, the use and abuse of the tongue, the need for endurance, and the importance of prayer. The letter, C. L. Mitton writes, "is largely a series of exhortations to true Christian holiness of life, that is, to perfect love towards God and man."[40] James "saw very clearly that a true Christian, once converted, must set himself the goal of true holiness."[41] Mitton sees a parallel between James's use of his favorite adjective, "perfect," and John Wesley's doctrine of Christian perfection.

---

38. *Hebrews,* p. 216.

39. BBC, 10:181.

40. *The Epistle of James* (Grand Rapids: William B. Eerdmans Publishing Co., 1966), p. 8.

41. Ibid. Cf. the review of Mitton by Marcus Ward, *Expository Times,* vol. 68, no. 5 (February, 1967), p. 140.

A. Perfect and Complete, Jas. 1:4

Jas. 1:4 sets the tone of the letter: "And let steadfastness have its full effect, that you may be perfect and complete, lacking in nothing" (RSV). Writes Mitton:

> The word "perfect" (Greek *teleios*) is a favourite one with James. Besides its repeated use in this verse, it occurs also in 1:17, 25; 2:22; 3:2. Here James urges that his readers will set before them the goal of becoming PERFECT AND COMPLETE, LACKING IN NOTHING. There is no escaping, however disconcerting it may be, this lofty uncompromising summons, sounded here as elsewhere in the New Testament, to what has come to be called "Christian Perfection", as God's purpose for His Christian people. James emphasizes this call to perfection by adding the word "complete" (Greek *holokleros*) and the phrase "lacking in nothing". "Perfect" means "having reached full development". "Complete" means "having no unfinished part".[42]

B. The Double-minded, Jas. 1:8

James's term "double-minded" ("he is a double-minded man, unstable in all he does"—1:8) is, from its use in 4:8, the equivalent of the "carnal" man Paul describes in 1 Cor. 3:1-3, KJV. The word is *dipsuchos*, literally "two-souled." He has the mind of Christ, but is pulled by the mind of the flesh (Rom. 8:5-8; Gal. 5:17, 24). He has never experienced an answer to the prayer of Ps. 86:11, "Give me an undivided heart." The result of double-mindedness is instability, *akatastatos*, fickle, staggering, reeling like a drunken man. The remedy in 4:8 is heart purity.

C. The Nature of Temptation, Jas. 1:14-15

Jas. 1:14-15 is the writer's definition of temptation and his statement of its relation to sin in both heart and life: "But each one is tempted when, by his own evil desire, he is dragged away and enticed. Then, after desire has conceived, it gives birth to sin; and sin, when it is full-grown, gives birth to death."

It is to be questioned whether "evil desire" is the best translation here for *epithumias* ("strong desire of any kind").[43] The RSV is preferable here: "But each person is tempted when he is lured

---

42. Ibid., p. 24.
43. EDNTW, 3:25.

and enticed by his own desire. Then desire when it has conceived gives birth to sin; and sin when it is full-grown brings forth death."

Desire itself is not sin. It may arise from human instincts and needs. The temptations of the pure in heart come through the avenue of desires that are a natural and legitimate part of our humanness. This is the way Jesus was tempted. It is when the will of the individual yields to desire at the expense of obedience to God's known will that desire conceives and gives birth to sin. The result of sin "full-grown"—that is, accepted again as a principle of action—is spiritual death. Leo G. Cox writes:

> In these verses are clearly three categories. First, in temptation one's own desire allures him. This is true of the sanctified life. Second, this alluring desire can conceive and bring forth sin. Here it becomes a polluted, heart desire as found in the believer not entirely sanctified, or who has lost the blessing. Third, when this desire that has become sinful becomes full-grown—gains full consent of the will—it quenches all spiritual life. Here is the picture of the backslider, or the sinner who willfully transgresses.[44]

D. Pure Religion, Jas. 1:27

In 1:27, James speaks of "religion that God our Father accepts as pure and faultless." "Religion" is a word rarely used in the New Testament, and always except here in the sense of false religion. It stands for the external expression of piety. To be religious in the Greek sense was to be careful in the externals of divine service. Here James uses the term "religion" ("religious" in v. 26) in the sense of the proper and necessary outward expression of inner devotion to God. A "pure heart" must be reflected in "religion that God our Father accepts as pure and faultless" (*amiantos;* "free from contamination").[45]

"To a Christian," writes Burton Scott Easton, "**keep oneself unstained** from the world would mean 'avoid the pollution of sin of any kind.'"[46] And Alexander Ross adds, "In the discharge of such charitable tasks there might sometimes be a danger of moral and spiritual pollution, and, therefore, the Christian is also ex-

---

44. In Geiger, comp., *Further Insights into Holiness,* pp. 189-90.
45. EDNTW, 4:168.
46. IB, 12:34.

horted by James to keep himself unspotted from 'the contagion of the world's slow stain.'" Ross continues, "There must be no selfish isolation of himself from all contact with the woes of humanity, but, at the same time, he must seek earnestly to maintain personal purity in all his intercourse with others."[47]

E. Wisdom, Jas. 3:13-17

James speaks not only of a pure heart and pure religion, he also speaks of "the wisdom that comes from heaven [that] is first of all pure; then peace loving, considerate, submissive, full of mercy and good fruit, impartial and sincere" (3:17). This is in contrast to the false wisdom that is "earthly, unspiritual, of the devil" and evidenced by "envy and selfish ambition" (vv. 13-16).

Pure wisdom is peace-loving, considerate (forbearing, not contentious, "equitable, fair, moderate, not insisting on the letter of the law"[48]), submissive ("conciliatory," Moffatt; "open to reason," RSV; "willing to yield," Goodspeed; lit., ready to obey, compliant), full of mercy and good fruit ("full of compassion and produces a harvest of good deeds," TEV), impartial (free from prejudice; lit., not judging) and sincere (without pretense, not playacting). James Moffatt writes:

> **Wisdom** originally and essentially was the knowledge of duties and dangers in the moral life, as revealed in the law of God, and as this study was directed to practical ends, it involved practical qualities in those who professed to teach it. The bearing of **pure** here is best seen in the use made of the verb in iv.8 or by Peter in 1 Peter 1.22 f. It suggests a life unsullied because it is inspired and influenced by God above, free from impure motives and methods, especially from aggressiveness and quarrelsomeness.[49]

James A. Robertson is quoted by Alexander Ross to the effect that such wisdom "is pure because it has its origin in an all-holy God and it comes forth from His holy throne, and it always inspires in its recipient a desire to live a holy life."[50]

---

47. "The Epistles of James and John," NICNT (Grand Rapids: William B. Eerdmans Publishing Co., 1970), p. 43.

48. EDNTW, 2:144.

49. "The General Epistles," *The Moffatt New Testament Commentary* (New York: Harper and Brothers, Publishers, n.d.), p. 53.

50. *Epistles of James and John,* p. 70.

F. God's Greater Grace, Jas. 4:5-8

Jas. 4:5 is admittedly one of the most difficult verses in the letter: "Or do you think Scripture says without reason that the spirit he caused to live in us tends toward envy . . . ?" The statement is given as a saying of Scripture. Yet there is no biblical passage that can be recognized as its source. It is possible that James is summarizing what he understands as the whole sweep of Scripture.

The statement itself is difficult to interpret. Translators and commentators are divided as to what it means. A number take "the spirit he caused to live in us" to be the Holy Spirit, who strives within God's people to keep them loyal to Him. This is Weymouth's understanding: "The Spirit which He has caused to dwell in us yearns jealously over us"; and one alternative of the NIV margin, "The Spirit he caused to live in us longs jealously."

Others take the verse to mean that God yearns for the complete loyalty of the human spirit He has placed within us. This is Moffatt's understanding: "He yearns jealously for the spirit he set within us"; and the other alternative of the NIV margin, "God jealously longs for the spirit that he made to live in us." The RSV also accepts this understanding.

A third possibility is suggested by the KJV rendering, "The spirit that dwelleth in us lusteth to envy," to which the NEB and NIV virtually return: "The spirit which God implanted in man turns toward envious desires" (NEB); "The spirit that God placed in us is filled with fierce desires" (TEV); "The spirit he caused to live in us tends toward envy" (NIV text). This is the human spirit, created by God but corrupted by sin and controlled by the lusts arising from the carnal condition of the unsanctified soul. It is "The sinful nature [that] desires what is contrary to the Spirit" (Gal. 5:17) or "the sinful nature" that results in "minds set on what that nature desires," the "sinful mind [that] is hostile to God . . . [and] does not submit to God's law, nor can it do so" (Rom. 8:5, 7).

Mitton opts for the second interpretation (with Moffatt and the RSV) but admits that the third (NEB, TEV, NIV) alternative prepares more satisfactorily for "the sentence which follows since, if this verse is an affirmation of the corruption which infests the human heart, the reference to God's still more abundant supply of grace to counter this prevalent evil (in verse 6) is very appropriate."[51]

The answer to the problem of man's corrupted spirit is therefore "But he gives us more grace" (v. 6). The Greek is literally, "He gives greater [or, a greater] grace." It is a grace withheld from the proud and self-sufficient. It is given abundantly to the humble. The way to greater grace is "Submit yourselves, then, to God. Resist the devil, and he will flee from you. Come near to God and he will come near to you. Wash your hands, you sinners, and purify your hearts, you double-minded" (vv. 7-8).

The term "submit" is a translation of *hupotassō*. It is primarily a military term. It means "to rank under," to be of lower rank; to be subject to or under obedience to. It is almost a synonym for Paul's great term "offer" (NIV), "yield," or "present" (Rom. 6:13, 19; 12:1), words that carry the meaning we ordinarily attach to "consecrate" or "consecration."

"Purify your hearts" is *hagnisate kardias*. *Hagnizō* means "to purify, cleanse from defilement." It is used in a ceremonial sense in John 11:55; Acts 21:24, 26; 24:18. But it is also used in a moral sense for cleansing the soul (1 Pet. 1:22) or oneself (1 John 3:3). It is akin to *hagnos*, "pure from carnality," "immaculate," "chaste."[52] It means "free from defilement."[53] When used in the ethical sense, it is as comprehensive a term for cleansing from all sin as the Greek language affords.

A pure heart is the answer to double-mindedness: "Come near to God and he will come near to you. Wash your hands, you sinners, and purify your hearts, you double-minded." The parallel with Ps. 24:3-4 is apparent: "Who may ascend the hill of the Lord? / Who may stand in his holy place? / He who has clean hands and a pure heart" (cf. also Ps. 73:13). "Inwardly and outwardly a man must be clean," says William Barclay, "for only the pure in heart shall see God (Matthew 5:8)."[54] "Everything inside must be on God's side." Adam Clarke writes:

> *Separate* yourselves from the world, and consecrate yourself to God: This is the true notion of sanctification. . . . There

---

51. *James*, p. 155. Cf. Purkiser, BBE, 11:155-56.
52. EDNTW, 3:233; 1:183.
53. G. B. Stevens in *Hastings' Bible Dictionary*; quoted ibid., 2:227.
54. *James*, DSB, p. 127.

are, therefore, two things implied. . . . 1. That he separates himself from evil ways and evil companions, and devotes himself to God. 2. That God separates guilt from his conscience, and sin from his soul, and thus makes him internally and externally *holy.* . . . As a man is a *sinner,* he must have his *hands cleansed* from wicked works; as he is *double-minded,* he must have his *heart sanctified. Sanctification* belongs to the *heart,* because of *pollution of the mind; cleansing* belongs to the *hands,* because of sinful acts.[55]

III. THE LETTERS OF PETER

First and Second Peter come from approximately the same period of time as Paul's letters to Timothy and Titus. They were probably written shortly after A.D. 63, for the threat of a larger persecution such as that under the Emperor Nero is clearly seen. It is even possible that the place of origin was Rome itself, if the tradition that fixes Peter's martyrdom there shortly after is valid.

First Peter has been called "The Epistle of Hope." It has been dubbed the best commentary ever written on the beatitude, "Blessed are those who are persecuted because of righteousness, for theirs is the kingdom of heaven" (Matt. 5:10).

A. The Sanctifying Work of the Spirit, 1 Pet. 1:1-2

As with Paul, Peter is concerned that the Christians under his care shall be worthy of their high calling. He addresses himself "to God's elect, strangers in the world, scattered throughout Pontus, Galatia, Cappadocia, Asia and Bithynia, who have been chosen according to the foreknowledge of God the Father, by the sanctifying work of the Spirit, for obedience to Jesus Christ and sprinkling by his blood" (1:1-2).

Archibald Hunter notes "the trinitarian sound and symmetry of Peter's words" and the parallel here with 2 Thess. 2:13-14. He calls the idea of God expressed here "the trinity of experience" from which came later creedal statements. The early Christians, he says, "found by experience that they could not express all that they meant by the word 'God' till they had said, 'Father, Son, and Spirit.'" Christians were then, he says, "as they still are, people who

---

55. *The New Testament of Our Lord and Saviour Jesus Christ* (New York: Abingdon-Cokesbury Press, n.d.), 2:820. Cf. Albert F. Harper, BBC, 10:233.

are seeking, finding, and doing the Father's will with the companionship of his Son by the strength and guidance of the Spirit."[56]

John Wick Bowman remarks that "the sanctifying work of the Spirit" is "a phrase suggestive of the central teaching of the letter as a whole, which is to the effect that the Christian way is one of holiness or sanctification like that of God (1:15, 16)." "Obedience to Jesus Christ" and "sprinkling by his blood" suggest major themes in the letter. Obedience in v. 14 is contrasted with "the evil desires you had when you lived in ignorance" and Bowman notes that "in verse 22 this obedience is further related to the subject of purification or sanctification and is defined as 'obedience to the truth.'"[57]

Roy S. Nicholson notes that the sanctification here described includes "both the process and the result of that operation of the Holy Spirit whereby man's heart is cleansed from moral evil, and the self is totally adjusted to the will of God."[58]

Like Paul, Peter recognizes the Spirit as the Agent through whom sanctification occurs in the human heart. "It is the Spirit of God [who] cleanses our inner selves from sin."[59] Peter's reference to "sprinkling by his blood" has in view the Old Testament act of sprinkling sacrificial blood on the people, confirming God's covenant (Exod. 24:1-8), and the ritual in which the leper was cleansed (Lev. 14:12-18).

B. As God Is Holy, 1 Pet. 1:14-16, 22

Peter takes an Old Testament imperative that in its Leviticus context had reference both to ceremonial and ethical holiness, and relates it directly to Christian conduct: "As obedient children, do not conform to the evil desires you had when you lived in ignorance. But just as he who called you is holy, so be holy in all you do; for it is written: 'Be holy, because I am holy'" (1:14-16; cf. Lev. 11:44-45; 19:2; 20:7). James Moffatt writes:

> Holiness, "deepest of all words that defy definition" (Lord Morley), implies here as elsewhere a renunciation of what is

---

56. IB, 12:90.

57. LBC, 24:123.

58. BBC, 10:265.

59. A. R. C. Leaney, *The Letters of Peter and Jude* (Cambridge: Cambridge University Press, 1967), p. 14.

worldly and corrupting, in the strength of some higher conception of God. **You shall be holy because I am holy** now means
for Christians the call to reproduce what is the real nature of
God, His goodness, justice, and moral purity.[60]

Nor is the holy conduct here in any way a human accomplishment, however much its realization depends on our recep-
tivity. Bo Reicke comments:

> Holiness is not an attribute of man, and man cannot attain
> it by himself, nor progressively sanctify himself, and then tri-
> umphantly present the result to God. Rather, holiness belongs
> to God; he is the only Holy One. Inasmuch as he is holy, his
> people must live a holy life before him. This God-centered
> doctrine of sanctification differs from the view that man,
> through holy living, can develop a holy personality.[61]

Hunter comments on the Old Testament quotation here:
"Christianity, no less than Judaism, summons to holiness; but the
holiness it demands is not ritual and outward, but inner—the
holiness of 'the pure in heart' who shall 'see God' because they are
like him."[62] Peter "understands holiness or purity as entirely
moral."[63] And Alan M. Stibbs writes, "It is, therefore, the revelation
of God's character and the call to be intimately related to Him that
makes holiness an obligation. Religion and ethics are thus in biblical revelation fundamentally welded together."[64]

The idea of inner purity is carried through in v. 22: "Now that
you have purified yourselves [your souls, RSV, Moffatt] by obeying
the truth so that you have sincere love for your brothers, love one
another deeply, from the heart [or with some early manuscripts,
from a pure heart]." To have "purified your souls" (KJV) is, as
Moffatt says, "the other side of the holiness mentioned in ver. 15."[65]
Hunter paraphrases: "Your obedient acceptance of the [gospel]
truth has cleansed your souls and made them ready for true love of
the brethren: so let your love for one another be spontaneous and
fervent."[66] And Reicke says, "It is to be assumed that this cleansing

---

60. *General Epistles*, p. 105.

61. AB, 37:84.

62. IB, 12:101.

63. Leaney, *Peter and Jude*, p. 24.

64. "The First Epistle General of Peter," TNTC (Grand Rapids: William B.
Eerdmans Publishing Co., 1959), p. 88.

65. *General Epistles*, p. 109.

66. IB, 12:104.

or purification involves deliverance from evil lusts. For its result is said to be a guileless or sincere brotherly love which is not possible to the old carnal nature."[67]

C. The Holy Priesthood, 1 Pet. 2:4-5, 9-12

A concept stated by Paul in 1 Cor. 3:16 and Eph. 2:19-22 is reiterated by Peter in 2:4-5: "As you come to him, the living Stone—rejected by men but chosen by God and precious to him—you also, like living stones, are being built into a spiritual house to be a holy priesthood, offering spiritual sacrifices acceptable to God through Jesus Christ." The context in which the holiness of the priesthood is placed is moral and ethical (2:1-3) and contrasts with the way of unbelief (vv. 7-8). The Old Testament priesthood must be ritually and ceremonially holy; the priesthood of the New Testament must be ethically righteous and personally holy.

The Church as the "New Israel" realizes on a spiritual plane what the Old Israel was meant to exemplify on a geographical and political plane. Peter applies the great statement of Exod. 19:6 to his readers and as a consequence urges them to holy living (2:11 ff.)—"But you are a chosen people, a royal priesthood, a holy nation, a people belonging to God, that you may declare the praises of him who called you out of darkness into his wonderful light" (2:9).

D. Partakers of the Divine Nature, 2 Pet. 1:3-4

Second Peter includes two passages of special significance for our theme. One is 1:3-4: "His divine power has given us everything we need for life and godliness through our knowledge of him who called us by his own glory and goodness. Through these he has given us his very great and precious promises, so that through them you may participate in the divine nature [come to share in the very being of God, NEB] and escape the corruption in the world caused by evil desires."

Here "the apostle is making their divine call the ground for his appeal for holy living. . . . The point is that the One who calls, enables."[68] He stresses both the "divine power" and the "divine

---

67. AB, 37:86.
68. Michael Green, "The Second Epistle of Peter," TNTC (Grand Rapids: William B. Eerdmans Publishing Co., 1968), p. 63.

nature." The divine power—a Hebraism for God through the Holy Spirit—has given us everything necessary for life and godliness, a gift mediated "through our knowledge of" the Savior both as the Jesus of history and the Christ of faith—a knowledge both historical and existential.[69]

Through God's "very great and precious promises" we become partakers—we share in—"the divine nature." The reference to God's promises parallels Paul's statement in 2 Cor. 7:1, "Since we have these promises, dear friends, let us purify ourselves from everything that contaminates body and spirit, perfecting holiness out of reverence for God." Elmer G. Homrighausen writes:

> To partake of God's **nature** . . . means an intimate relation with God's Spirit: His moral character, his holy purpose, his saving love, his healing light, his yearning concern for justice, his suffering compassion, his pure righteousness, his victorious and universal rule. In this sense, the Christian life is not an imitation of Christ, as though he were a sort of copybook pattern. . . . We partake of Christ's nature. We do not take Christ as an external model; we receive him as an internal power. Paul put it thus: "I live, yet not I, but Christ liveth in me" (Gal. 2:20).[70]

The idea of being partakers of Christ's divine nature—the nature He shares with the Father and the Spirit—is breathtaking in scope. B. T. Roberts offers an interpretation and caution that are essential. He reminds us that holiness in man is derived. It is not innate or original. It is the image of God's holiness. Holiness in man, Roberts says, "resembles His holiness, though it falls infinitely short of it." The resemblance lies in possessing "in a limited degree, the hatred of sin, the sincerity, the veracity, the justice, the love, the goodness, and all the other virtues which constitute in all their fulness the holiness of God." The comparison is as a glass of water taken from the ocean, possessing all the chemical properties of the ocean without the sublimity, grandeur, and power of its source.[71]

Coordinate with partaking of the divine nature is escape from "the corruption in the world caused by evil desires"—"the cor-

---

69. Cf. Elmer G. Homrighausen, IB, 12:174.

70. Ibid.

71. *Holiness Teachings* (1893; reprint ed., Salem, Ohio: H. E. Schmul, 1964), p. 21.

ruption that is in the world because of passion" (RSV). These words admit of a sociological interpretation: society is corrupt because of the operation within it of *epithumia*—in this context, evil desires. But the words also admit of a subjective or psychological application. We escape the corruption of our own natures (as in Eph. 4:22) by the inner working of the divine power and an impartation of the divine nature.

The grace that ministers the divine power and the divine nature is the motivation for "every effort to add to your faith goodness; and to goodness, knowledge; and to knowledge, self-control; and to self-control, perseverance; and to perseverance, godliness; and to godliness, brotherly kindness; and to brotherly kindness, love" (vv. 5-7). These virtues form the basis of the exposition by T. M. Anderson titled *After Holiness, What?*[72] From Peter's use of "unproductive" (*akarpous*, lit., without fruit) in v. 8, these graces constitute his summary of the fruit of the Spirit.

E. Holy and Godly Lives, 2 Pet. 3:9-14, 17-18

As did Paul in 1 Thessalonians, Peter sets the call to holiness in an eschatological context. In a pregnant passage in c. 3, the author refers to a prevalent skepticism about the return of Christ. He admits the possibility of delay and affirms that God's calendar is not limited as ours. But the very delay is evidence of God's patience, "not wanting anyone to perish, but everyone to come to repentance" (3:9).

"But the day of the Lord will come like a thief," the apostle continues. "The heavens will disappear with a roar; the elements will be destroyed by fire, and the earth and everything in it will be laid bare.

"Since everything will be destroyed in this way, what kind of people ought you to be? You ought to live holy and godly lives as you look forward to the day of God and speed its coming. . . .

"So then, dear friends, since you are looking forward to this, make every effort to be found spotless, blameless and at peace with him" (3:10-12, 14).

Hunter writes that "**lives of holiness** (11, RSV) refer to ways in which holy living manifests itself. The reference is fundamentally to 'life and godliness' (1:3) for which Christ endows

---

72. (Kansas City: Nazarene Publishing House, 1929).

men."[73] "Holiness of life, worship of God and service to men are the three practical conclusions he draws from the study of the advent."[74]

Peter's last word is a warning against presumption and an exhortation to spiritual growth: "Therefore, dear friends, since you already know this, be on your guard so that you may not be carried away by the error of lawless men and fall from your secure position. But grow in grace and knowledge of our Lord and Savior Jesus Christ. To him be glory both now and forever! Amen" (3:17-18). The two, security and growth, are closely related.

This has often been said and should be repeated. William McDonald writes, "Unless the soul pants for more of God, pants for more of the fullness of which he was made a partaker in the hour that he was made pure; unless faith seeks and secures enlargement, and love increases in intensity, one not only will not grow, he will not maintain the grace he has attained."[75]

J. A. Wood makes the same point: "The Christian who does not grow becomes peevish, fretful and unhappy, like a child that has ceased to grow. Is not this the reason why so many professors of religion have become weak, uneasy and dissatisfied? In nature, when growth ceases, decay and death are at hand. . . . not to progress is to regress and regression is destruction."[76]

IV. First John

The close connection between 1 John and the Gospel of John has long been noted. It has been argued both that the letter was "written to accompany and introduce the Gospel"[77] and that it was written as a postscript to the Gospel—the Gospel having been written to explain how men might have eternal life, and the letter to show how they might know it.[78]

There is a background of controversy reflected in 1 John. The

---

73. IB, 12:202.

74. Green, *Second Peter,* p. 140.

75. *The Scriptural Way of Holiness* (Chicago: The Christian Witness Co., 1907), pp. 319-20.

76. *Purity and Maturity* (Chicago: S. K. J. Chesbro, 1903), p. 197.

77. E. M. Blaiklock, *Faith Is the Victory: Studies in the First Epistle of John* (Grand Rapids: William B. Eerdmans Publishing Co., 1959), p. 9.

78. Hunter, *Introducing the New Testament,* p. 175.

controversy concerned a form of docetic Gnosticism which taught that salvation was through a special kind of knowledge and that the Incarnation was only an appearance. Put together, these ideas could lead to rank licentiousness. John's opposition on both points is consistent and clear.

J. A. Robertson has made the suggestion that the Epistle is organized around three definitions of God, to which are added three tests for the possession of eternal life. The first definition is "God is light" (1:5), and the test is "Are we walking in the light?" The second definition is "God is life" (2:25), and the testing question is "Are we born of God?" The third definition is "God is love" (4:8), and the corresponding test is "Are we dwelling in love?"[79]

A. Cleansing from All Sin, 1:5-10

A major passage is found in 1:5-10:

> This is the message we have heard from him and declare to you: God is light; in him there is no darkness at all. If we claim to have fellowship with him yet walk in the darkness, we lie and do not live by the truth. But if we walk in the light, as he is in the light, we have fellowship with one another, and the blood of Jesus, his Son, purifies us from every [better, as with the margin and RSV, *all*] sin.[80]

> If we claim to be without sin, we deceive ourselves and the truth is not in us. If we confess our sins, he is faithful and just and will forgive us our sins and purify us from all unrighteousness. If we claim we have not sinned, we make him out to be a liar and his word has no place in our lives.

The symmetry of affirmation followed by refutation of a false claim is apparent and is important for a proper interpretation:

Affirmation	*Refutation of false claim*
No. 1: "God is light; in him there is no darkness" (v. 5).	"If we claim to have fellowship with him yet walk in the darkness, we lie and do not live by the truth" (v. 6).
No. 2: "But if we walk in the light, as he is in the light, we have fellowship with	"If we claim to be without sin, we deceive ourselves and the truth is not in us" (v. 8).

---

79. Quoted, Hunter, ibid., p. 176 f.

80. The Greek phrase standing by itself could be translated "every sin." "All sin" fits the context better (i.e., vv. 8-9). *Apo pasēs hamartias* (from all sin) in v. 7 is paralleled by *Apo pasēs adikias* (from all unrighteousness) in v. 9.

Affirmation	*Refutation of false claim*
one another, and the blood of Jesus, his Son, purifies us from all sin" (v. 7, marg.).	
No. 3: "If we confess our sins, he is faithful and just and will forgive our sins and purify us from all unrighteousness" (v. 9).	"If we claim we have not sinned, we make him out to be a liar and his word has no place in our lives" (v. 10).

As we have seen, recognizing the pattern is important for the proper interpretation of this passage. In each case, the refuted false claim that follows the affirmation is a denial or evasion of the truth that has been affirmed.

In No. 1, the truth is that God is light. The false notion is that one may have fellowship with the One who is light and yet walk in darkness. When this claim is made, it is a lie and is evidence that the claimant is not living by the truth.

In No. 2, the truth is that the blood of Jesus, God's Son, purifies us from all sin. The false claim is that we have no sin from which we need to be cleansed. When this claim is made, it is out of self-deception and total failure to apprehend the truth.

In No. 3, the truth is that the faithful and just God forgives our sins and cleanses us from all unrighteousness. The false claim is that we have not sinned and therefore need no forgiveness. When this claim is made, the result is to make God out to be a liar (cf. Rom. 3:23), and the evident fact is that His Word has no place in our lives.

It has often been argued that v. 8 destroys any idea of freedom from inner sin. It would indeed except for its context and its position in the section in which it is found. Verse 8 not only contradicts the Gnostic notion that esoteric knowledge purifies the soul, it also contradicts any teaching that would equate entire sanctification with justification (as Wesley understood Zinzendorf to teach) or any view that minimizes the biblical concept of original sin (as is apt to characterize a liberal optimistic theology).

Brooke Foss Westcott makes a strong statement concerning the cleansing by the blood of Jesus described in 1:7. The Blood, he says, "brings about that real sinlessness which is essential to union with

God." The thought is not just forgiveness of sin, but the *removal* of sin. "The sin is done away; and the purifying action is exerted continuously. . . . The thought here is of 'sin' and not of 'sins': of the spring, the principle, and not of the separate manifestations."[81]

While he disavows what he understands by "perfectionism," Alexander Ross writes: "The righteous God cleanses us from all unrighteousness, removing the pollution of sin, so that the new life of holiness is begun in the soul which is to issue in complete conformation to the image of God's Son (Rom. 8:29), who is called in 2:1 'the Righteous One'."[82]

Daniel Steele quotes Henry Alford with respect to the difference between "forgive us our sins" and "purify us from all unrighteousness": "In verse 9 'to cleanse us from all unrighteousness' is plainly distinguished from 'to forgive us our sins;' distinguished as a further process; as, in a word, sanctification, distinct from justification." Alford points out that the two verbs are aorists, explained, he says, "because the purpose of God is to do each as one great complex act—to justify and to sanctify wholly and entirely."[83]

B. Freedom from Sin, 2:1-6

John carries his emphasis on into the second chapter:

> My dear children, I write this to you so that you will not sin. But if anybody does sin, we have one who speaks to the Father in our defense—Jesus Christ, the Righteous One. He is the atoning sacrifice for our sins, and not only for ours but also for the sins of the whole world.
>
> We know that we have come to know him if we obey his commands. The man who says, "I know him," but does not do what he commands is a liar, and the truth is not in him. But if anyone obeys his word, God's love is truly made complete in him. This is how we know we are in him: Whoever claims to live in him must walk as Jesus did *(vv. 1-6)*.

The normal Christian life, in John's view, is free from acts of sin. "I write this to you so that you will not sin" presupposes such a life to be possible and expected. There is no allowance for sin in

---

81. *The Epistles of St. John* (London: Macmillan and Co., 1883), pp. 20-21.

82. *James and John*, p. 146.

83. *Half-hours with St. John's Epistles* (Chicago: Christian Witness Co., 1901), p. 16. Cf. Henry Alford, *Greek New Testament*, 4:430.

the Christian life. But if it should occur, there is provision for it. Even the provision, however, acknowledges the standard: "If anybody does sin" is not the same as "When we sin." Dr. Samuel Young expresses it clearly:

> But what does the Christian do who is overtaken in a sin? He turns to God quickly for forgiveness and help. He doesn't wait for public services or for special revival meetings. Perhaps he looks up some older Christian or his pastor to pray with him. But it would be even better to pray alone rather than to delay. John wrote clearly at this point: "And if any man sin, we have an advocate with the Father, Jesus Christ the righteous" (1 John 2:1). This is not a provision for a sinning religion; rather, it is a provision for the cure of sin. John points out that Jesus is the atoning Sacrifice for our sins. He also reveals that what he had written he had done so to keep them from sinning. A man cannot sin every day and repent every night. He will either lose his sincerity (for repentance involves a break with sin) or his sanity (for a man cannot play with his own mind in the turn-about on sin). The whole purpose of God is the gift and death of his Son to save us from our sins.[84]

R. Newton Flew writes, "Once again we hear the austere note of absolute freedom from sin as the mark of a believer. . . . There may be a fall from this ideal standard (I.ii.1). But this is evidently regarded as altogether exceptional. The possibility of fulfilling the commands of God is set forth later in the epistle (I.iii.22)."[85]

Daniel Steele adds, "The tense indicates a single act into which the regenerate person may be suddenly carried against the real purpose and tenor of his life (i.7), in contrast with a career or habitual state of sin."[86]

When the emphasis of 1:7 and 9 on cleansing "from all sin" and "from all unrighteousness" (RSV) is related to 2:1-2, the propriety of Major Allister Smith's exposition is apparent:

> In I John 2:1, we read, "If any man sin, we have an advocate with the Father, Jesus Christ the righteous." It is important that we flee at once to Christ for cleansing. When a sheep falls into the mud, it is unhappy and cries for deliverance. But a pig is happy in the mud, and does not seek for deliverance. May we be spotless lambs, because we walk with the Lamb of God day

---

84. *Temptation* (Kansas City: Beacon Hill Press of Kansas City, 1967), pp. 64-65.

85. *The Idea of Perfection in Christian Theology* (London: Oxford University Press, 1934), pp. 109-10.

86. *Half-hours with St. John's Epistles,* p. 28.

by day. The more we walk with Him, the longer we go on in the sanctified life, the less likely we are to sin. But we shall never be able to say that we do not need the blood of Christ.[87]

It should be made clear that John is not talking here about the premeditated sin that betrays a backslidden heart. He deals with such sin in 1 John 3:8-9. This is rather what classic holiness writers called a "surprise sin," the result of momentary yielding to unexpectedly strong temptation. Such sin must be immediately renounced and confessed. To fail to do so is to lapse into continued disobedience and unbelief.

C. As Christ Is Pure, 3:2-11

As did both Paul and Peter, John sets the holiness imperative in an eschatological context in 3:2-3: "Dear friends, now we are children of God, and what we will be has not yet been made known. But we know that when he appears, we shall be like him, for we shall see him as he is. Everyone who has this hope in him purifies himself, just as he is pure."

Scholars differ in understanding "when he appears, we shall be like him, for we shall see him as he is." Some read in this the transformation or "glorification" of our mortality as in Phil. 3:21. Others point out that such an interpretation would require "become like him" rather than "be like him" and relate v. 2 to the conclusion in v. 3: it is "the pure in heart" who shall see God (Matt. 5:8).

In either case, the hope of seeing Christ is the supreme incentive for purifying oneself. The standard and measure of that purity is "just as he is pure." This is an empirical holiness, not a positional holiness.

No self-sanctification is indicated here. While seeing in this verse progressive holiness despite the punctiliar (aorist) form of the verb, Ross writes: "Though it is only the blood that can clease (1:7), on each of us rests the responsibility of seeking that cleansing with all our hearts; cf. Paul's words in 2 Cor. 7:1."[88] And Westcott says, "The believer's act is using what God gives."[89]

---

87. *Ideal of Perfection,* p. 71.
88. *James and John,* pp. 180-81.
89. *Epistles of St. John,* p. 98.

The verb translated "purifies" and the adjective "pure" are respectively *hagnizei* and *hagnos.* The *hagnos* family of words is related to but not identical with the *hagios* family. It is used to describe both ceremonial cleanness as well as moral or spiritual purity (John 11:55; Acts 21:24, 26; 24:18 as compared with Jas. 4:8; 1 Pet. 1:22; and 1 John 3:3). Its generic meaning is "pure from defilement, not contaminated."[90] Harvey J. S. Blaney writes:

> No man can thus keep himself pure by his own will and effort, but he can continually walk in the light; and this light— the revealed truth of God in Christ—serves as the purifying ray. The light will search a man's innermost being and it will burn its way into his very conscience and will. John further dares to assert that we are pure **as he is pure.** He can make this bold assertion because it is God who does the cleansing. It is because of this purifying that **we shall be like him.**[91]

John's polemic against "sinning sainthood" is continued in 3:3-11. The heart of the passage is v. 9: "No one who is born of God will continue to sin, because God's seed remains in him; he cannot go on sinning, because he has been born of God." The translation quoted here fairly represents the force of the verbs used.

Further, what John has in mind is indicated by his statement that "sin is lawlessness" (v. 4). It is not the result of inadvertent and unconscious human frailty; it is disobedience to and rebellion against God. Under the influence of Augustine and Calvin, those in the Reformed tradition often classify as sins all acts, thoughts, and words that deviate from an absolute standard of perfection. The result is to make quite unintelligible such passages as this and 2:1, 4; 5:18 (together with John 8:34, 36; Rom. 5:8; 6:1, 15, 18, 22; 8:2-3; Gal. 2:17-18; 1 Thess. 2:10; Heb. 9:26; 10:26-29; and others).

D. Love Perfected, 4:16-18

In 4:16-18, John turns to the positive principle in holiness that underlies all of cc. 3 and 4: "God is love. Whoever lives in love lives in God, and God in him. Love is made complete [*teteleiōtai,* has been perfected] among us so that we will have confidence on the day of judgment, because in this world we are like him. There is no fear in love. But perfect love drives out fear, because fear has to do

---

90. EDNTW, 3:231.
91. BBC, 10:377.

with punishment. The man who fears is not made perfect in love" (cf. v. 12).

Fear in this context is neither the instinctive psychological response to danger that is essential to our human well-being, nor the reverential awe denoted by the scriptural phrase "fear of the Lord" (Acts 9:31; cf. Rom. 3:18; 2 Cor. 7:1). It is, as the context shows, fear of God's judgment—the fear of an unsanctified heart in the presence of divine holiness (e.g., Isa. 6:5). Such fear is banished by perfect love.

Edwin C. Lewis makes a discerning comment on the meaning of "perfect love":

> The nature of love remains always the same, but it may always deepen in quality and increase in range. At a given time, the perfection of holy love may obtain in Christian experience. The acme is reached. But time moves on, bringing new possibilities, new demands, new experiences. If the acme still remains where it was, it is the acme no longer. It can be kept only as it is exceeded. This is the logic of love. Perfect love is therefore perfect love only as it is a continual *going on unto* perfect love.[92]

The result of true love is Christlike conduct: "in this world we are like him" (v. 17). John consistently emphasizes the fact that the only genuine evidence of true love is obedience. This aspect of Christ's teaching caught John's ear and is recorded in the Gospel (14:15, 21, 23; 15:10). It reappears in 1 John 5:3. It underlies John's insistence on a holy life (2:4-6, 15-17; 3:18; 4:19-21; 5:18).

V. THE BOOK OF REVELATION

The Book of Revelation is a book for times of crisis. It was written against the background of persecution arising from the demands of Roman emperor worship. It is the supreme New Testament example of the apocalyptic style of writing: prophecy concerning the end of the age expressed in vivid but veiled symbolism. Notorious for the variety of interpretations that have been given it, Revelation is still crystal clear in its insistence that however fierce the battle may be, the final victory of righteousness is assured.

---

92. "The Ministry of the Holy Spirit," *The Revival Pulpit,* August/September, 1944, p. 158; quoted by C. William Fisher, *Don't Park Here* (New York: Abingdon Press, 1962), p. 158.

In harmony with its emphasis, the last book of the New Testament is not primarily a doctrinal work. It does, however, continue the theme of the preceding books emphasizing the holiness of God and His requirement for His people.

The salutation is another great Trinitarian formula with a unique designation for the Holy Spirit: "Grace and peace to you from him who is, and who was, and who is to come, and from the seven spirits [the sevenfold Spirit, marg.] before his throne, and from Jesus Christ, who is the faithful witness, the firstborn from the dead, and the ruler of the kings of the earth" (1:4-5). The seven spirits, it has been noted, are operations or aspects of the One Spirit of God. Those seven operations include regeneration (John 3:5-6), assurance (Rom. 8:16), sanctification (2 Thess. 2:13), guidance (Rom. 8:14), intercession (v. 26), healing, and resurrection (v. 11).

The messages to the seven churches (cc. 2—3) emphasize aspects of Christian living in a world in turmoil. Only two of the churches (Smyrna and Philadelphia) are praised without note of concern (2:8-11; 3:7-13). Dangers to be avoided include loss of the first love (2:4), compromise with error and evil (vv. 14-15, 20-23), spiritual deadness and lethargy (3:1-3), and lukewarmness (vv. 15-16).

The holiness of God is celebrated by the heavenly hosts in a manner reminiscent of Isaiah's Temple vision (4:6-11; Isa. 6:1-8). The worshipping throngs of the redeemed before God's throne "have washed their robes and made them white in the blood of the Lamb" (7:14, cf. 9-17). The prayers of the saints (lit., the sanctified) are offered with incense before God (8:3-4). When the seventh angel sounds (the last trumpet, 1 Cor. 15:23-28, 52), loud voices in heaven proclaim that

> *The kingdom of the world has become the kingdom of*
> *our Lord and of his Christ,*
> *and he will reign for ever and ever* (11:15).

In a great parenthesis (12:1—14:30), the victory over "the accuser" is seen to be

> *by the blood of the Lamb*
> *and by the word of their testimony* (12:10-11).

"This calls for patient endurance and faithfulness on the part of the saints" (13:10) "who obey God's commandments and remain faithful to Jesus" (14:12).

The "song of Moses" and "the song of the Lamb" also hymn the holiness of God:

> *Great and marvelous are your deeds,*
> *Lord God Almighty.*
> *Just and true are your ways,*
> *King of the ages.*
> *Who will not fear you, O Lord,*
> *and bring glory to your name?*
> *For you alone are holy.*
> *All nations will come*
> *and worship before you,*
> *for your righteous acts have been revealed* (15:3-4).

At the wedding of the Lamb, the Bride is arrayed in purity:

> *For the wedding of the Lamb has come,*
> *and his bride has made herself ready.*
> *Fine linen, bright and clean,*
> *was given her to wear.*

(Fine linen stands for the righteous acts of the saints) (19:7-8).

"Blessed and holy are those who have part in the first resurrection. The second death has no power over them, but they will be priests of God and of Christ and will reign with him for a thousand years" (20:6). The redeemed are gathered home at last to the city in which "there will be no more night. They will not need the light of a lamp or the light of the sun, for the Lord God will give them light. And they will reign for ever and ever" (22:5). But of that heavenly city of God it is said that "nothing impure will ever enter it, nor will anyone who does what is shameful or deceitful, but only those whose names are written in the Lamb's book of life" (21:27).

John is instructed not to "seal up the words of the prophecy of this book, because the time is near. Let him who does wrong continue to do wrong; let him who is vile continue to be vile; let him who does right continue to do right; and let him who is holy continue to be holy" (22:10-11).

For those who do wrong and are vile, the invitation of v. 17 is recorded: "The Spirit and the bride say, 'Come!' . . . Whoever is thirsty, let him come; and whoever wishes, let him take the free gift of the water of life." The righteous and the holy must continue in the way of righteousness and holiness if they are to be assured of their final reward.[93]

So the Bible comes full circle with the completed cycle of the ages. It began in a garden in fellowship with God, marred by the entrance of sin and the curse, the devastating effects of evil. It ends in a garden with the tree of life, the worship of God and the Lamb, the banishment of sin, and the eternal reward of righteousness and holiness in God's presence forever.

---

93. Cf. Martin Rist, IB, 12:546.

Bibliography

I. Books

Abbott-Smith, G. *A Manual of the Greek Lexicon of the New Testament.* 3rd edition. Edinburgh: T. and T. Clark, 1937.

Agnew, Milton S. *More than Conquerors: The Message of Romans—Chapters 1—8.* Chicago: The Salvation Army, 1959.

Amplified New Testament. Grand Rapids: Zondervan Publishing House, 1958.

Anderson, T. M. *After Holiness, What?* Kansas City: Nazarene Publishing House, 1929.

———, comp. *Our Holy Faith: Studies in Wesleyan Theology.* Kansas City: Beacon Hill Press of Kansas City, 1965.

Arndt, William F., and F. Wilbur Gingrich. *A Greek-English Lexicon of the New Testament and Other Early Christian Literature.* Chicago: University of Chicago Press, 1957.

Atkinson, J. Baines. *The Beauty of Holiness.* London: Epworth Press, 1953.

Barclay, William. *The Apostles' Creed for Everyman.* New York: Harper and Row, Publishers, 1967.

———. *The New Testament: A New Translation.* 2 vols. London: Collins, 1969.

———. *The Promise of the Spirit.* Philadelphia: Westminster Press, 1960.

———. *The Mind of Saint Paul.* New York: Harper and Brothers, 1958.

Barker, John H. J. *This Is the Will of God: A Study in the Doctrine of Entire Sanctification as a Definite Experience.* London: Epworth Press, 1956.

Barth, Karl. *Prayer and Preaching.* Naperville, Ill.: SCM Book Club, 1964.

Baxter, Batsell Barrett. *I Believe Because . . . : A Study of the Evidence Supporting Christian Faith.* Grand Rapids: Baker Book House, 1971.

Baxter, J. Sidlow. *Christian Holiness Restudied and Restated.* Grand Rapids: Zondervan Publishing House, 1977.

———. *A New Call to Holiness.* Grand Rapids: Zondervan Publishing House, 1973.

Bishop, James R. *The Spirit of Christ in Human Relationships.* Bangarapet, Mysore State, India: South India Bible Institute, 1964.

Blaney, Harvey J. S. *Speaking in Unknown Tongues: The Pauline Position.* Kansas City: Beacon Hill Press of Kansas City, 1973.

Bowman, John Wick. *Prophetic Realism and the Gospel.* Philadelphia: Westminster Press, 1955.

BOYD, MYRON F., and MERNE A. HARRIS, comps. *Projecting Our Heritage.* Kansas City: Beacon Hill Press of Kansas City, 1969.

BRENGLE, SAMUEL LOGAN. *Helps to Holiness.* London: Salvationist Publishing, 1896.

BROWN, CHARLES EWING. *The Meaning of Sanctification.* Anderson, Ind.: Warner Press, 1945.

BRUNER, FREDERICK DALE. *A Theology of the Holy Spirit.* Grand Rapids: William B. Eerdmans Publishing Co., 1970.

BUTTRICK, GEORGE ARTHUR, ed. *The Interpreter's Dictionary of the Bible.* Nashville: Abingdon Press, 1962. 4 vols.

CATTELL, EVERETT LEWIS. *The Spirit of Holiness.* Grand Rapids: William B. Eerdmans Publishing Co., 1963.

CHADWICK, SAMUEL. *The Way to Pentecost.* Kansas City: Beacon Hill Press of Kansas City, n.d.

CHAMBERS, OSWALD. *If Thou Wilt Be Perfect . . . Talks on Spiritual Philosophy.* London: Simpkin Marshall, Ltd., 1949 reprint.

COLEMAN, ROBERT E. *The Spirit and the Word.* Wilmore, Ky.: Asbury Theological Seminary, 1965.

COX, LEO G. *John Wesley's Concept of Perfection.* Kansas City: Beacon Hill Press, 1964.

CULLMANN, OSCAR. *The Christology of the New Testament.* Translated from the German by Shirley C. Guthrie and Charles A. M. Hall. Philadelphia: Westminster Press, 1959.

DAVIDSON, ROBERT F. *Rudolf Otto's Interpretation of Religion.* Princeton: Princeton University Press, 1947.

DEAL, WILLIAM S. *Problems of the Spirit-filled Life.* Kansas City: Beacon Hill Press, 1961.

DEWOLF, L. HAROLD. *A Theology of the Living Church.* New York: Harper and Brothers, 1953.

DRUMMOND, HENRY. *The Greatest Thing in the World,* and other addresses. London: Collins' Cleartype Press, n.d.

EDERSHEIM, ALFRED. *The Bible History: Old Testament.* Grand Rapids: William B. Eerdmans Publishing Co., 1949 reprint.

EDMAN, V. RAYMOND. *They Found the Secret.* Grand Rapids: Zondervan Publishing House, 1968.

EICHRODT, WALTHER. *Theology of the Old Testament.* Vol. 1. Translated by J. A. Baker. Philadelphia: Westminster Press, 1961.

FISHER, C. WILLIAM. *Don't Park Here.* New York: Abingdon Press, 1962.

FLETCHER, JOHN. *Works.* 4 vols. New York: Phillips and Hunt, 1883.

FLEW, R. NEWTON. *The Idea of Perfection in Christian Theology.* An Historical Study of the Christian Ideal for the Present Life. London: Oxford University Press, 1934.

FORSYTH, PETER T. *Positive Preaching and the Modern Mind.* New York: George H. Doran Company, 1907.

————. *The Work of Christ.* London: Hodder and Stoughton, 1910.

GEIGER, KENNETH, comp. *Insights into Holiness.* Kansas City: Beacon Hill Press, 1962.

————, comp. *Further Insights into Holiness.* Kansas City: Beacon Hill Press, 1963.

GREEN, MICHAEL. *I Believe in the Holy Spirit.* Grand Rapids: William B. Eerdmans Publishing Co., 1975.

GREEN, THOMAS SHELDON. *A Greek-English Lexicon to the New Testament.* New York: Macmillan and Co., 1890.

GRUBB, NORMAN P. *The Liberating Spirit.* Fort Washington, Pa.: Christian Literature Crusade, 1955.

HARPER, ALBERT F. *Holiness and High Country.* Kansas City: Beacon Hill Press of Kansas City, 1964.

HARRISON, EVERETT F. *A Short Life of Christ.* Grand Rapids: William B. Eerdmans Publishing Co., 1968.

————, ed. *Baker's Dictionary of Theology.* Grand Rapids: Baker Book House, 1960.

HASTINGS, JAMES, ed. *Encyclopedia of Religion and Ethics.* New York: Charles Scribner's Sons, 1951.

HORDERN, WILLIAM. *New Directions in Theology Today.* Vol. I, Introduction. Philadelphia: Westminster Press, 1966.

HOWARD, RICHARD E. *Newness of Life.* Kansas City: Beacon Hill Press of Kansas City, 1975.

HUGHES, PHILIP E. *But for the Grace of God: Divine Initiative and Human Need.* Philadelphia: Westminster Press, 1964.

HUNTER, ARCHIBALD M. *The Gospel According to Saint Paul.* Revised edition of *Interpreting Paul's Gospel.* Philadelphia: Westminster Press, 1966.

————. *Introducing the New Testament.* London: SCM Press, 1951.

INGE, WILLIAM R. *Faith and Its Psychology.* New York: Charles Scribner's Sons, n.d.

JACOB, EDMOND. *Theology of the Old Testament.* New York: Harper and Brothers, 1958.

JONES, E. STANLEY. *Mastery: The Art of Mastering Life.* New York: Abingdon Press, 1955.

————. *Victory Through Surrender.* New York: Abingdon Press, 1966.

JONES, OWEN ROGER. *The Concept of Holiness.* New York: Macmillan Co., 1961.

KEIR, THOMAS H. *The Word in Worship.* The Warrick Lectures, Aberdeen and Glasgow. London: Oxford University Press, 1962.

KENNEDY, GERALD. *The Preacher and the New English Bible.* New York: Oxford University Press, 1972.

KITTEL, GERHARD, ed. *Theological Dictionary of the New Testament.* Geoffrey W. Bromiley, trans. and ed. Grand Rapids: William B. Eerdmans Publishing Co., 1964.

KNIGHT, GEORGE A. F. *A Christian Theology of the Old Testament.* Richmond, Va.: John Knox Press, 1959.

KÖHLER, LUDWIG. *Old Testament Theology.* A. S. Todd, trans., from 3rd revised edition. Philadelphia: Westminster Press, 1957.

LAWSON, JOHN. *Introduction to Christian Doctrine.* Wilmore, Ky.: Francis Asbury Publishing Co., Inc. 1980.

MARTY, MARTIN E., ed. *New Directions in Biblical Thought.* New York: Association Press, 1960.

MCDONALD, WILLIAM. *The Scriptural Way of Holiness.* Chicago: Christian Witness Co., 1893.

METZ, DONALD S. *Studies in Biblical Holiness.* Kansas City: Beacon Hill Press of Kansas City, 1971.

MOODY, DWIGHT L. *Secret Power.* Chicago: Fleming H. Revell Co., 1881.

MURRAY, ANDREW. *The New Life: Words of God for Young Disciples of Christ.* Translated from the Dutch by Rev. J. P. Lilley, M.A. Minneapolis: Bethany Fellowship, Inc., 1965 (reprint from 1903 edition, slightly abridged, grammatical changes made, and copyrighted).

NEILL, STEPHEN. *The Interpretation of the New Testament, 1861-1961.* The Firth Lectures, 1962. London: Oxford University Press, 1964.

New Grolier Webster International Dictionary of the English Language, The. New York: Grolier, 1976.

NICHOLSON, ROY S. *The Arminian Emphases.* Owosso, Mich.: Owosso College, n.d. M. L. Goodman Lecture Series, vol. I.

NIEBUHR, REINHOLD. *Christianity and Power Politics.* New York: Charles Scribner's Sons, 1952.

ORR, JAMES, general ed. *The International Standard Bible Encyclopedia.* 5 vols. The original 1915 edition. Wilmington, Del.: Associated Publishers and Authors, reprint edited by Jay Green, n.d.

OTTO, RUDOLF. *The Idea of the Holy.* John W. Harvey, trans. London: Oxford University Press, 1957.

PERKINS, HAROLD WILLIAM. *The Doctrine of Christian or Evangelical Perfection.* London: Epworth Press, 1927.

PHILLIPS, J. B. *The New Testament in Modern English.* Revised edition. New York: Macmillan Publishing Co., Inc., 1972.

PURKISER, W. T. *The Gifts of the Spirit.* Kansas City: Beacon Hill Press of Kansas City, 1975.

―――. *Sanctification and Its Synonyms.* Kansas City: Beacon Hill Press, 1961.

―――, Richard S. Taylor, and Willard H. Taylor. *God, Man, and Salvation: A Biblical Theology.* Kansas City: Beacon Hill Press of Kansas City, 1977.

RALSTON, THOMAS W. *The Elements of Divinity.* Nashville: Publishing House of the Methodist Episcopal Church, South, 1919.

REES, PAUL S. *Don't Sleep Through the Revolution.* Waco, Tex.: Word Books, 1969.

RICHARDSON, ALAN, ed. *Theological Word Book of the Bible.* London: SCM Press, 1950.

RINGGREN, HELMER. *Faith of the Psalmists.* Philadelphia: Fortress Press, 1963.

ROBERTS, B. T. *Holiness Teachings.* Salem, Ohio: H. E. Schmul, 1964 reprint. First published, 1893.

ROBERTSON, A. T. *Word Pictures in the New Testament.* New York: Harper and Brothers, 1931. 6 vols.

ROBINSON, H. WHEELER. *The Christian Experience of the Holy Spirit.* New York: Harper and Brothers Publishers, 1928.

ROWLEY, HAROLD H. *The Faith of Israel: Aspects of Old Testament Thought.* Philadelphia: Westminster Press, 1956.

————. *The Unity of the Bible.* Philadelphia: Westminster Press, 1953.

RYLAARSDAM, J. C. *Revelation in Jewish Wisdom Literature.* Chicago: University of Chicago Press, 1946.

SANGSTER, W. E. *The Path to Perfection.* New York: Abingdon-Cokesbury Press, 1943.

SCHOFIELD, J. N. *Introducing Old Testament Theology.* Naperville, Ill.: SCM Book Club, 1964.

SCHULTZ, HERMANN. *Old Testament Theology.* 2 vols. J. A. Paterson, trans. Edinburgh: T. and T. Clark, 1909.

SMITH, ALLISTER. *The Ideal of Perfection.* London: Oliphants, Ltd., 1963.

SMITH, C. RYDER. *The Bible Doctrine of Man.* London: Epworth Press, 1951.

SNAITH, NORMAN H. *The Distinctive Ideas of the Old Testament.* Philadelphia: Westminster Press, 1946.

STARKEY, LYCURGUS M., JR. *The Work of the Holy Spirit: A Study in Wesleyan Theology.* New York: Abingdon Press, 1962.

STEELE, DANIEL. *Milestone Papers.* New York: Phillips and Hunt, 1878.

STEVENSON, DWIGHT E. *Preaching on the Books of the New Testament.* New York: Harper and Brothers, 1956.

STOLEE, H. J. *Speaking in Tongues.* Reprint of *Pentecostalism: The Problem of the Modern Tongues Movement,* 1936. Minneapolis: Augsburg Publishing House, 1963.

STOTT, JOHN R. W. *The Baptism and Fullness of the Spirit.* Downers Grove, Ill.: InterVarsity Press, 1964.

STRONG, JAMES. *A Concise Dictionary of the Words in the Hebrew Bible* in *Strong's Exhaustive Concordance of the Bible.* Nashville: Abingdon Press, reprint of 1890 edition.

STRUNK, ORLO, JR. *The Choice Called Atheism.* Nashville: Abingdon Press, 1968.

SYNAN, VINSON. *The Holiness-Pentecostal Movement in the United States.* Grand Rapids: William B. Eerdmans Publishing Co., 1971.

TAYLOR, J. PAUL. *Holiness the Finished Foundation.* Winona Lake, Ind.: Light and Life Press, 1963.

TAYLOR, RICHARD S. *Life in the Spirit: Christian Holiness in Doctrine, Experience, and Life.* Kansas City: Beacon Hill Press of Kansas City, 1966.

——. *Tongues: Their Purpose and Meaning.* Kansas City: Beacon Hill Press of Kansas City, 1973.

TAYLOR, VINCENT. *Forgiveness and Reconciliation.* London: Macmillan and Co., 1956.

TEMPLE, WILLIAM. *Nature, Man, and God.* London: Macmillan, Ltd. First edition, 1934.

THAYER, JOSEPH. *Greek-English Lexicon of the New Testament.* New York: American Book Co., 1889.

THOMAS, G. E. *A Pocket Book of Discipleship.* Nashville: The Upper Room, 1960.

THOMPSON, CLAUDE H. *Theology of the Kerygma: A Study in Primitive Preaching.* Englewood Cliffs, N.J.: Prentice-Hall, Inc., 1962.

THOMSON, JAMES G. S. S. *The Old Testament View of Revelation.* Grand Rapids: William B. Eerdmans Publishing Co., 1960.

TOOMBS, LAWRENCE. *The Old Testament in Christian Preaching.* Philadelphia: Westminster Press, 1961.

TURNER, GEORGE ALLEN. *The Vision Which Transforms.* Kansas City: Beacon Hill Press of Kansas City, 1964.

UNGER, MERRILL F. *The Baptism and Gifts of the Holy Spirit.* Chicago: Moody Press, 1974.

VAN DUSEN, HENRY P. *Spirit, Son and Father: Christian Faith in the Light of the Holy Spirit.* New York: Charles Scribner's Sons, 1958.

VINE, W. E. *An Expository Dictionary of New Testament Words.* 4 vols. London: Oliphants, Ltd., 1940.

VRIEZEN, TH. C. *An Outline of Old Testament Theology.* Boston: Charles T. Branford Company, 1958.

WEATHERSPOON, JESSE BURTON. *Sent Forth to Preach: Studies in Apostolic Preaching.* New York: Harper and Brothers, 1954.

WESLEY, JOHN. *A Plain Account of Christian Perfection.* As believed and taught by the Reverend Mr. John Wesley from the year 1725 to the year 1777. Reprinted from the complete original text as authorized by the Wesleyan Conference Office in London, England, in 1872. Kansas City: Beacon Hill Press of Kansas City, 1966.

——. *Explanatory Notes upon the New Testament.* Naperville, Ill.: Alec R. Allenson, Inc., 1958 reprint.

——. *Sermons on Several Occasions.* 2 vols. New York: Lane and Scott, 1852.

WILEY, H. ORTON. *Christian Theology.* 3 vols. Kansas City: Nazarene Publishing House, 1940.

WILLIAMS, DANIEL DAY. *The Minister and the Care of Souls.* New York: Harper and Brothers, Publishers, 1961.

WILSON, A. S. *Concerning Perplexities, Paradoxes and Perils in the Spirit-led Life.* London: Marshall, Morgan and Scott, Ltd., 1935.

WOOD, J. A. *Purity and Maturity.* Chicago: S. K. J. Chesbro, 1903.

WOOD, LAURENCE W. *Pentecostal Grace.* Wilmore, Ky.: Francis Asbury Publishing Company, Inc., 1980.

WRIGHT, G. ERNEST, and REGINAL H. FULLER. *The Book of the Acts of God.* New York: Doubleday and Co., Inc., 1957.

WYNKOOP, MILDRED BANGS. *A Theology of Love.* Kansas City: Beacon Hill Press of Kansas City, 1972.

YOUNG, ROBERT. *Analytical Concordance of the Bible.* 22nd American edition, revised. Grand Rapids: William B. Eerdmans Co., n.d.

YOUNG, SAMUEL. *Temptation.* Kansas City: Beacon Hill Press of Kansas City, 1967.

II. COMMENTARIES

ALFORD, HENRY. *The Greek Testament,* with revisions by Everett F. Harrison. 4 vols. Chicago: Moody Press, 1958.

ARCHER, GLEASON L., JR. *The Epistle to the Romans: A Study Manual.* Grand Rapids: Baker Book House, 1959.

BARCLAY, WILLIAM. *The Gospel of Matthew.* 2 vols. "The Daily Study Bible." Edinburgh: Saint Andrew Press, 1957.

———. *The Gospel of Mark.* "The Daily Study Bible." Edinburgh: Saint Andrew Press, 1956.

———. *The Gospel of John.* 2 vols. "The Daily Study Bible." Edinburgh: Saint Andrew Press, 1956.

———. *The Letter to the Romans.* "The Daily Study Bible." Edinburgh: Saint Andrew Press, 1962.

———. *The Letters to the Galatians and Ephesians.* "The Daily Study Bible." Edinburgh: Saint Andrew Press, 1960.

———. *The Letters to the Philippians, Colossians and Thessalonians.* "The Daily Study Bible." Edinburgh: Saint Andrew Press, 1961.

BARRETT, C. K. *The Epistle to the Romans.* "Black's New Testament Commentaries." London: Adam and Charles Black, 1957.

BEST, ERNEST. *The Letter of Paul to the Romans.* "The Cambridge Bible Commentary: New English Bible." Cambridge: University Press, 1967.

BLAIKLOCK, E. M. *Faith Is the Victory: Studies in the First Epistle of John.* Grand Rapids: William B. Eerdmans Publishing Co., 1959.

BRUCE, F. F. *The Book of Acts.* "New International Commentary on the New Testament." Grand Rapids: William B. Eerdmans Publishing Co., 1974.

————. *The Epistle to the Ephesians.* New York: Fleming H. Revell, 1969.

————. *The Epistle to the Hebrews.* "The New International Commentary on the New Testament." Grand Rapids: William B. Eerdmans Publishing Co., 1964.

————. *Colossians.* "The New International Commentary on the New Testament." Grand Rapids: William B. Eerdmans Publishing Co., 1957.

BUTTRICK, GEORGE ARTHUR. *The Interpreter's Bible.* 12 vols. New York: Abingdon Press, 1952.

CLARKE, ADAM. *The Holy Bible with a Commentary and Critical Notes.* 6 vols. New York: Abingdon Press, n.d.

DAVIDSON, FRANCIS, ALAN M. STIBBS, and ERNEST F. KEVAN. *The New Bible Commentary.* Second edition. Grand Rapids: William B. Eerdmans Publishing Co., 1956.

DODD, C. H. *The Epistle of Paul to the Romans.* "The Moffatt New Testament Commentary." New York: Harper and Brothers, 1932.

EARLE, RALPH. *Word Meanings in the New Testament: Romans,* vol. 3. Kansas City: Beacon Hill Press of Kansas City, 1974.

ERDMAN, CHARLES R. *The Epistle of Paul to the Romans.* Philadelphia: Westminster Press, 1925.

————. *The Epistle to the Hebrews: An Exposition.* Philadelphia: Westminster Press, 1934.

FOAKES-JACKSON, F. J., and KIRSOPP LAKE, *The Acts of the Apostles. Part I, The Beginnings of Christianity.* 5 vols. London: Macmillan and Co., 1922.

GODET, FREDERICK. *St. Paul's Epistle to the Romans.* A. Cusin, trans. Edinburgh: T. and T. Clark, 1884.

GREATHOUSE, WILLIAM M. *Search the Scriptures.* Vol. 6. "Romans." Kansas City: Nazarene Publishing House, n.d.

GREEN, MICHAEL. *The Second Epistle of Peter.* "The Tyndale New Testament Commentaries." Grand Rapids: William B. Eerdmans Publishing Co., 1968.

GRIFFITH THOMAS, W. H. *Through the Pentateuch Chapter by Chapter.* Grand Rapids: William B. Eerdmans Publishing Co., 1957.

HARPER, ALBERT F., general ed. *Beacon Bible Commentary.* 10 vols. Kansas City: Beacon Hill Press of Kansas City, 1964-1969.

HEWITT, THOMAS. *The Epistle to the Hebrews: An Introduction and Commentary.* "Tyndale New Testament Commentaries." Grand Rapids: William B. Eerdmans Publishing Co., 1960.

HILLS, A. M. *Holiness in the Book of Romans.* Reprint of *The Establishing Grace.* Kansas City: Beacon Hill Press, 1937 and 1950.

HODGE, CHARLES. *Commentary on the Epistle to the Ephesians.* Grand Rapids: William B. Eerdmans Publishing Co., 1950.

HOSKYNS, EDWIN CLEMENT. *The Fourth Gospel.* Francis Noel Davey, ed. London: Faber and Faber, 1947.

KELLY, BALMER H., ed. *The Layman's Bible Commentary.* 25 vols. Richmond, Va.: John Knox Press, 1959.

KNOX, JOHN. *Life in Christ Jesus.* Greenwich, Conn.: Seabury Press, 1961.

LEANEY, A. R. C. *The Letters of Peter and Jude.* Cambridge: Cambridge University Press, 1967.

LEENHARDT, FRANZ J. *The Epistle to the Romans: A Commentary.* Cleveland: World Publishing Company, 1961.

MANSON, WILLIAM. *The Epistle to the Hebrews: An Historical and Theological Reconsideration.* The Baird Lecture, 1949. London: Hodder and Stoughton Ltd., 1951.

MEYER, F. B. *The Way into the Holiest: Expositions of the Epistle to the Hebrews.* New York: Fleming H. Revell, 1893.

MITTON, C. L. *The Epistle of James.* Grand Rapids: William B. Eerdmans Publishing Co., 1966.

MOFFATT, JAMES. *The General Epistles.* "The Moffatt New Testament Commentary." New York: Harper and Brothers, Publishers, n.d.

MORGAN, G. CAMPBELL. *An Exposition of the Whole Bible.* Westwood, N. J.: Fleming H. Revell Company, 1954.

MOULE, HANDLEY C. G. *Ephesians Studies.* Second edition. London: Pickering and Inglis, Ltd., n.d.

NEIL, WILLIAM. *The Epistle to the Hebrews.* Introduction and Commentary. "Torch Bible Commentaries." London: SCM Press, Ltd., 1955.

———. *St. Paul's Epistles to the Thessalonians.* "Torch Bible Commentaries." New York: Macmillan Co., 1957.

Oxford Annotated Bible, RSV, The. New York: Oxford University Press, 1962.

PURKISER, W. T. *Hebrews, James, Peter.* "Beacon Bible Expositions." Kansas City: Beacon Hill Press of Kansas City, 1974. Vol. 2.

REES, PAUL S. *The Adequate Man: Paul in Philippians.* Westwood, N.J.: Fleming H. Revell Company, 1959.

———. *Prayer and Life's Highest.* Grand Rapids: William B. Eerdmans Publishing Co., 1956.

ROSS, ALEXANDER. *The Epistles of James and John.* "The New International Commentary on the New Testament." Grand Rapids: William B. Eerdmans Publishing Co., 1970.

SANDAY, WILLIAM, and A. C. HEADLAM. *A Critical and Exegetical Commentary on the Epistle to the Romans.* "International Critical Commentary." New York: Charles Scribner's Sons, 1923.

SCOTT, E. F. *The Epistles of Paul to the Colossians, to Philemon and to the Ephesians.* "The Moffatt New Testament Commentary." New York: Harper and Brothers, Publishers, 1930.

————. *The Pastoral Epistles.* "The Moffatt New Testament Commentary." New York: Harper and Brothers, Publishers, n.d.

STEELE, DANIEL. *Half Hours with St. John's Epistles.* Chicago: Christian Witness Co., 1901.

STIBBS, ALAN M. *The First General Epistle of Peter.* "The Tyndale New Testament Commentaries." Grand Rapids: William B. Eerdmans Publishing Co., 1959.

TAYLOR, VINCENT. *The Epistle to the Romans.* London: Epworth Press, 1956.

VINCENT, MARVIN R. *Epistles to the Philippians and to Philemon.* "International Critical Commentaries." Edinburgh: T. and T. Clark, 1897.

————. *Word Studies in the New Testament.* Grand Rapids: William B. Eerdmans Publishing Co., 1965 reprint.

Wesleyan Bible Commentary. Grand Rapids: William B. Eerdmans Publishing Co., 1965.

WESTCOTT, BROOKE FOSS. *The Epistles of St. John.* London: Macmillan and Co., 1883.

WICKHAM, E. C. *The Epistle to the Hebrews.* "Westminster Commentaries." London: Methuen and Co., Ltd., 1910.

WILEY, H. ORTON. *The Epistle to the Hebrews.* Kansas City: Beacon Hill Press, 1959.

WOOD, A. SKEVINGTON. *Life by the Spirit.* Formerly published as *Paul's Pentecost.* Grand Rapids: Zondervan Publishing House, 1963.

WUEST, KENNETH S. *Romans in the Greek New Testament.* Grand Rapids: William B. Eerdmans Publishing Co., 1955.

III. ARTICLES

AIRHART, ARNOLD E. "The Baptism with the Holy Spirit." *Preacher's Magazine,* vol. XXXVIII, no. 5 (May, 1963).

ANDERSON, BERNHARD W. "From Analysis to Synthesis." *Journal of Biblical Literature,* vol. 97, no. 1 (March, 1978), pp. 23-29.

BERKOUWER, GERRIT C. "What Difference Does Faith Make?" *Christianity Today,* vol. XIV, no. 5 (Dec. 5, 1969).

DAVIES, W. D. "A Quest to Be Resumed in New Testament Studies." *New Directions in Biblical Thought.* Martin E. Marty, ed. New York: Association Press, 1960.

DAYTON, DONALD W. "Asa Mahan and the Development of American Holiness Theology." *Wesleyan Theological Journal,* vol. 9 (1974), pp. 60-69.

————. "The Doctrine of the Baptism of the Holy Spirit: Its Emergence and Significance." *Wesleyan Theological Journal,* vol. 13 (1978), pp. 114-26.

DEASLEY, ALEX R. G. "Entire Sanctification and the Baptism with the Holy Spirit: Perspectives on the Biblical View of the Relationship." *Wesleyan Theological Journal,* vol. 14, no. 1 (Spring, 1979).

DE VRIES, SIMON J. "The Fall." *Interpreter's Dictionary of the Bible,* George Arthur Buttrick, ed. Nashville: Abingdon Press, 1962. 2:235-37.

GREATHOUSE, WILLIAM M. "The Baptism with the Holy Spirit." Unpublished paper, 1979.

GRIDER, J. KENNETH. "Spirit-baptism the Means of Entire Sanctification." *Wesleyan Theological Journal,* vol. 14, no. 2 (Fall, 1979), pp. 31-50.

HARRISON, EVERETT F. "Historical Problems in the Fourth Gospel." *Bibliotheca Sacra,* vol. 116, no. 463 (July, 1959).

ISBELL, CHARLES D. "Glossolalia and Propheteialalia: A Study in 1 Corinthians 14." *Wesleyan Theological Journal,* vol. 10 (1975), pp. 15-22.

LYON, ROBERT W. "The Baptism of the Spirit—Continued." *Wesleyan Theological Journal,* vol. 15, no. 2 (Fall, 1980).

MCGONIGLE, HERBERT. "Pneumatological Nomenclature in Early Methodism." *Wesleyan Theological Journal,* vol. 8 (1973), pp. 61-72.

MIKOLASKI, SAMUEL J. *The Triune God.* "Fundamentals of the Faith," Essay no. 4. Washington, D.C.: Christianity Today, 1966.

MUILENBERG, JAMES. "Holiness." *Interpreter's Dictionary of the Bible.* George Arthur Buttrick, ed. Nashville: Abingdon Press, 1962. Pp. 616-25.

PROCKSCH, OTTO. "*Hagios,* etc." *Theological Dictionary of the New Testament.* Gerhard Kittel, ed. Geoffrey W. Bromiley, trans. and ed. Grand Rapids: William B. Eerdmans Publishing Co., 1964. 1:88-115.

RHODES, ARNOLD B. "The Message of the Bible." *The Layman's Bible Commentary.* Balmer H. Kelly, ed. Richmond, Va.: John Knox Press, 1959. Pp. 67-118.

SMITH, TIMOTHY L. "The Doctrine of the Sanctifying Spirit in John Wesley and John Fletcher." The *Preacher's Magazine,* vol. 55, no. 1 (Sept., Oct., Nov., 1979).

————. "How John Fletcher Became the Theologian of Wesleyan Perfectionism." *Wesleyan Theological Journal,* vol. 15, no. 1 (Spring, 1980), pp. 68-87.

TURNER, GEORGE ALLEN. "An Evaluation of John R. W. Stott's and Frederick Bruner's Interpretations of the Baptism of the Holy Spirit." *Wesleyan Theological Journal,* vol. 8 (1973), pp. 45-51.

WOUDSTRA, MARTEN H. "Circumcision." *Baker's Dictionary of Theology.* Everett F. Harrison, editor-in-chief. Grand Rapids: Baker Book House, 1960. Pp. 127-28.

Subject Index

Author Index

Index of Scripture References